Practitioner Agency and Identity in English for Academic Purposes

New Perspectives for English for Academic Purposes

Series editors: Alex Ding, Ian Bruce and Melinda Whong

This series sets the agenda for studies in English for Academic Purposes (EAP) by opening up research and scholarship to new domains, ideas and perspectives as well as giving a platform to emerging and established practitioners and researchers in the field.

The volumes in this series are innovative in that they broaden the scope of theoretical and practical interests in EAP by focusing on neglected or new areas of interest, to provide the EAP community with a deeper understanding of some of the key issues in teaching EAP across the world and in diverse contexts.

Advisory Board:

Jigang Cai, Fudan University, China
Nigel Caplan, University of Delaware, USA
Greg Hadley, Niigata University, Japan
Nigel Harwood, University of Sheffield, UK
Azirah Hashim, University of Malaya, Malaysia
Carole Macdiarmid, University of Glasgow UK
Jennifer MacDonald, Dalhousie University, Canada
Geoffrey Nsanja, University of Malawi, The Polytechnic, Malawi
Brian Paltridge, The University of Sydney, Australia
Diane Pecorari, The City University of Hong Kong, Hong Kong
Nadezda Silaski, University of Belgrade, Serbia
Christine Tardy, University of Arizona, USA
Jackie Tuck, Open University, UK

Also available in this series

What Is Good Academic Writing?: Insights into Discipline-Specific Student Writing, edited by Melinda Whong and Jeanne Godfrey

Pedagogies in English for Academic Purposes, edited by Carole MacDiarmid and Jennifer J. MacDonald

Social Theory for English for Academic Purposes, edited by Alex Ding and Michelle Evans

Contextualizing English for Academic Purposes in Higher Education, edited by Ian Bruce and Bee Bond

Forthcoming in the series

Linguistic Approaches in English for Academic Purposes, edited by Milada Walková

Practitioner Agency and Identity in English for Academic Purposes

Edited by

Alex Ding and Laetitia Monbec

BLOOMSBURY ACADEMIC
LONDON • NEW YORK • OXFORD • NEW DELHI • SYDNEY

BLOOMSBURY ACADEMIC

Bloomsbury Publishing Plc, 50 Bedford Square, London, WC1B 3DP, UK
Bloomsbury Publishing Inc, 1359 Broadway, New York, NY 10018, USA
Bloomsbury Publishing Ireland, 29 Earlsfort Terrace, Dublin 2, D02 AY28, Ireland

BLOOMSBURY, BLOOMSBURY ACADEMIC and the Diana logo are trademarks of
Bloomsbury Publishing Plc

First published in Great Britain 2024
Paperback edition published 2026

Copyright © Alex Ding, Laetitia Monbec and Contributors, 2024, 2026

Alex Ding, Laetitia Monbec and Contributors have asserted their right under the Copyright,
Designs and Patents Act, 1988, to be identified as Editors of this work.

For legal purposes the Acknowledgements on p. xvii constitute an extension of this
copyright page.

Series design: Charlotte James
Cover image © Tuomas Lehtinen/Getty Images

All rights reserved. No part of this publication may be: i) reproduced or transmitted in any form, electronic or mechanical, including photocopying, recording or by means of any information storage or retrieval system without prior permission in writing from the publishers; or ii) used or reproduced in any way for the training, development or operation of artificial intelligence (AI) technologies, including generative AI technologies. The rights holders expressly reserve this publication from the text and data mining exception as per Article 4(3) of the Digital Single Market Directive (EU) 2019/790.

Bloomsbury Publishing Plc does not have any control over, or responsibility for, any third-party websites referred to or in this book. All internet addresses given in this book were correct at the time of going to press. The author and publisher regret any inconvenience caused if addresses have changed or sites have ceased to exist, but can accept no responsibility for any such changes.

A catalogue record for this book is available from the British Library.

A catalog record for this book is available from the Library of Congress.

ISBN: HB: 978-1-3502-6323-9
PB: 978-1-3502-6327-7
ePDF: 978-1-3502-6324-6
eBook: 978-1-3502-6325-3

Series: New Perspectives for English for Academic Purposes

Typeset by Deanta Global Publishing Services, Chennai, India

For product safety related questions contact productsafety@bloomsbury.com.

To find out more about our authors and books visit www.bloomsbury.com and sign up
for our newsletters.

This volume is dedicated to all those practitioners seeking a better understanding of the field.

Contents

List of Figures	ix
List of Tables	x
List of Contributors	xi
Series Editors' Foreword	xv
Acknowledgements	xvii
Introduction *Alex Ding*	1

Part I: Mesocosms

1	A Socio-Analysis of English for Academic Purposes *Alex Ding and Laetitia Monbec*	11
2	An Exploration of the Ethics of Scholarship in EAP: Collegial Connections and Ethical Entanglements *Bee Bond*	47
3	EAP Practitioners in the Global South: Participation, Positioning and Agency in the Context of 'Peripheral' Scholars and Scholarship *Namala Lakshmi Tilakaratna*	67

Part II: Microcosms

4	EAP Practitioners' Agency and Identity in Pakistan: From Social Class to Social Capital *Tanzeela Anbreen and Samina Ayub*	91
5	Trials and Tribulations of EAP Practitioners in Zimbabwe *Tambawoga C. Muchena*	108
6	'Be More Pirate': Harnessing the Power of Liminal Spaces in Creating Academic Literacy Practitioner Identity and Agency *Michelle Joubert and Sherran Clarence*	122
7	Finding Space and Voice: Duoethnographic Exploration of Teacher Agency in EAP *Iwona Winiarska-Pringle and Ania Rolińska*	136
8	Respected Teachers or a Marginalized, Stigmatized Profession? An Exploration of UK EAP Practitioner Identity *Sarah Taylor*	155

9   EAP Teacher Agency in a Digital Age *Blair Matthews*   173
10 'Changing Lanes': Balancing between Roles of EAP Lecturer
    and Researcher in a Teaching Institution towards a Research
    University *Eric Cheung*   186
11 Responding to Students' Disciplinary Writing in a University-Wide
    Writing Requirement: Negotiating Agency through Positioning
    Shari Dureshahwar Lughmani and Svetlana Chigaeva-Heddad   205
12 Power and the Canadian EAP Practitioner: Multiethnography as
    Resistance? *James N. Corcoran, Jennifer J. MacDonald,
    Jonathan Mendelsohn and Leonardo Gomes*   222

Conclusion: Engaging with Identity and Agency in a Collaborative
    Project *Laetitia Monbec*   240

Index   245

Figures

4.1	WhatsApp message	98
5.1	Specialization plane	111
12.1	Our professional intersections	224

Tables

2.1	Iterative ethical questions	63
4.1	Different types of capital possessed by elite-class and middle-class EAP practitioners	101
5.1	Translation device	114
5.2	Summary of qualifications of participants	116
8.1	Overview of participants	161
9.1	Participants	177
11.1	Four types of positioning	210
11.2	The grammar of agency	211

Contributors

Alex Ding is Associate Professor of English for Academic Purposes and Director of Scholarship at the University of Leeds. He has a long-standing interest in the EAP practitioner and has published in this area. He co-wrote with Ian Bruce a book entitled *The English for Academic Purposes Practitioner: Operating on the Edge of Academia* (2017). He has also published work on practitioner identity and agency, education and development as well as practitioner scholarship. He is co-editor of the Bloomsbury series 'New Perspectives for English for Academic Purposes'.

Laetitia Monbec is Senior Lecturer of English for Academic Purposes at the National University of Singapore. She has an academic background in education and applied linguistics, with a particular interest in Systemic Functional Linguistics and Legitimation Code Theory approaches to academic literacy and EAP. She has fifteen years' experience in EAP in a range of higher educational settings in France, Hong Kong and Singapore and has published in journals such as the *Journal of English for Academic Purposes*, the *Journal for Academic Language and Literacy* and the *Journal of Assessment and Evaluation in Higher Education*.

Namala Lakshmi Tilakaratna is Senior Lecturer at the Centre for English Language Communication at the National University of Singapore. She teaches an Ideas and Exposition module in the Residential Colleges programme on nations and nationalism. She was awarded a PhD in linguistics from the University of Sydney in 2017 where she focussed on Systemic Functional Linguistic approaches to national identity. She is currently co-editing (with Dr Eszter Szenes) a book titled *Demystifying Critical Reflection: Improving Pedagogy and Practice with Legitimation Code Theory* for the Routledge series on legitimation code theory edited by Professor Karl Maton due for publication in 2023.

Bee Bond is Associate Professor of EAP at the University of Leeds, UK. She is the author of *Making Language Visible in the University: English for Academic Purposes and Internationalisation* (2020). You can follow her on Twitter @BeeBond1.

James N. Corcoran is Assistant Professor of English as a Second Language and Applied Linguistics in the Department of Languages, Literatures and Linguistics at York University in Toronto, Canada. He teaches 'sheltered' undergraduate EAP courses, TESOL certificate courses and graduate applied linguistics courses to York University students. His research interests include language teacher education, (critical) English for Specific/Academic Purposes and relations of power in global academic knowledge production. His active research projects include investigations into (i) the political economy of post-secondary EAP; (ii) the long-term impact of research writing interventions; and (iii) EAP teachers' pedagogies for supporting diverse students' academic literacies. James spends large amounts of time with his cat, Genius.

Dr. Jennifer J. MacDonald is an EAP practitioner-researcher whose work focuses on topics at the intersection between EAP, critical applied linguistics and the internationalization of higher education. Her latest research tackles the challenges of language policies, politics and pedagogy in the linguistically-diverse context of internationalized Canadian higher education. Her books include Academic Inquiry 1, Sentences and Paragraphs (with Marcia Kim, Oxford University Press, 2017) and Pedagogies in English for Academic Purposes: Teaching and Learning in International Contexts (with Carole MacDiarmid, Bloomsbury, 2021). Dr. MacDonald was Director and Associate Director/Head Teacher of English Language Studies at Dalhousie University from 2012-2023 and has been an adjunct faculty member in the Faculty of Education at Saint Mary's University, and the Faculty of Education at Mount Saint Vincent University, all in Halifax, Canada. She sits on the board of EduNova and is a past board member of Languages Canada and TESL Nova Scotia.

Eric Cheung is Lecturer of the Division of Languages and Communication in the College of Professional and Continuing Education at Hong Kong Polytechnic University. His major research interests include Systemic Functional Linguistics, Legitimation Code Theory, academic discourse analysis, literacy pedagogy and metaphor. He is also associate editor of *Linguistics and the Human Sciences*.

Blair Matthews is a Teaching Fellow at the University of St Andrews. He teaches on the MSc TESOL and is the module convenor for Technology for Teaching and English for Academic Purposes. He is interested in language education, social theory and learning technology.

Sarah Taylor is a Learning Developer and EAP practitioner at the London School of Economics and Political Science. She has taught EAP for about twenty-three years at universities in Turkey, the USA and the UK. She completed an undergraduate degree in journalism and English literature in South Africa, a master's in language teaching in the USA and a Doctorate in Education (EdD) in the UK. Her EdD thesis examines how EAP practitioners in the UK construct their professional identities.

Tambawoga C. Muchena is Lecturer in the Department of English and Communication at Midlands State University, Zimbabwe. He holds a BA (Honours) in linguistics, an MA in applied English linguistics and is currently pursuing a PhD in applied linguistics. His research interests cover English for

Academic Purposes, Legitimation Code Theory, genre analysis, appraisal theory, critical discourse analysis theory, occupational discourse, discourse analysis and semiotics.

Michelle Joubert is head of an academic literacy unit embedded in the Centre for Teaching and Learning at the University of the Free State in South Africa and has worked in the EAP field in the United Kingdom. She has also taught English in the United States while on a Fulbright Scholarship in Washington DC. Her research interests lie in curriculum and materials development and student engagement, as well as the identity of EAP practitioners. She is also Fellow of the Higher Education Academy (UK).

Sherran Clarence is Research Associate and an academic developer based at the Centre for Higher Education, Research, Teaching and Learning (CHERTL) at Rhodes University in Makhanda, South Africa. Her work focusses on academic writing at postgraduate and postdoctoral level and developing theorized, practical approaches to helping students to create more successful written texts and achieve greater success. Her research looks at how student success can be enhanced through theorizing pedagogic practice and supervisions using academic literacies and feminist theory and legitimation code theory. She supervises students in higher education and gender studies and holds a Y2 rating from the National Research Foundation.

Shari Dureshahwar Lughmani is Senior Teaching Fellow at the English Language Centre at Hong Kong Polytechnic University and coordinates the English Language Enhancement Initiatives including a university-wide, collaborative writing programme. Shari manages collaborative disciplinary literacy projects funded by internal and external grants. Her research encompasses academic literacy, collaborative writing programmes and genre-based feedback in disciplinary writing. She has given invited talks at Coventry University London and the Chinese University of Hong Kong and keynote talks at SUSTech, SPEED and the British Council. She was a visiting scholar at Coventry University and Kings College London in 2018 and 2019.

Svetlana Chigaeva-Heddad is Assistant Professor and English Team Leader at the School of General Education and Languages, Technological and Higher Education Institute of Hong Kong, where she coordinates a range of English language modules and initiatives. Prior to this, she worked at the Hong Kong Polytechnic University where she contributed to the development and coordination of advanced academic language courses and literacy programmes. Her research interests include academic literacy development, writing across the curriculum, writing in the disciplines, teacher feedback practices and early-career staff development.

Tanzeela Anbreen holds a PhD in applied linguistics from the University of Bedfordshire, an MA from the University of Reading and a CELTA from the

University of Cambridge. She is an experienced EAP practitioner. She has worked for Cambridge English Assessment, the British Council and IDP Australia. She is a faculty member of Lahore College for Women University (LCWU) in Pakistan. She is a recipient of the Aptis research award and Charles Wallace Trust.

Samina Ayub holds an MS (MPhil) in English literature with distinction (Gold Medal). She is a full-time EAP practitioner at Lahore College for Women University, Pakistan. She has eight years of EAP teaching experience to her credit. She is a teacher trainer and is a Higher Education Commission of Pakistan (HEC)-approved professional. She also sits on the English language curriculum committee. She has also received training in Turkey.

Ania Rolińska is Lecturer at the Glasgow School of Art, teaching English and study skills to foundation students during the academic year and coordinating a bespoke pre-sessional course for the creative disciplines in summer. On top of her ELT qualifications, she holds an MSc in digital education and is keen to use technology to support learning and teaching. In her practice, she tries to blend art education and EAP pedagogies and help her students develop the communication skills needed to thrive in the studio.

Iwona Winiarska-Pringle teaches on the summer pre-sessional course at the University of Glasgow. She graduated with a master's degree in TESOL and translation from Warsaw University and taught on a range of English language courses until in 2004. She worked in the public sector, obtaining a Graduate Diploma in Information Governance from the University of Bath. She is an IELTS examiner and a Higher Education Academy Fellow. Her professional interests are the internationalization of HE, oracy skills, interactional and intercultural competences and socially engaged academia.

Leo Gomez is a freelance researcher, teacher, and educator with over 23 years of EAL experience. He is also a founding member of Learn YOUR English, a grassroots educational organization aiming at bridging the gap between research and practice. Leo's research interests include humanistic education, psychology of learning, critical pedagogy, Task-based education, and podcasting as tool for professional and personal development.

With degrees in Creative Writing and Applied Linguistics, **Jonathan Mendelsohn** teaches in both the Writing and the Languages and Linguistics departments. He taught at Doshisha University in Kyoto, Japan and the University of Toronto before teaching at York University over 10 years ago. Jonathan also works as a professional writer. He has published fiction in Prism International and Litbreak Magazine, as well as creative non-fiction in a variety of publications including The Globe and Mail, The Toronto Star, The Toronto Review of Books and Today's Parent.

Series Editors' Foreword

English for Academic Purposes practitioners, until recent years, have been almost invisible agents in their own field. Their roles have been defined functionally in terms of the needs of universities and their programmes. Practitioners have been required to be needs analysts, course creators, knowledge brokers and providers of bridging into the requirements of universities that are anxious to recruit and acculturate students from 'other' linguistic and cultural backgrounds. However, issues relating to the practitioner's own personal role, agency, identity and their own intersections with their working contexts have been largely ignored. The books by Hadley (2015) and Alex Ding and myself (Ding and Bruce, 2017) marked the beginning of a new focus on the practitioner, but those works were mainly preoccupied with the influences of the macro-level aspects of the contexts within which EAP practitioners work. Detailed, contextualized accounts of the individual working lives of practitioners have remained scarce, and those that have been offered have tended to focus on EAP practitioners in 'inner-circle' country contexts with 'inner-circle' country concerns. In contrast, the achievement of this volume, contributing to the 'new perspectives' theme of our series, is to provide richness and depth through accounts of the working lives of practitioners in diverse contexts, and specifically how the structural elements, issues and challenges of those contexts shape the identity and agency of practitioners.

The contributors' accounts reinforce the fact that EAP can no longer be considered to be an 'inner-circle' country activity, with a comfortable inner-circle country literature built around certain luminaries. Rather, EAP has jumped those boundaries and, under various designations, is found in multiple contexts. The differing realities of those contexts have been clearly described in the various accounts of the contributors to this volume. However, regardless of context, each contribution provides a nuanced portrayal of an author's working identity and agency within the affordances and constraints of their particular situation.

When Alex Ding and I wrote *The English for Academic Purposes Practitioner* and chose the subtitle *Operating on the Edge of Academia*, the characterization of the field by the latter phrase was seen as somewhat negative, perhaps pejorative by some. They saw it as not being apt or applicable to many EAP contexts. However, I would argue that the accounts of this volume validate our words. What emerges, sadly, is the depths of marginalization faced by practitioners in some contexts and the differing challenges faced within all contexts. For me, the rich ethnographic accounts of the volume are arguments for the need for an ethical framework for EAP, one that is discussed and developed across national boundaries. Having established the liminal, perhaps marginalized position of EAP, there now needs to be the development of a consensus through a cross-border debate about what EAP should and should not be. This is an argument for a debate that has not yet taken place but is long overdue.

I wish to acknowledge the work of the editors, Alex Ding and Laetitia Monbec, for their work on this volume, for the monthly meetings with contributors and for the editorial support that they provided. However, above all, I acknowledge the work of those who contributed each individual chapter. Your chapters are enlightening and make a great contribution to the field of EAP. Creating this volume has not been an easy process for all involved, but it has been an extremely worthwhile one, and one that begins important conversations that need to continue.

Ian Bruce
On behalf of the series editors

References

Ding, A. and I. Bruce (2017), *The English for Academic Purposes Practitioner*, Cham, Switzerland: Palgrave Macmillan.

Hadley, G. (2015), *English for Academic Purposes in Neoliberal Universities: A Critical Grounded Theory*, Heidelberg: Springer.

Acknowledgements

We would like to thank all the authors who contributed to this volume. They were generous with their time to share, discuss and help each other. We would also like to thank our family, friends and colleagues who showed an interest and encouraged us in our work.

INTRODUCTION

Alex Ding

On hearing that there is yet another publication on identity and agency one could and should expect a collective shrug of indifference. Applied linguistics and TESOL (and many other fields too) are saturated with publications exploring agency and identity, perhaps to the point where the impact and rewards of publishing for authors far outweigh any benefit for readers. The frequency of reading 'agency' and 'identity' has a potentially numbing effect, and any potential these terms may have had in any given publication for providing insights, novelty or leading to educational transformations risks being buried in an ever-growing pile of publications.

The sheer number of publications is not the only issue to contend with: there is also the matter of the myopic theoretical hegemony within applied linguistics and TESOL to contend with. Theories of identity and agency are, inevitably, largely parasitical on existing (and past) debates and frameworks drawn from philosophy, politics and social theory. However, rather than suggesting a plethora of richly diverse theoretical sources and inspiration taken from elsewhere, two associated theories dominate research: post-structuralism and postmodernism. Identity and agency are largely reworkings and reiterations of post-structural and postmodern theories and, to use a post-structural trope, operate as theoretical hegemony in discourse on identity and agency and thus potentially censor other promising avenues of research. One is repeatedly informed that identities, for example, are *dynamic, multiple, negotiated, shifting, conflicting, situated, unstable* (see Gladjo, 2016: 5, Cheng et al., 2014: xvi, and Varghese et al., 2005: 22–3 for typical examples of this). Not only are these words almost obligatory when discussing identity, the focus of much of the research in this area tends to focus on race, gender and sexual orientation. Applied linguists have spent considerably less energy on investigating social class (Block, 2014). *Scholastic fallacy* may go some way to explain this:

> An important aspect of researcher's life stories and trajectories is their middle-class condition, it is not surprising that there is often a tendency to impose on a view of the world that emanates from and reflects middle class position ... This means that when focusing on identity, as a lot of applied linguists have done in recent years, there is a strong tendency to focus on issues around gender, race, religion, and sexuality because these are dimensions of identity that are

most salient to applied linguists in their daily lives and middle-class people in multicultural societies. (Block, 2014: 170)

The refusal to see or consider fully the economic and material conditions of identity and agency and instead focus on specific features of identity chimes too with a focus on recognition at the expense of redistribution:

> Recognition at the level of discourse and attitudes is of course important, but it is not enough, and at worst may be tokenistic. It is easy for the dominant to grant discursive recognition and civility to the dominated or socially excluded; giving up some of their money and other advantages to them another matter. (Sayer, 2005: 64)

Identity, conceived in applied linguistics and TESOL, because of its debt to post-structuralism and postmodernism, is more a paralogical impulse *against identity*. To counteract claims of essentialism, ever finer demarcations and distinguishing features of identity are sought to capture the experience of a given group, leading to ever-diminishing group affiliations and ever-increasing incommensurate identities and voice. This has the effect of dissolving groups to individuals and weakening social ties and political solidarity. It is no surprise that post-structuralism and postmodernism are highly congruent with neoliberalism and individualism, and it is no coincidence that both have flourished at the same moment. An attendant risk in research on agency and identity lies in hermeneutic narcissism where 'knowledge claims shrink into ever-decreasing circles, leading to authors telling us only about themselves, for they feel unable to tell us anything about anyone else' (Maton, 2003: 55). Worse, there is a risk that

> the privileged always make an effort to point out their own unprivileged features and elevate them above all those many other aspects on the basis of which they would have to consider themselves privileged. Here, a potential truth becomes ideological as a result of being used to conceal many other truths that are perceived as being embarrassing. One seeks to realign one's own alleged moral misalignment as a privileged individual in a narcissistic way through self-imagination as victim. (Pfaller, 2022: 38)

Presented in this way, these are not promising antecedents for this volume. Yet, one of the peculiarities of EAP as a discipline is that there has been so little interest historically in the practitioner although there is a growing but still very small number of accounts of EAP agency and identity. How can this rather remarkable historical lack of interest in the EAP practitioner be accounted for? And how can a much more recent, if still minor, interest be explained? And can EAP, as a field, perhaps take heed of some of the shortcomings of the bloated research on identity and agency in applied linguistics and forge ahead with more productive and innovative accounts of identity and agency?

The historical lack of interest in the practitioner is discussed in some detail in Chapter 1 (Ding and Monbec), but it is worth making a few comments here. Historically, the ideational domain of EAP has been (and still is) dominated by researchers who, by and large, have, through journals such as the *Journal of English for Academic Purposes*, focussed their attention on academic communication, texts and genre. Because practitioners lack cultural capital, resources and time (but may also resist the call to contribute to scholarship), their interests and concerns struggle to reach a readership and impact or interest the field. Largely, but not wholly, erased from the ideational domain, it is as if practitioners are simply classroom executors of theories and research drawn from the discipline. However, Hadley's (2015) landmark publication on EAP managers within neoliberal universities triggered a small but significant shift to interest in the lives of practitioners. His characterization of 'professional disarticulation' to signal professional anomie was timely. My premise is that recent interest in identity and agency in EAP is an articulation of threats to the self and group. In other words, concern about practitioner identity and agency has emerged through *crisis*. This may seem counter-intuitive as EAP *as a discipline* 'has done a good job of consolidating a position at the forefront of language education' (Hyland, 2012: 30) with all the 'paraphernalia of journals, monographs, conferences, and research centres: all the trappings, in fact, of a full-fledged educational practice' (Hyland, 2018: 389). One can discern too a current within EAP where there is a pride in its perceived applied, pragmatic, business-oriented nature, focussing on students' needs and texts and a reticence to engage with politics, identity and agency, especially, but not uniquely, by those who perceive the field as congruent with their capitals, expectations, successes, recognition and opportunities. Yet there is also a disconcerting undercurrent:

> [F]rom its outset, it [EAP] has accepted the role as an economic and intellectual short-cut . . . [i]t seems that maximum throughput of students with minimum attainment levels in the language in the shortest possible time was the conceptual framework within which EAP was conceived. (Turner, 2004: 96–7)

This led Hadley to describe EAP centres as 'student processing units' (Hadley, 2015: 39). My argument is that there is a growing existential unease within the field of practice and among a growing number of practitioners regarding the status of the profession and a sense of lack of value, reward and recognition within and beyond EAP as well as practitioners having to grapple with the purposes of their practices within neoliberal regimes of avaricious profit extraction from their endeavours. The stark realization and reality for many in the UK and similar contexts is that EAP, *for practitioners and as a practice*, would barely exist without neoliberal education policies and practices. This uncomfortable truth emphasizes that EAP is essential to a neoliberal university but certainly not of its essence. This explains, in a reductive way no doubt, the emergence of crisis among a growing number of practitioners and a growing interest in agency and identity. However, one of the purposes of this volume is to correct what seems like a universal assertion of professional anomie due to nefarious neoliberal policies and instead to render the ideational domain less parochial by acknowledging that these concerns are not shared everywhere nor in the same way and, as such, we hope to engender greater solidarity and understanding for practitioners across contexts and microcosms whatever the challenges they face.

One could characterize the field of EAP as in transition from *collective amnesia* to *anamnesis*. Anamnesis conjures the idea of both reminiscence/recalling and of a medical case history. Anamnesis in the field offers practitioners the first steps to a rupture with the unsaid, the unthought thought, the implicit, the doxas that permeate the field and then trigger resistance to domination, orthodoxy and injustices. What binds all the chapters in this book, despite their many differences, is their contribution to a *collective anamnesis*. Underpinning all the chapters in this volume, perhaps very obliquely in some cases, is the fundamental existential and ethical imperative to account for professional anomie through examining who we are as agents in the field and where we might have some freedom or agency to resist or transform. Who we are is a 'matter of what we care about most and the commitments we make accordingly' (Archer, 2003: 120). This collective anamnesis reveals the existential danger of a rupture between self-worth and social identity with the potential consequence of alienated practitioners becoming 'passive executors of minimalistic and enforceable expectation' (Archer, 2000: 304).

Much that is significant in the lives of practitioners never reaches the pages of a book; much of what impacts practitioners remains unwritten. There are fears and taboos in what should be in the public domain. To exemplify this, I want to briefly mention how I came to ask Laetitia Monbec to co-edit this volume. I knew Laetitia Monbec's work and respected her contribution to EAP. However, what prompted me to contact her was a social media post by someone who had some social capital within EAP in the UK but who was seemingly unaware of having little capital beyond. The post was an ill-tempered reaction to an article authored by a UK-based practitioner. Two reactions came to mind; firstly, the critique was not directed at the author but rather at Laetitia Monbec as the author of a cited work. Secondly, the attack was highly personal suggesting that Laetitia Monbec had no right or status to comment on the field, a positioning both appalling and ludicrous to Laetitia and the many practitioners in her part of the world. Myopic, parochial, personal and ill-informed as it was, it is just one example, more visible admittedly, of what occurs in the field everyday but generally goes unrecorded. This is a reminder that the field of EAP, like all fields, is a social arena where politics, power, domination, legitimacy, status, ambition and recognition are integral to the field and the everyday lives of practitioners. This episode not only prompted me to collaborate with Laetitia Monbec on this volume, but it also motivated me to ensure that the authors selected to contribute to this volume were not chosen because of social capital, status or power but, rather, what they could contribute to the volume.

We have organized this volume in two sections. The first, 'Mesocosms', consists of three chapters that we have positioned here because they offer a wide lens on agency and identity and also because they offer, we believe, innovative accounts that will disrupt reader expectations. Moreover, combined, these three chapters also offer lens or frameworks through which the chapters in the second part, 'Microcosms', can be read, analysed or critiqued.

'Mesocosms' opens with a very lengthy chapter by Ding and Monbec entitled 'A Socio-Analysis of English for Academic Purposes'. In this chapter we undertake a socio-analysis of EAP by operationalizing concepts taken from Bourdieu. In particular, we focus on a reflexive account of the field and its agents, and our ambition is to effect a *metanoia*, a transformation of how we see the field of EAP; to repudiate past practices and doxas; to adopt a new gaze and to break with illusio. We identified three key research questions, focussing on the historical, social and cultural determinants which have traditionally been valued and have shaped different positioning in the field; the types, volume and configuration of capital characterize EAP practitioners; and how practitioners perceive and explain their positions in the field. From these questions, we collected data through a survey and analysis of publicly available documents. Our results focus on analysis of practitioners' backgrounds, language(s), qualifications, scholarship, funding, editorial roles and roles within the academy. We continue with a historical analysis of the beginnings of EAP and identify the high priests, missionaries and diplomats before moving on to exploring the minor prophets and heretics in the field. Our research finishes with a short discussion of practitioners' ethics.

Chapter 2, 'Collegial Connections and Ethical Entanglements: An Exploration of the Ethics of Scholarship in EAP', by Bee Bond, connects theoretical considerations with the reality of EAP scholarship and practice. Using a case study, she explores the ethical reflexivity required in scholarship when the practices and people under investigation are tightly woven into the professional life and identity of the researcher, and when the participants are also co-researchers and colleagues within the same institution. Power dynamics and differing perceptions of power, agency and identity within an EAP unit reveal issues and conflicts around practitioner identity, leadership and professional hierarchies.

Chapter 3, 'EAP Practitioners in the Global South: Participation, Positioning and Agency in the Context of "Peripheral" Scholars and Scholarship', by Namala Lakshmi Tilakaratna, argues that, while existing research in the field has provided eloquent and important critiques of EAP scholarship in the West and raises questions about how and why scholars from the 'Global South' are excluded from academic publishing and research, these studies can be critiqued for 'knowledge blindness' or a lack of systematic engagement with knowledge practices. Drawing on the dimension of Specialization from Legitimation Code Theory to uncover the underlying principles of knowledge practices presents an important opportunity to examine how periphery practitioners engage with the theory/practitioner dichotomy in EAP, institutional challenges in contexts beyond the hegemonic West and how they engage with being positioned as 'peripheral' and 'marginalized' in debates and discussions with centre scholarship.

Part II, 'Microcosms', opens with two chapters by authors from Pakistan and Zimbabwe respectively. The first, Chapter 4, 'EAP Practitioners' Agency and Identity: From Social Class to Social Capital', by Tanzeela Anbreen and Samina

Ayub, offers a powerful account, drawing on Bourdieu, of the role of social capital in the lives of EAP practitioners in Pakistan. They argue that social class in the context of Pakistan is important as it contributes to inculcating various characteristics among the members and these same characteristics impact practitioners' understanding of who they are. Using Bourdieu's notion of field, capital and habitus, they explore the impact of previous education on the working lives of the privileged and less privileged practitioners.

In Chapter 5, 'Trials and Tribulations of EAP Practitioners in Zimbabwe', Tambawoga C. Muchena employs an autoethnographic approach, triangulated with questionnaires and content analysis, to explore the identity and predicaments of EAP practitioners in Zimbabwe. EAP practitioners' lives within the academic terrain are explored using the Specialization dimension of Legitimation Code Theory. EAP practitioners, with varied social backgrounds and divergent educational interests, tend to be dominated by the academic field despite having similar contracts and promotion routes as other academics.

In Chapter 6, '"Be More Pirate": Harnessing the Power of Liminal Spaces in Creating Academic Literacy Practitioner Identity and Agency', Michelle Joubert and Sherran Clarence explore the marginalized field of EAP in South African higher education, where practitioners are typically positioned within the periphery due to a misrecognition of the value of EAP to student learning. The focus of their chapter is on the ways in which practitioners work out how to, in effect, be (or not be) pirates – working out their role and identity in conversation with their environment and with themselves, their goals and ambitions.

In Chapter 7, 'Finding Space and Voice: Duoethnographic Exploration of Teacher Agency in EAP', Ania Rolińska and Iwona Winiarska-Pringle investigate two EAP practitioners' lived experience of transitioning to EAP scholarship and English for specific academic purposes (ESAP) teaching through the lens of agency. Focussing on time, space and caring collaborations as potentially determining factors, this chapter discusses agentic successes and failures in the context of becoming an EAP scholar and an ESAP teacher.

In Chapter 8, Sarah Taylor asks the question, 'Respected Teachers or a Marginalized, Stigmatized Profession? An Exploration of UK EAP Practitioner Identity'. She examines data from interviews with EAP practitioners in the UK in an attempt to understand how EAP practitioners may construct their identities in response to positioning labels, such as 'tutor', 'support service' and so on, whereby they may perceive their identities as stigmatized. Using symbolic interactionist theories, she examines how practitioners 'manage impressions' when discussing their identities as a means of effecting agency.

In Chapter 9, 'EAP Teacher Agency in a Digital Age', Blair Matthews investigates the agency of five EAP teachers relating to technology, observing its emergence from an assemblage of technical objects, practices and discourses. He argues there is a need to decentre humans and see our natural state as being together, embedded in complex relations, all of which condition how we engage in certain practices. His chapter brings to the fore the complex relations of technology and agency.

In Chapter 10, '"Changing Lanes": Balancing between Roles of EAP Teacher and Researcher in a Teaching Institution towards a Research University', Eric Cheung focusses on the EAP lecturers in a Hong Kong university changing to the 'research lane' branching from the teaching track. Lecturers reflected on their precarious, complex and liminal identities in the college and critiqued the influence of an increasingly 'managerial' institutional culture on teaching and research, in response to the significant changes that they experienced at the personal, collegiate and institutional levels. Claiming scholarly identities, seeking alignment and collaboration with the broader academic community, finding meanings of research in their EAP teaching careers and personal dispositions such as determination, passion and resilience are considered key in achieving some success in challenging circumstances.

In Chapter 11, 'Responding to Students' Disciplinary Writing in a University-Wide Writing Requirement: Negotiating Agency through Positioning', Shari Dureshahwar Lughmani and Svetlana Chigaeva-Heddad explore how teacher agency is defined by institutional policies, expectations and constraints in a Hong Kong university and how it is exercised within the context of this highly standardized and regulated programme. Despite the contextual constraints and a general feeling of limited agency among language teachers, they exercise some agency from various given, negotiated or contested positions.

'Power and the Canadian EAP Practitioner: Multiethnography as Resistance?', by James N. Corcoran, Jennifer J. MacDonald, Jonathan Mendelsohn and Leonardo Gomes, concludes Part II. Their study adopts a critical storytelling approach that considers four practitioners' experiences working across Canadian institutions of higher education with an eye towards better understanding how they navigate an educational sector perceived as rife with precarity and marginalization and with an interest in reconciling social structures with EAP practitioners' perceived professional agency. Their aims are to better understand the material conditions of EAP practitioners and challenge asymmetrical social relations of power in Canadian EAP.

In the conclusion, Laetitia Monbec provides some final thoughts on the volume.

References

Archer, M. S. (2000), *Being Human: The Problem of Agency*, Cambridge: Cambridge University Press.

Archer, M. S. (2003), *Structure, Agency and the Internal Conversation*, Cambridge: Cambridge University Press.

Block, D. (2014), *Social Class in Applied Linguistics*, London: Routledge.

Cheng, Y. L., S. B. Said and K. Park (2014), 'Expanding the Horizon of Research in Language Teacher Identity', in Y. L. Cheng et al. (eds), *Advances and Current Trends in Language Teacher Identity Research*, xv–xxi, Abingdon: Routledge.

Glodjo, T. (2016), 'Deconstructing Social Class Identity and Teacher Privilege in the Second Language Classroom', *TESOL Journal*, 8 (2): 342–66.

Hadley, G. (2015), *English for Academic Purposes in Neoliberal Universities: A Critical Grounded Theory*, Heidelberg: Springer.

Hyland, K. (2012), 'The Past is the Future with the Lights On: Reflections on AELFE's 20th Birthday', *Iberica*, 42: 29–42.

Hyland, K. (2018), 'Sympathy for the Devil? A Defence of EAP', *Language Teaching*, 51 (3): 383–99.

Maton, K. (2003), 'Reflexivity, Relationism and Research: Pierre Bourdieu and the Epistemic Conditions of Social Scientific Knowledge', *Space and Culture*, 6 (1): 52–65.

Pfaller, R. (2022), 'The Dubious Wonder of Identity', in E. L. Lange and J. Pickett-Depaolis (eds), *The Conformist Rebellion: Marxist Critiques of the Contemporary Left*, 25–42, London: Rowman and Littlefield.

Sayer, A. (2005), *The Moral Significance of Class*, Cambridge: Cambridge University Press.

Turner, J. (2004), 'Language as Academic Purpose', *Journal of English for Academic Purposes*, 3: 95–109.

Varghese, M., B. Morgan, B. Johnston and K. A. Johnson (2005), 'Theorizing Language Teacher Identity: Three Perspectives and Beyond', *Journal of Language Identity and Education*, 4 (1): 21–44.

Part I

MESOCOSMS

Chapter 1

A SOCIO-ANALYSIS OF ENGLISH FOR ACADEMIC PURPOSES

Alex Ding and Laetitia Monbec

Introduction

The practitioner in the field: From ephemeral concern to disarticulation

Throughout the history of EAP, interest in EAP practitioners and their concerns, conditions of practices, struggles, status, identities, trajectories, development and agency, in the ideational domain at least, can be characterized as sporadic, marginal, ephemeral, fleeting and largely invisible. One can point to fleeting glimpses of disquiet – rather than systematic investigation – as early as Johns (1981), Ewer (1983), Raimes (1991) and Robinson (1991) where concerns were raised about the status of practitioners and their neglected developmental needs. From these early signs of disquiet within the field, sporadic and unsystematic commentaries and small-scale studies continued, with a small number of publications exploring the vexed question of credentials and qualifications to teach EAP (cf. Erray and Ansell, 2001; Krzanowski, 2001; Roberts, 2001). Alongside these studies, the question of transitioning into EAP from 'General English' emerged as a minor theme in the field (cf. Campion, 2016; Elsted, 2012; Martin, 2014; Post, 2010) as did intermittent comments and concerns on the affective challenges for practitioners working with unfamiliar disciplines, practices and texts (cf. Strevens, 1988; Hyland, 2012), summed up as 'reluctant dwellers in a strange and unchartered land' (Hutchinson and Waters, 1987: 152).

Despite these and a few other glimpses of disquiet within the field of EAP, Belcher's claim that the 'community that ESP professionals know the least about is their own' (Belcher, 2013: 544) remains true for much of the history of EAP. Ding and Bruce (2017) characterized the marginalization of the interests and concerns of the practitioner as a

> lacuna [that is] is symptomatic of the continued marginalisation of practitioners both within their own discipline and beyond in the academic community where the consequences are material (in terms of status, recognition, and power). (Ding and Bruce, 2017: 117)

However, despite continued marginalization of the practitioner, Hadley's 2015 landmark publication *English for Academic Purposes in Neoliberal Universities: A Critical Grounded Theory* signalled a small but noticeable shift within the field. His striking expression of 'professional disarticulation' to characterize a collective *anomie* among practitioners within the field serves as a trope and a trigger that frame many subsequent publications by, about and for the practitioner. Although these subsequent publications represent a still fragmented and marginal body of work and are still overshadowed by an ever-increasing and increasingly esoteric body of work exploring largely textual features of academic communication, they do, nonetheless, indicate a growing and critical interest in practitioners. This also provides a useful second indication: the field of practitioners is largely subservient and submissive to the disciplinary interests of EAP. Indeed, one can point to a rupture or disjunction (Ding, 2022) where the disciplinary field – revealing its own scholastic bias and doxas – has little interest and concern for the practitioner and practice, including pedagogy (cf. Bruce, 2021; Cheng, 2019; Swales, 2019).

Ding and Bruce (2017) offered the first systematic account of the agency and identity of practitioners; the marginalization of practitioners and the structural neoliberal forces that shape and constrain their practices and development; the struggles to define an academic identity with sufficient cultural capital to exercise power in academia; and the fight against the encroachment of commercialization and profit-seeking in EAP. Disarticulation is also visible, for example, in attempts to locate EAP in a liminal third space (cf. MacDonald, 2016); a critique of the development and education of practitioners (Ding and Campion, 2016); accounts of the many challenges for practitioners of undertaking and publishing their scholarship and research (Davis, 2019 and Webster, 2022); attempts to analyse practitioner status (cf. Bell, 2021); an analysis of power within the field of practitioners (Flowerdew, 2019); an exploration of practitioner identity within neoliberal universities (Ding, 2019); an attempt to operationalize Bourdieu's concept of field in EAP (Ding, 2022); and critical analyses of the roles associations could or should play in the material and ideational struggles of practitioners (Ding and Bruce, 2022 and Ding, Bond and Bruce, 2022). The Bloomsbury Series 'New Perspectives for English for Academic Purposes' with edited volumes published on social theory (Ding and Evans, 2022), politics and policy (Bruce and Bond, 2022) and this volume on identity and agency are all testimony to this increased focus on making sense of professional disarticulation. Further evidence can be found in the British Association of Lecturers of English for Academic Purposes (BALEAP) conference held at the University of Leeds in 2019 where the theme was the practitioner, and it can also be found in a growing number of critical PhDs exploring aspects of the practitioner.

Practitioner disarticulation could be better characterized or translated as hysteresis where

> practices are always liable to incur negative sanctions when the environment with which they are objectively confronted is too distant from that in which they are objectively fitted. (Bourdieu and Passeron, 1977: 78)

This brings us to the purpose and theoretical framing of this chapter: to employ concepts and tools from Bourdieu to provide a socio-analysis of the practitioner field of EAP thereby extending previous practitioner studies and accounting for practitioner hysteresis. In this chapter, we begin with a discussion of socio-analysis, what it entails and what it promises for those undertaking a socio-analysis of a field. We continue with a discussion of field and how field is central to socio-analysis and the whole sociological enterprise of Bourdieu. We then narrow the discussion to analysing the key features of the field of EAP. From this analysis of the field, we then identify three key research questions that inform our socio-analysis of EAP. In our methodology section we describe how we operationalized our socio-analysis drawing mainly on Bourdieu and on critical discourse analysis. Our results focus on analysis of practitioners' backgrounds, language(s), qualifications, scholarship, funding, editorial roles and roles within the academy. We continue with a historical analysis of the beginnings of EAP and identify the high priests, missionaries and diplomats before moving on to exploring the minor prophets and heretics in the field. Our research section finishes with a short discussion of practitioners' ethics. Our chapter concludes with some final remarks outlining where we hope to pursue further research to add further substance to our socio-analysis of EAP.

Elements of socio-analysis

To undertake this socio-analysis, we first have to reveal a number of counter-intuitive precepts that inform, direct and motivate our analysis. These are anything but axiomatic, and in keeping with the spirit of Bourdieu (if not the letter) one of our ambitions is to effect a *metanoia* (see Bourdieu and Wacquant, 1992, and Grenfell, 2023, for a discussion of metanoia): a transformation of how we see the field of EAP; to repudiate past practices and *doxas*; to adopt a new gaze; and to break with *illusio* – 'the enchanted circle of collective denial' (Bourdieu, 2000a: 5). Our rhetorical strategy is to 'twist the screw the other way' (Bourdieu, 1990: 53) in order 'to emphasise the truth very strongly' (Bourdieu, 2000a: 173) and by doing so we hope there is

> [a] small chance of knowing what game we play and of minimizing the ways in which we are manipulated by the forces of the field in which we evolve . . . [Sociology] allows us to discern the sites where we do indeed enjoy a degree of freedom and those where we do not. (Bourdieu and Wacquant, 1992: 198–9)

Socio-analysis *as metanoia* is triggered first by a sense of crisis – a 'disruption between the habitus of a social agent and his location in the field' (Frangie, 2009: 218) – and this leads to a break with common-sense beliefs and assumptions about the field. Socio-analysis is above all a never-ending *collective reflexive practice*, and it is equally a remedy to crisis. It is a way of grounding and enacting collective *reflexivity* which 'aims at discovering the historical and field-dependent social influences that coalesce to form the individual specific habitus' (Frangie, 2009:

220). Identification of the features and mechanisms of field crises then enables practitioners to intervene in the field to contain, resist or mitigate domination. Reflexivity, as enacted through socio-analysis, endangers shattering the very *illusio* of the field (Bourdieu, 2000a: 12) and risks disillusionment with feelings of, for example, 'blighted hope' or 'frustrated promise' (Bourdieu, 1984: 150). However, through reflexivity, limitations to knowledge production can be revealed in three aspects: social position, the field and the *scholastic* point of view where 'the social and political unconscious [is] embedded in analytical tools and operations' (Bourdieu and Wacquant, 1992: 36). Socio-analysis aims at identifying and challenging the social and political unconscious that undermines the objectivity of knowledge. Reflexivity, through socio-analysis, is a collective investment (itself a form of *illusio*) which emerges through institutionalizing reflexivity in processes of training, dialogue and critical evaluation (Bourdieu and Wacquant, 1992: 40). Reflexivity therefore becomes part of the *habitus* of the social scientist and part of the cognitive system of the agent. As such, what is transformed is both the habitus of the field agents and, as importantly, if not more, the social organization of the field itself. This transformation must focus on and be set against the *doxas* in the field: 'a set of fundamental beliefs which do not even need to be asserted in the form of an explicit, self-conscious dogma' (Bourdieu, 2000a: 16), and by doing so reflexively we can break with 'the enchanted circle of collective denial' (Bourdieu, 2000a: 5).

Identifying the *illusio* of the field, why and how practitioners are 'taken in and by the game' (Bourdieu and Wacquant, 1992: 116), what makes investing in a field 'worth the candle' and what gives agents a 'feel for the game' (Bourdieu, 1998: 76), is key to socio-analysis. *Illusio* is

> the enchanted relation to a game that is a product of a relation of ontological complicity between mental structures and the objectives structures of social space... games which matter to you are important and interesting because they have been imposed and introduced in your mind, in your body, in a form called the feel for the game. (Bourdieu, 1998: 77)

Yet, it should be clear to readers that the moment one stops to think about what *illusio* might be in the field of EAP this task is far from easy not least because our own investments, habitus and interests tend to lead us to define the field in ways that promote our own interests/position in the field. Socio-analysis requires the difficult task of confronting and acknowledging the desire to impose the definition of the profession most favourable to what we are (Bourdieu, 2000a: 158). In addition, what are viable and visible as options within a field depends on our current (objective) position in a field and the histories that we bring to the field. Combined with a scholastic fallacy (Bourdieu, 1990) produced in academic space where understanding is theoretical in nature – 'made possible by the situation of skholè, of leisure' (Bourdieu, 1990: 381) in which we 'forbid ourselves to understand practice as such' (Bourdieu, 1990: 382) – we risk confusing things of logic for the logic of things. These risks and obstacles to socio-analysis are compounded as it is more apt to speak of *collusio* (Bourdieu, 2007: 7; 2000a: 145) entailing a collective complicity in a shared purpose and investment.

Buried beneath this notion of *illusio* lies an important, and universal, philosophical/anthropological statement that can explain the profound power, impact and hold of *illusio*. Bourdieu (2000a: 239) – highly influenced by Blaise Pascal's *Pensées* (1670) – asserts that man is 'haunted' because 'he is a being without reason'; he knows that he is mortal, and knowledge of this is unbearable. Because there is no inherent meaning to life, humans must search for and find their own meaning and this is to be found *in the world* (see Atkinson, 2020: 42–3, for a discussion of this issue). And this is why investment and *illusio* are so important: fields give meaning and purpose to life and not only this, through struggles within fields to establish power, to transform or preserve a field, agents can accrue symbolic capital: that is, 'glory, honour, credit, reputation, fame – the principle of an egotistical quest for satisfactions of *amour propre*, which is, at the same time, a fascinated pursuit of the approval of others' (Bourdieu, 2000a: 166). The approval or recognition from others gives 'reasons for being. It is capable of giving meaning to life' (Bourdieu, 2000a: 240). Conversely, 'there is no worse dispossession, no worse privation, perhaps, than that of the losers in the symbolic struggle for recognition, for access to a socially recognised social being, in a word, to humanity' (Bourdieu, 2000a). The stakes are high in all fields and for all their agents. And this can in some ways explain why *disarticulation* is such a powerful metaphor for the field of EAP and its practitioners.

We have evoked metanoia, hysteresis, *illusio*, reflexivity, habitus, doxas, power, recognition, legitimation and symbolic capital, all drawn from Bourdieu's lexis and concepts, and all these terms are burdened with underlying (and often crypto-) ethical and normative critique. Despite Bourdieu's own ambivalence around ethics (see Wacquant, 1989: 14) and the widespread disagreement on Bourdieu's ethical and political engagement(s) and its relationship to his work (see Pellandini-Simányi (2014) for a useful summary of this discussion), our desire, through socio-analysis, is 'to reveal the sacred as profane' (Maton, 2005: 102) and as such not only to contribute to a more truthful and scientific account of the field of EAP for its practitioners but also to reveal the forms of injustices and domination inherent in the field and thereby enable an informed resistance to dominant forces and contribute to the transformation of the field by its practitioners. This is why we wish to twist the screw the other way: our ultimate concern is with the ethics of knowledge, the field and its agents.

The field

In socio-analysis the primary focus is on the field:

> the characteristics of a field are: it is a structured social space; it contains agents (people[1] and institutions) who dominate and who are dominated; the field is a permanent relationship of inequality; field agents struggle to transform or preserve the field; all agents harness the powers they have in this

struggle; and power defines agents' positions in the field and their strategies. (Ding, 2022: 157)

What draws agents to a particular field is an expectation of obtaining the 'highest profit' based on their habitus and their own configuration of capitals (Bourdieu, 1996) and if habitus and field align, practitioners achieve 'subjective expectations of objective probabilities' (Bourdieu, 1990: 59). This makes both believing and participating in the game worth the candle. But agents are also drawn to a field because of the field *illusio* that presupposes and promises an ethos, values and normative orientation. Fields are laden with ethical doxas and *illusio* that promise rewards and recognition and fulfilling aspirations but also they are arenas for (widespread) 'blighted hope' or 'frustrated promise' (Bourdieu, 1984: 150).

In Bourdieu's work the struggle for power and legitimating power through accruing various forms of field-dependent capital (cultural, social and economic) combine to give symbolic capital and power to specific agents and institutions, that is, a recognition, a distinction and a 'socially recognized authority to act' (Swartz, 2013: 102) upon agents in the field.

> Symbolic capital enables forms of domination which imply dependence on those who can be dominated by it, since it only exists through the esteem, recognition, belief, credit, confidence of others, and can only be perpetuated so long as it succeeds in obtaining belief in its existence. (Bourdieu, 2000a: 166)

This socially recognized authority to act, built on struggles between agents, relies on the achievements and qualities valued and imposed within the field. In other words, there is an ethical evaluation attached to recognition, esteem, credit and having the confidence of others. Once values are introduced, and one could argue that they are foundational for all fields, then, necessarily, there are certain consequences. The first is that there is a hierarchy of values – for every distinction there is a corresponding vulgarity, 'for every form of the sacred has its profane complement' (Bourdieu, 1990: 196.), and this includes hierarchies of competing ethos and ethics in the field.

With the struggles to establish and maintain domination and legitimation within a field and the attendant symbolic power and capital that come with domination (temporary – as all fields are dynamic), there are also agents who are dominated within fields. Lacking in sufficient capitals, or the right configuration of capitals, there are agents who do not have enough (perceived) value and power to impose their values and practices. These dominated agents risk suffering a 'sense of incompetence, failure or cultural unworthiness' (Bourdieu, 1984: 389).

Antagonism within all fields is between orthodoxy and heresy. The struggle is between conservation and domination on one side and heresy, rupture, subversion and critique on the other (Bourdieu, 1996: 234). As such, values, ethics and politics may be harnessed to either preserve or transform a field. Bourdieu (2000a: xvii–xviii) makes the striking counter-intuitive claim that it is *not* 'political stances which determine people's stances on things academic, but it is their positions within the academic field which inform the stances that they adopt on political issues in general as well as on academic problems'. This complicates a potentially simplistic analysis where one might be tempted to see only abstracted/decontextualized ethical discourses and positions within fields and not to see the interests invested in these positions and discourses.[2] We may object that we sincerely believe that our (pre-) dispositions, propensities and inclinations – *habitus* – drive our actions within a field and these may be driven by values, for example, to accrue epistemic capital (knowing and knowledge have intrinsic value) or, for example, to be the best practitioner or teacher for our students, but, *objectively*, this (apparent) *disinterestedness* is also a means to acquiring power (Pellandini-Simányi, 2014). Rather than concluding that all actions and values are simply strategies in a cynical game for distinction and power (which they may well be by some agents) we need to undertake a sociological account of fields, not to condemn or resign ourselves to playing a game without (ethical) value, but, rather, as Bourdieu has argued, the aim is to render the field more objective, scientific and truthful, to rectify practices that distort a field and to allow agents greater freedom to transform the field. In addition, an absence of socio-analysis has political and ethical consequences for fields and their agents in terms of reproducing social injustices:

> the blindness of intellectuals to the social forces which rule the intellectual field, and therefore their practices, is what explains that, collectively, often under very radical airs, the intelligentsia almost always contribute to the perpetuation of dominant forces. (Wacquant, 1989: 18)

The field of EAP

Having initially explored the growing but still marginal concern for the practitioner in the ideational domain, from initial fleeting asides on the status of practitioners to a growing sense of disarticulation and hysteresis, and then having discussed the motivation and reasons for undertaking a socio-analysis of the field of EAP, we now turn our attention to a closer examination of the field of EAP.

Our first precept is the assertion that EAP is an ill-defined field and, as such, this may enable great(er) lucidity for practitioners. Bourdieu characterizes an ill-defined field as:

> Because these posts ill-defined and ill-guaranteed but open and 'full of potential' as the phrase goes, leave their occupants the possibility of defining them by bringing the embodied necessity which is constitutive of their habitus, their future depends on what is made of them by their occupants, or at least those of them who, in the struggles with the 'profession' and in confrontations with neighbouring and rival professions, manage to impose the definition of the profession most favourable to what they are. (Bourdieu, 2000a: 158)

Blighted hope and frustrated promise are also likely to feature in the field of EAP: being an ill-defined field (Ding, 2022), where the rules and rewards of the game as well as access, credentials and capitals are nebulous and contested and are as likely to lead to a sense of confusion as lucidity where practitioners feel dissonance between their dispositions and the demands of their positions. Each position in a field is also a perspective on the field, and it can be difficult for agents to see the world and other agents within it from a different vantage point than their own. Dominant agents then can see their position as being fully, meritocratically deserved and see the dominated as justly awarded for their (lesser or less valuable) abilities (Bhopal and Myers, 2023: 47). This is true for those who benefit from the field's existing structure and legitimation systems and may perceive this advantage as a natural state of things which happens to value their capital and comfort and fully justify their legitimacy.

In mapping the field of EAP, Ding (2022) begins with tracing the field's autonomy in relation to the broader field of higher education (HE), highlighting the uncomfortable relation between EAP and the neoliberal push to increase internationalization as a means to finance universities. This in turn relegates EAP to a dominated position within higher education serving the avaricious university and influences the rules of the game both within EAP and in its relation to other, more powerful, fields. Ding argues that while some scholars within EAP align with traditional academic research fields (with accompanying symbolic capital such as publications, research activities, academic titles, funding, social capital, etc.), practitioners lack symbolic capital to impact the field. This is partly due to EAP being an ill-defined field which sees a number of agents feeling dissonance between their dispositions and the demands of their positions. While many other academic fields are defined by clear entry requirements, EAP is vague in this respect (Ding and Bruce, 2017) and this reinforces a dominated, agentless position for practitioners in a HE field where cultural capital is key. Other characteristics of an ill-defined field as shown in EAP are the variety of location within the university, the titles, career trajectories, opportunities and agency all of which 'condemns EAP to the edge of academia' (Ding, 2022: 163). Managers in EAP are seen as equally ill-defined in terms of capital and do not seem to require more academic capital to occupy their position (although they undoubtedly accrue significant economic capital). In the UK context, partly drawing on Davis (2019), Ding also highlights serious hurdles to scholarship through hostile or unsupportive management as well as no material (time/resource) support.

Ding also describes linguistic and pedagogical (expertise in teaching) capital as part of EAP practitioners' habitus, drawing on their habitus as language educators (rather than academics, for example). This, he argues, has ambiguous consequences, because linguistic capital is contested, dismissed or simply misrecognized in higher education. When little is understood about language by agents in academia (including some or possibly many EAP practitioners), claiming linguistic capital can be counter-productive and can be associated with pointless formalism, problematic language ideologies and intellectual vacuousness (cf. Turner, 2004). The same is true of claiming legitimacy based on teaching expertise, when a short teaching qualification cannot give access to the prestigious positions and titles in teaching and learning centres which are awarded to academics with significant cultural and social capital rather than practitioners.

Collective habitus is also key to understanding the field of EAP as collective habitus implies mastery of a common code, '[a] sense of one's space but also a sense of the place of others' (Bourdieu, 1989: 19). Group habitus generates common-sense (and unthought) responses and actions in a specific context. It leads to a 'distinctive social identity' which shapes common dispositions and actions. Actions by agents are positively sanctioned if they conform to the logic of doxic practice. Dispositions, beliefs, tendencies and ethos (doxas and collusio) might be recognizable in EAP practitioners in different contexts, and, within the generic and somewhat abstract EAP practitioner group, there might be a very different collective habitus too, revealing that EAP practitioners are not a completely homogeneous group and heterodoxy is as much a part of the field as orthodoxy.

There are two questions we need to answer. One is to understand, through field analysis, the degree of agency that practitioners enjoy. The second is to find ways to move from this understanding of the patterns and tendencies in the field, in habitus and different valued capital to ways social change might be achieved. The objective relations that constitute a field are perceived by agents as independent from their intentions and will and are felt as opaque and uncontrollable. In fact, each position is associated with its own space of the possible: some agents sail upwind, while others have the wind in their sail, but many perceive this as the natural state of things. This state of things can be further legitimized by notions such as meritocracy. Agents have different structural weights, and so different impacts on the field (Bourdieu, 2022: 582). Some agents have more agency through their position and can act on the structure (and themselves), modify the constraints and change the structure in order to conquer or safeguard a dominant position. Ones who possess large volumes of capital can impose upon the logic of the field, for example controlling the cost of entry and excluding new entrants. Agency depends on agents' structural position. However, Bourdieu argues that agents in dominated positions still have some power, as existing in a field is to be capable of producing effects on this field, to cause reactions (Bourdieu, 2022: 590). In Olúfẹ́mi O Táíwò's words:

> Despite all our social programming, we can just do things. We can, to some extent at will, ignore what social structures have told us to do [. . .] We can do the thing that will be punished; we can ignore the potential reward, choose the smaller prize. Moreover, we can accept the rewards and the punishments without accepting the 'lessons' they are meant to teach us about who and what is worthy. (Táíwò, 2022: 101–2)

Based on the discussion above, our three research questions are:

1. What are the historical, social and cultural determinants which have traditionally been valued and have shaped different positioning in the field? In other words, what is the narrative of origin about EAP practitioners?

2. What types, volume and configuration of capital characterize EAP practitioners?
3. How do practitioners perceive and explain their positions in the field? What do they see as valuable or not?

Before moving on to the methods section we would like to make one final point. The process of raising awareness about these relations and legitimation mechanisms can be perceived as arrogant and hostile – a sacrilege (Bourdieu, 2007: 112). Bourdieu discusses this reservation in *Homo Academicus*, a book which turned his theoretical concepts on his own academic field and colleagues, and explains that this led him to keep the manuscript unpublished for years (for fear of consequences, and perhaps to wait until his capital had accrued sufficiently to make him professionally 'safe'). Like Bourdieu, we too 'have made no concessions in writing this chapter, but [we] trust that it bears no malice, for it comprises, as the reader will have guessed, a considerable proportion of self-analysis by proxy' (Bourdieu, 1988: xxvi).

Methodology

The study

We devised a mixed qualitative study to survey the field through an online questionnaire and publicly available information on various EAP actors. The field analysis we conducted lies within a critical discourse approach, specifically inspired by Fairclough (1995) and by Riesigl and Wodak's (2016) discourse-historical approach (DHA) in the sense that it is interdisciplinary – it combines sociological (Bourdieusian field theory) and linguistics tools to provide a historical perspective on some of the data. It relies on several data types, and it aims to serve a practical application. In his field analyses, Bourdieu collected similar data and applied a multi-correspondence analysis (MCA) statistical approach, which we could not do for lack of resources. We detail our approach below with the steps we adopted to operationalize Bourdieu's concepts.

Data and participants

The construction of a field representation is iterative and involves collecting a range of data about agents and institutions.

First, we paid attention to **publicly available texts** constructing the EAP practitioner identity, specifically important actors at the beginning of their careers ('luminaries') on various websites such as BALEAP, platforms such as uefap.net and in various publications such as blogs, obituaries and theses.

We also explored agents' practices and attitudes through an online **questionnaire** with a range of open-ended questions to access perceptions and understandings of professional values, trajectories, experience with scholarship and aspirations.

Following Bourdieu, part of the questionnaire also collected demographic and credential information to access indicators of the types, volume and configuration of various capitals. We used a *convenience sampling* survey approach and circulated the questionnaire online to colleagues and the wider community through professional mail lists, emails and Twitter. Forty-seven replied: twenty-seven women, seventeen men, and one non-binary. Of these forty-seven, only five answered from outside the UK: two in HE institutions in Kazakhstan, one in Saudi Arabia, one in Italy and one in South Korea. We also obtained ten Singapore-based responses. We kept the two data sets separate to identify any salient differences in both sub-fields.

Representativeness: the rich qualitative data we collected from the open-ended questions from this empirical sample enables us to approach the demographic details, professional situations, beliefs, dispositions and values of a non-negligible, if not necessarily representative, part of the population (Martin, 2017: 18).

Analysis and operationalizing Bourdieu

Thematic and theoretical analysis

Analysis of informational data collected on publicly available texts: we recorded qualifications, some indications of powerful roles in committees and professional associations, agents' specific capital and their symbolic capital (fame, global impact). We also conducted a discourse analysis of the representations of EAP to trace valued capital in the EAP practitioner, especially in the infancy of the field.

Questionnaire responses: the responses provided demographic information, linguistic background and a range of dispositions. We analysed the questionnaire data through open thematic coding to start with, and then through axiological coding, engaging an operationalization of Bourdieusian capital and habitus concepts. These concepts included, for example, embodied cultural capital in the form of linguistic background (diverse L1, diverse accents) and institutional cultural capital in the form of qualifications, awards and professional credentials. Indications of symbolic capital (academic power and prestige) took the form of membership in professional bodies, awards in teaching or scholarship, research supervision and academic production in terms of publications, editorial positions, h-indexes and consultation roles. Social capital took the form of connections to specific powerful communities, access to sub-groups and social relations.

The role of language

Bourdieu discussed language at length as key to social reproduction, a source of inequality in schooling for example, in publications such as *Language and Symbolic Power (1991)*. He sees language as social action and argues that 'the whole social structure is present in each interaction (and thereby in the discourse uttered)' (1991: 67). In Bourdieu's work, language is key to the symbolic representation of the social world, a main mediator in social reproduction. Bourdieu also uses discourse analysis as a method (to supplement multi-correspondence analysis): in *Homo Academicus* (1988) for example he tracks linguistic indicators which reveal deep academic classifications, systems of perceptions and appreciations. He mostly focusses on *evaluative language* through *epithets* (clumsy, dull, sincere); *nuanced/restrictions of meaning* ('fluent but nervous delivery', 'conscientious but servile') (Bourdieu, 1988: 197–225); and *euphemisms* where negative evaluation is invoked and "intended for equals able to read between the lines" (1988: 209). These indicators are then cross-referenced with objective indicators of position in the field and social origins. Bourdieu argues that these classifications shape a mental schema which is 'generative of practice' (1988: 224).

To analyse the discursive data, we engaged in a detailed linguistic operationalization of Bourdieusian concepts grounded in a broad social theory of language and semiotics, including elements of systemic functional linguistics (SFL). Systemic functional linguistics offers a theoretical architecture which is well suited to exploring the discursive strategies actors employ to construct their self-representation and to legitimize their beliefs and their positions in the field (Hodge, 2017). Bourdieu's views on the social role of language are in several ways similar to systemicists' (Bartlett, 2014; see Hasan, 1998, for a discussion on this). SFL sees language as social action and theorizes context as part of its architecture. Bourdieu argues that language is to be analysed within its social context as it is 'formed by, and comes saturated with, the moral ethos of its field context, and thus carries with it all the doxa and interest (illusio) of that field' (Grenfell, 2023: 130). Systemic functional linguistics' proponents argue that language both reflects ideational meanings and interpersonal meanings (power relations and evaluation), as well as construes them. The concept of construal is (somewhat) present in Bourdieu's discussion of language as 'worldmaking' through its function of categorization and labelling. SFL is a common approach in critical discourse studies, and we found SFL's various theoretical elements/systems deployed in research on identity and affiliation (Bednarek and Martin, 2010), evaluation and appraisal (Martin and White, 2005), agency and power (Bartlett, 2014) and ideology (Lukin, 2019) very useful to track Bourdieu's concepts in the discursive data. For example, Bartlett shows how power and legitimation are construed through transitivity and evaluative meanings. We also used Van Leeuwen's (2008) Social Actors Theory , a major analytical tool in critical discourse analysis, which draws on SFL to show that inclusion and exclusion are expressed linguistically and that agents and activities are represented according to the doxa of the field, through specific linguistic and multimodal strategies. In this way, for example, silence and absence also tell us much about doxa and world construal (Venkataraman, 2018).

Some of these discursive strategies are visible to careful readers, but many are deeply buried under the text surface, representing practices and beliefs that have become common sense. Paying close attention to these linguistic realizations gives us a clearer insight into agents' worldview. An SFL/social semiotics analysis is therefore a powerful complement to a Bourdieusian analysis of *illusio*, or 'collective denial' (Bourdieu, 2000a: 5).

Positionality, self-socio analysis

We need to 'tak[e] a point of view on one's own point of view' (Bourdieu, 2000a: 284). Positionality or reflexive statements are increasingly common in research publications now. Declarations of identity are supposed to alert the reader in a more transparent way to any possible cognitive (and perhaps ethical) limitations the author(s) may have regarding their research (Savolainen et al., 2023). Yet, despite positionality statements becoming increasingly doxic in academia, we both feel uncomfortable making such a statement. Once the performative declaration of identity is made, it can appear as if analysis can continue as normal. In just one sentence the burden of biography can give way to unfettered enlightenment. In a very important sense, the whole of this chapter reveals our position(s); socio-analysis is making visible our processes of making sense of positions, including ours, in the field. In addition, 'the discovery that someone who has discovered the truth had an interest in doing so in no way diminishes his [sic] discovery' (Bourdieu, 2000: 3) should come as no surprise. We both have a vested interest, as agents in the field, as practitioners, in positioning the field as we do. What we hope though is that our interests are objective or can be objectified, and we try to objectify the field through socio-analysis. We do this by providing a rigorous analysis of our data, engaging in a careful use of Bourdieu's theoretical concepts and tracking their realization in discourse through a detailed linguistics analysis.

A thorough, truthful and objective positionality statement would require a whole socio-analysis in itself,[3] and what is more important than a positionality statement is a comment on the social conditions of producing this chapter. One of us, Alex Ding, has sufficient cultural capital in the field to edit and shape this book series and make decisions about this volume, what to include and exclude. Ding can also use his cultural capital to some degree to engage in skholé – the privilege of having some agency over time and relations to practice and to writing. The position Ding occupies in the field enables him to make this and other contributions to the field that many others simply cannot because they lack the opportunity, dispositions, cultural capital and contingent histories that combine to allow this kind of agency. The second author, Laetitia Monbec, brings cultural capital related to her areas of expertise, scholarship and publications, as well as her professional experience outside of the UK, mainly in Asia. The Senior Lecturer position she occupies in her institution allows her time for research and agency to initiate and develop individual and collective scholarship projects within her institution and beyond.

Ethics

The study was reviewed by the Institutional Review Board (NUS-IRB) at the National University of Singapore which approved it (NUS-IRB Reference Code: NUS-IRB-2021-1012). As this study involved voluntary participation in surveys and interviews, and excluded student data or uneven power relations, it was

Results

The results first provide a snapshot of EAP practitioners' capitals, based on the data we collected and publicly available information. We then use some of Bourdieu's *Homo Academicus* nomenclature to 'categorise' practitioners (with a broad brush). An analysis of the narratives of origins of EAP reveals the construction of *the high priests*; The analysis of the questionnaire responses reveals *the minor prophets* and *the heretics*.

Anglicarum academica professor

In the UK, over 50 per cent of the respondents list British as their nationality; the rest listed the US, Bulgaria, Italy, Ireland, Poland, Australia and Greece. Sixty per cent are women, 38 per cent men, 2 per cent non-binary.

In the UK, the field is overwhelmingly white: only two of the participants indicated a non-white identity (African, mixed-Asian). In the Singapore sample there are nine women and two men and ethnicity labels reflect the multicultural nature of the Singaporean society: Chinese Singaporean (four), Caucasian/white/Italo-American (four), Indian (two) and Malayalee (one) (this distribution is not representative of EAP practitioners in Singapore, where white practitioners are a minority).

Home background

We took as parental professions as a broad indicator of class origin, although this is a reductive approach (Crew, 2020; Bourdieu, 1984), as we did not have the scope to investigate economic, cultural and social capitals in participants' childhoods. **Home backgrounds** tended to be of middle-class origin, with parental professions including teachers, civil servants, nurses and typists, but also farmers, factory workers, cleaners, bartenders and labourers. Only a small minority listed professions in the upper-middle class, such as engineers (five) and veterinary surgeon (one). Sixty-three per cent indicate an English monolingual home background. The rest indicate multilingual backgrounds including languages such as English, Scot, Irish, Italian, French, Thai, Urdu, Bengali, Telegu, Marathi, Punjabi, Pashto, Pashto, Persian and Arabic (the same person for the last nine languages in the list). A few indicated Kiswahili and Kichagga (one), Polish (two), Bulgarian (one), Spanish (one), Scots and Italian (two) as their first language. While English dominates as a first language, and in the professional realm, the large majority of participants also indicate a more multilingual environment in their adult lives, with multilingual homes or an interest in second language learning while living abroad, for travel or film and literature appreciation.

Qualification

The large majority of practitioners indicated in the survey that they had an undergraduate degree, mostly from non-elite UK universities, although a few indicated Oxford (two) and St Andrews (three). Undergraduate qualifications were mostly in English literature and modern languages, but also in philosophy, film studies, fine arts, theology and political sciences indicating a rich knowledge base and experience with academic discourse. In our sample, only a few indicated a field outside of the humanities or social sciences (chemistry, home economics and real estate).

Seventy-six per cent (thirty-six) held a master's qualification, in less diverse fields than BAs: MEd in language teaching, MA in teaching English for academic purposes (TEAP), teaching English to speakers of other languages (TESOL), applied linguistics and English literature. Additionally, fourteen had the Diploma in English language teaching (DELTA) and three the RSA Diploma. About 20 per cent (ten) had PhDs in English (literature), English language teaching, EAP linguistics or EdDs.

In terms of contract types, over 85 per cent were in full-time, permanent employment. The rest were part-time/fractional (two), fixed terms (three), self-employed (one) and zero hours (one). Forty-four per cent indicated professional experience abroad, but there are no long lists as we will see with the luminaries below. in 4.2.

Scholarship

Scholarship is part of their professional role for half of the participants. Several wish it was a formal part of their duties and indicate the lack of support in the form of time allocation as a reason for lack of engagement. A large proportion of EAP practitioners are not seeking or benefitting from funding for scholarship (only 20 per cent have sought funding). The majority indicate no institutional expectations of publications because of their department not being linked to REF requirements, but a few explain that, on the educator track, scholarship is well regarded by their department. They note that the expectations are vague. The large majority (90 per cent) do not have any editorial roles (four said yes). Only very few state that they peer-reviewed papers, often for colleagues.

For a brief comparison, in **the Singaporean data** (eleven respondents), home background origin was similar, mostly middle class. Most spoke English as a first language in a multilingual environment which included Teochow, Cantonese, Mandarin, Malayalam and Tamil. One indicated Mandarin as a first language, another Cantonese and Mandarin as first languages. In the context of Singapore, a first language indicates a stronger home language (mostly due to family origins). English is taught at school from kindergarten along with the other commonly used languages of the country (Malay, Mandarin, Tamil) (Wong, 2014). As expected, these practitioners speak a range of languages even in the professional setting, conversing with different colleagues in their language of choice. Six had PhDs (literature, linguistics) and ten had a master's (MA literature, MSc, MA TESOL) in universities from the region, the US and the UK. All were full time on the educator track (teaching). In terms of scholarship, practitioners indicate this is a requirement on the teaching track, and that they can access internal educational enhancement grants.

The EAP practitioner: Capital and cleft habitus

Within academia, EAP practitioners then do not tend to accumulate traditionally valued capital. Many do not hold PhDs, or post-doc experience, very few graduated from elite universities and few hold professorships (although this is changing with the implementation of educator or teacher career progression tracks in some institutions). Very few can demonstrate prestige bestowed through publishing records and committee memberships; doctoral supervision is rare. Family backgrounds and qualifications indicate a field where many have experienced upward class mobility or different educational achievement compared with their parents. These shifts create a cleft habitus in the practitioner and are well known for the challenges they present in terms of identity, agency and well-being (Crew, 2020). Bourdieu (1984) talks about the struggles of the self-taught which relate to feelings of possessing inadequate knowledge of the dominant and high-brow culture when one has not been socialized to relate to this culture (Bourdieu argues it is not as much a matter of volume of cultural knowledge that distinguishes agents, than it is a matter of confidence in one's familiarity with the high-brow culture). The same phenomenon affects practitioners' relations to knowledge and to the academic community (Monbec, 2022). These broad observations, however, do not necessarily imply a marginal position. Conditions all across the neoliberal university have changed, workloads have increased, and many academic departments rely more and more on teaching-track staff. So, the position of the EAP practitioner within academia is also shifting and is always renegotiated within specific contexts. Within EAP, also, there are struggles for distinction and resources. As seen in the data above, agents differ in the types and volume of capital which position them differently in the field. Dominant agents tend to be more senior, having accumulated the necessary capital. Newcomers 'typically arrive empty-handed' (Salo, 2017: 34) and either try to legitimize their capitals, thereby subverting the established order, or simply recognize the legitimacy of the current dominant group (Salo, 2017).

A historical analysis of the beginnings: The high priests

The first step in this socio-analysis was to look at the history of the field and more particularly at how practitioners are represented in *narratives of origin*. These stories constitute the field's heritage and frame our understanding of the field. Bourdieu (1990) explains how our habitus is shaped by a collective memory which partly reproduces itself through the ways social actors are represented. The analysis below is based on a collection of texts that represents the social practice '*starting out in the field*'.

The history of EAP is usually told through its intellectual development and its theoretical influences. Dudley-Evans and St-John (1998), Jordan (1997) and Hyland and Hamp-Lyons (2002) for example detail successive approaches or key pedagogical resources. Some historical accounts also describe the field from a political and economic perspective, relating it to colonial power and the globalization of English as the language of academia and business, extended in a post-colonial world by economic motives, soft power and the increase of international students in English-speaking countries and neoliberal universities (Philipson, 1992; Benesch, 2001; O'Regan, 2021; Pennycook, 2002). This expansion, Pennycook (2002) shows, has been assisted by a 'colonial celebratory' discursive construction of English (Pennycook, 2002), a positive portrayal of 'Global English' for its intrinsic (its nature) and extrinsic (its function) qualities (Pennycook, 2021: 66). Similarly, Benesch critiques the construction of the EAP field as neutral and ineluctable, rather than motivated by political ideology and economic drivers (Benesch, 2001: 33). This literature, however, does not pay much attention to practitioners themselves, although both Pennycook and Benesch's work surfaces useful information and data about the way (some) practitioners came to embody these ideologies. In order to trace the practitioner's representation in the early days of EAP, several sources proved very useful: the BALEAP website, in particular the history of BALEAP and the 'Using English for academic purposes' (UEFAP) archives page (http://www.uefap.com/baleap/), doctoral theses where accounts of lived experience are analysed, primary data in the form of interviews of 'luminaries' or recorded panel discussions between influential scholars/practitioners and even autobiographical and fictionalized accounts of EAP teachers. Following Bourdieu, we also used a selection of obituaries of significant EAP scholars as these texts detail these agents' contributions thereby highlighting what is considered valued capitals and dispositions. Representation of the practitioner in the early days of the field then provides an insight into the basis of legitimation of agents, purposes and values in EAP. The paragraphs below show in what ways the same political and economic context described in Benesch (2001) shaped the construction of the legitimate *EAP practitioner*.

Mobility

The first narrative of origin is one of **geographical expansion** and **practitioner's mobility**, characterized by what Pennycook calls 'expansionist rhetoric'. This is a discipline which grew along with globalization and which expanded through various channels, such as the British Council or Voluntary Service Overseas (VSO). Bartlett (2014) shows that circumstantial elements play an important role in construing events. Circumstances of place abound in the data through the sheer number of countries' names, often in the form of long lists. It is difficult to find a 'luminary' whose name is not soon followed by an inventory of (mostly) post-colonial countries: the United Arab Emirates, Hong Kong, Jordan, Kuwait, Libya, Saudi, Singapore, Sri Lanka, Venezuela and so on. Beyond these long lists that attest to a geographically varied professional experience, it is the surrounding discourse which gives it a distinctive colonial/imperialistic flavour. In Bell's (2016) thesis, for example, and several of the obituaries we consulted, cultural or economic symbols like 'British telecom', 'BP', references to 'the Royal Family', 'the year of the Queen's Silver Jubilee', 'the centre for British Teachers', 'VSO', 'petroleum companies' and

'Shell' and somewhat antiquated lexis such as 'cutting your teeth', 'coincidental careers', 'his Libyan period' and '3-year posting to the University of Kuwait' conjure the quaintness, charm and old-world nostalgia of an Agatha Christie novel (and incongruent images of EAP scholars in pith helmets). The world painted is one which today appears indulgent and privileged, a world of youth and adventure where the call of international travel was readily met by endless professional opportunities (bolstered by powerful institutions which 'posted' the practitioners and gave them status) and a prestigious aura upon return to the metropole. Unsurprisingly, this type of framing is not received in quite the same enthusiastic manner by practitioners originating from the countries themselves/the Global South (see Tilakaratna, this volume).

In the blurb for *English All over the Place*, Abbott and Jordan's (2001) account of their lives as EAP practitioners, beyond pointing to what might be an enjoyable non-academic read, shows an example of these discourse indicators (in italics) to describe the spread of English, in prose not unlike Paul Theroux, Bill Bryson or David Crystal's which Pennycook (2002) analysed.

> *The British Empire* is no more, but *the empire* of its language *flourishes*. This is in part because of the efforts of itinerant teachers in *far-flung corners* of what used to be called *British spheres of interest*. Enduring coups and odd customs, enjoying unexpected delights, two veterans of this life provide intimate recollections of what it was like to *ply their profession* during the decades of change between 1960 and 1990. (Abbott and Jordan, *English All over the Place*, 2001)

Expertise and agency

Another narrative in this data is that of **expertise and agency**, which invariably accompanies this geographical ambition. The significant social actors, or 'high priests' (a term used in *Homo Academicus*), are represented through 'activation' as powerful, agentive, dynamic experts (van Leeuwen, 2008). Bartlett (2014) explains how process types reveal the way actors' roles are construed and how they are positioned. Nominalizations are also useful in conflating different agents. In these accounts, EAP practitioners are **agents** in most clauses and act on the local educational world through material processes: **they** *set up* *centres and programmes*, **they** *build* *educational initiatives*, **they** *consult* on government educational plans or the large-scale professional development of school teachers. They '*advised on*', '*worked with* the education authorities to develop', '*led on government projects*'. When not active agents, they are a willing 'beneficialised' passivated social actor, working for a powerful institutional agent, as in: '*I was posted in . . . by the British Council*', '*further British Council postings*', and through the passive voice or nominalizations (*postings*), their missions become aligned with the broader linguistic expansion (see Abbott and Jordan's '*the efforts of itinerant teachers*', above). Similar accounts abound in the EAP literature. Swales (1977: 36) discusses the need for foreign experts because of a lack of local ones and describes the essential role of the British Council and UNESCO in recruiting those. Benesch quotes from a conference paper about English training in ARAMCO by Johnson (1971) which spells out that, beyond native expertise in the language, it is a civilizing, acculturating and modernizing capital which the 'native' English teacher is sought for.

This evokes a world where white English-speaking academics make use of their epistemic, cultural and racial (as well as gender) capital to develop the 'less fortunate', the 'linguistically deprived', and embody 'the onward march of the English language' (Pennycook, 2002: 136). In many instances, these narratives also imply generous financial compensation, secured by the rarity and prestige of the white, anglophone expert. Bourdieu (2008) explains powerfully the way groups form, reproduce agent legitimation patterns around a common habitus and so perpetuate the *illusio*:

> The grip of strongly integrated groups [. . .] is to a large extent due to the fact that they are linked by a collusio in the illusio, a deep-rooted complicity in the collective fantasy, which provides each of its members with the experience of an exaltation of the ego, the principle of a solidarity rooted in attachment to the group as an enchanted image of the self. It is indeed this socially constructed feeling of being a 'superior essence' which, together with the solidarities of interests and the affinities of habitus, does most to engender and support what must indeed be called an 'esprit de corps' – however strange the expression may seem when applied to a set of individuals persuaded of their perfect non-substitutability. (Bourdieu, 2008: 7)

The two main narratives above show how the 'collusio in the illusio' is construed through the grammar of the clause (in this analysis transitivity), creating a thematic motif of legitimation and agency (Bartlett, 2014: 44). The legitimation of this agent, however, is not complete without the next discursive strategy: erasure.

A pattern of absence

In the narratives of mobility and expertise, which construct a white anglophone speaker as the legitimate practitioner and expert, it is what is hidden from view which is the most problematic. In fact, arguably, this illusion of legitimacy cannot hold without constructing a parallel erasure of the local expertise. In the data, local scholars, their local expertise and knowledge, local academic literature and teaching practices are absent. Beyond the names of countries or government ministries which prop up the two narratives mentioned above, this erasure is shown by a complete absence of linguistic traces – a void or suppression (Stibbe, 2020; Venkataraman, 2018; van Leeuwen, 2008). A reader in 2023 wonders where the local expertise and knowledge, the qualified teachers, the published scholars, the students are. Mention of local contexts rarely go beyond an exotic description of wonderful sceneries, strange or amusing traditions and foods. The blurb from Abbott and Jordan's autobiographical account is a good example of this in non-academic prose. Hutchinson and Waters (1987) characterize the learners as *acquiescent non-agentive actors* in the whole ESP enterprise (Benesch, 2001: 25). The erasure of local agents has consequences for how they can be envisaged and envisage themselves as practitioners with agency to define issues, present solutions that are heard, let alone impactful, and contribute to shaping the field.

The 'luminaries' in the accounts above may not always be responsible for the narratives they are made to serve. With a Bourdieusian analysis, we want to draw attention not to the person, but rather to the epistemic agent, the position in the field and how this shapes the 'position holder's actions and beliefs'. There has been a developing awareness of these issues over the years. While Swales still attributes the start of his career to good fortune (Bell, 2016: 150), his 1997 'English as Tyrannosaurus Rex' article explains that reading Phillipson's (1992) book lifted the illusion that EAP was an apolitical endeavour: 'I have belatedly come to recognize a certain self-deception in my 30-year involvement with English for Academic Purposes [. . .] I also believed that working overseas in scientific English, as researcher, materials writer and teacher, was, in essence, a culturally and politically neutral enterprise' (Swales, 1997: 377). Interestingly, in Bell's thesis, the researcher frames this political awareness as 'a loss of a certain naiveté' (Bell, 2016: 286), which can be 'taken too far' and 'divert practitioners' attention from what I would consider to be much more immediate pragmatic and pedagogical concerns' (2016: 287). The above shows agents experiencing a form of hysteresis, when they perceive a shift in the rules of the game which appeared unproblematic – unproblematic because these rules bolstered the agents' capitals and habitus as dominant and were perceived as a natural state of things. Secondly, equally importantly, in this perspective, socio-political issues are isolated from EAP's 'pragmatic and pedagogical concerns' as if the first did not directly impact the nature of the second. The focus of this chapter is on practitioners, but we address the impact these narratives have on curriculum and pedagogy very briefly below.

While one might argue that 'in those days', these issues were not discussed, the reality is that there has long been a counter-hegemonic discourse available which has pushed back against the bold colonial and imperial foundational myths through critical sociolinguistics and critical linguistics publications, particularly addressing native-speakerism and linguistic imperialism (Ndebele, 1987; Phillipson, 1986; 1988; 1992; Pennycook, 1994; Braine, 1999; Canagarajah, 1999; Kirkpatrick, 2002 among others). But this has tended to be within broader ELT or TESOL-related literature, rather than EAP, except for Benesch (2001). And while today it would be increasingly difficult for an EAP practitioner to identify as a globe-trotting expert on a mission to help the less fortunate, these beliefs are far from absent in discourse and in practices. For example, although conditions and powers have shifted, we still find Global North experts in leadership positions where the local context would provide ample expertise. Many transnational collaborations for example still seem to value the L1 English-speaking, white and male practitioner over local expertise (based on staff lists at least). The BALEAP mailing list occasionally shows non-British practitioners construed as deficient: in Ding, Bond and Bruce (2022), a message on the mailing list dated 2011 makes the rather bold claim that 'outside the UK **we** are <u>very likely</u> to find "English" teachers who <u>are</u> *unqualified* or *poorly qualified*: **they** <u>may</u> be *qualified* as teachers, **but** <u>not</u> of English; **they** <u>may</u> *have a degree in*

English, **but** no *teacher training/educ coursework*' (Ding, Bond and Bruce, 2022: 8). Common discursive strategies include othering and generalizing '**they**', affiliation to a homogeneous superior UK practitioner '**we**' and a range of *appraisal* and subtle use of modality resources to dismiss expertise from outside the UK. Accounts of unequal relations still come up, for example when academics or practitioners construct jobs in faraway countries as a non-ideal but necessary notch on their professional trajectory belt. It is essential to pay attention to the ways local actors and knowledge are represented in discourse and to notice (and call out) when they remain occluded or inconsequential, mere props in a practitioner's negotiation of their own position in the field. This is particularly crucial in an environment where terms like inclusivity can be appropriated for institutional marketing purposes.

One pervasive and rarely discussed consequence of these narratives is its impact on the knowledge base and knowledge practices in EAP. Jansen argued that 'the newly dominant order always reflects in the curriculum, as codification of knowledge, vestiges from previous or alternative authorities' (Jansen, 2019: 58). Pennycook (2002) also discusses ways in which the cultural constructs of colonialism have shaped common myths in English language teaching, such as the belief that English is easy to learn and that it is a superior language for 'thinking'. Another example, which is now largely discredited, is the monolingual fallacy or the insistence on banning local/L1 languages from the English classroom (Tupas and Renandya, 2021; Renandya, Nguyen and Jacobs, 2023). This fallacy, working hand in hand with the erasure of local knowledge and agents, can be seen as having legitimized and empowered the monolingual anglophone teacher around the world. In the same way, the critical period hypothesis whereby starting to learn a language young ensures better fluency and a 'native-like' accent is also anchored in 'nativeness' ideology and has aided the 'young learner' industry in ELT as well as influenced educational policies and teaching practices. It is discredited both for its validity (Singleton and Muñoz, 2011) and for the educational aim it supports (native-speaker-like competence) (Kubota, 2015). The persistent (even sadly when well-intentioned) portrayal of multilingual teachers of EAP as lacking, struggling and agentless, and this despite decades of research and advocacy, shows that underlying ideologies are powerful and their reproduction patterns poorly understood. Remnants of the cultural constructs of colonialism are still part of an unquestioned doxa, and the way they adapt to modernity still needs to be explored if we want to halt these automatisms, these determined ways of thinking, and if we hope to address their impact on practice. Bourdieu presents reflexive analysis as the way to resist 'the postulates, axioms, which go without saying and require no inculcation' (Bourdieu and Wacquant, 1992: 168) and this whether we happen to be alternately victims or perpetrators, dominated or dominants:

> [i]t is difficult to control the first inclination of habitus, but reflexive analysis which teaches that we are the ones who endow the situation with part of the potency it has over us, allows us to alter our perception of the situation and thereby our reaction to it. It enables us to monitor, up to a certain point, some of the determinisms that operate through the relation of immediate complicity between position and dispositions. (Bourdieu and Wacquant, 1992: 136)

Shifting narratives: Experiencing hysteresis

We analysed the narratives of origin as a legitimation process of agents who claim legitimacy based on their language background, nationality, race, class and dispositions. These identities, hinting at Bourdieu's *Homo Academicus* classifications, include the high priests (those luminaries whose work has shaped the field in many corners of the world), the missionaries (those who aligned with the myths and illusion of ELT expansionism and associate their work with a mission, a service to populations in need) and the diplomats (those with closeted colonial views on global influence). This analysis points to what Bourdieu calls misrecognition: 'Misrecognition happens when we think that a system is based on a certain set of principles when it really works on the basis of another' (Yenn, 2022). Increasingly, discussions and new narratives are forming around the professionalization of EAP, scholarship, inclusivity, diversity, equity, anti-racism, decolonization, translanguaging and multilingualism which have destabilized these traditional narratives of legitimation and identities, relegating them to the past and causing certain agents to experience what Bourdieu calls hysteresis (when one's habitus and capital go out of synch with the evolving field and one feels the rules of the games are changing). The way participants are construed, erased, positioned as agents or passive actors is partly how dominance in the material world is perpetuated, and so, close attention to and deliberate use of language is a way, if not to transform the world, at least to lift the *illusio*.

Shifting values and capitals: The minor prophets and the heretics

In this section, we report on the questionnaire which aimed to gauge what practitioners see as valuable capital in the field. We show in what ways the shared collective narrative of the EAP practitioner seems to be shifting towards an identity that embraces diversity and knowledge under the influence of broader educational and social justice discussions as well as key influential practitioners: the minor prophets and the heretics.

Influences

As has been reported elsewhere, EAP practitioners are influenced by an eclectic range of theories and scholars confirming Cowley-Haselden and Monbec's (2019) findings. Some expected names appear as most influential, for example Hyland and Swales. In our sample, they are followed by Bruce, Ding, Halliday, Kirk, Street, Alexander, Lillis, Lea, Bond, Benesch and so on. Several names from a more EFL background such as Thornbury or Harmer appear. Several practitioners/scholars are mentioned, as seen above, and include Susie Cowley-Haselden, Michelle Evans, Laetitia Monbec and Milada Walková. Clearly this reflects our population sampling which we collected through the BALEAP mailing list and Twitter, therefore attracting people who are familiar with the activities of the BALEAP community over the years, willing to give their time generously to us, and perhaps sharing dispositions and orientations with the authors. The practitioners cited here do not have the global weight in the educational field which others on the list do have: Bruce, Pennycook, Gardner, Coffin, Halliday, Fairclough, bell hooks, Freire, Bieber, Hamp-Lyons, Biggs, Tuck, Foucault and Bourdieu (mentioned three times). Yet, this also indicates a population of EAP practitioners whose work is gaining more visibility and is beginning to influence the field because it concerns issues that matter to practitioners and their students. As one participant says:

> any EAP teacher reaches their point of saturation with articles on lexical bundles and starts to disengage with the endless papers on minute elements of academic writing.

Some participants report on a shift away from the more traditional ELT/EFL 'canon':

> In my current context, the canon of Thornbury, Harmer, Underhill, and Swan. Historically, they have provided a 'sound foundation' for generations of undergraduate trainee teachers in need of a basic introduction to TEFL and second language acquisition. There is a clear need, however, for a more critical approach to this field beyond these apparently 'neutral' approaches.

Others sense the field is changing but are constrained by a lack of access:

> I feel my current context is not very up to date with innovations in the field. This is a bit of an issue for me as there is this sense of 'well, this is how this has been done for years'.

This widening of influences to include practitioners themselves is a positive evolution in the field. It indicates a developing agency with regards to professional development and interest in engaging with theories and practices which can perhaps impact practices more effectively. Overwhelmingly, however, the influences still come from the centres of knowledge production of the Global North and are mostly white authors, with the exceptions of Suresh Canagarajah in nineteenth place, bell hooks (thirty-fifth) and Ruqaiya Hasan (101st). In Singapore, the top influences were Hyland, Swales, Halliday, Canagarajah and (Michelle) Lazar.

These results also provide a complementary image to the recent bibliometric studies conducted in EAP. Hyland and Jiang (2020), for example, index the concerns of the field and its historical development by analysing the most common research topics and most highly cited authors in the field. In this list of the fifteen most cited authors between 2001 and 2020, Hyland, Bourdieu, Swales, Dornyei, Vygotsky, Biber and Halliday take the first seven spots. There are, then, some commonalities with our participants' list, but Hyland and Jiang's lacks any mention of practitioners due to the nature of the research which calculates influence by citation counts in high-ranking journals. The same is true of the most influential publications listed, which are also calculated according to the number of citations they received in research papers: Swales's (1990) *Genre Analysis* comes first and Halliday's (1985)

Introduction to Functional Grammar is twelfth. Between 2001 and 2020, the first spots are taken by Vygotsky, Swales, Hyland and an increasing number of language acquisition and psycholinguistics scholars. As Hyland and Jiang recognize, this reflects the influence of researchers on researchers, not on EAP practitioners. As we saw above, practitioners may not be publishing much, or not in the journals analysed by Hyland and Jiang. This explains the differences in our findings and highlights a large, perhaps increasing, disjunction between the EAP research field and its practitioners (Ding, 2022).

Valued capital and dispositions

In this section, we show how practitioners define their roles and identities and describe their values. We first look at what is seen as valued capital for success in the field. Then, we explore the perceptions of valued skills and knowledge and finally practitioners' views on their specific contribution to students and subject lecturers.

First, participants perceived that specific professional experience is the **most valued capital in terms of promotions and prospects** (70 per cent), followed by qualifications (51 per cent see a PhD as useful). Scholarship output and length of service are next (40 per cent and 27 per cent respectively). Research funding and teaching awards are at the bottom of the list. Multilingualism in different forms is now clearly seen as a strong form of epistemic capital: this is shown through participants' deliberate detailing of their language skills at the beginning of the survey. Some stress that beyond these epistemic capitals, it is really social capital that shapes professional outcomes in the field: eight mention the 'lingering native speaker proximity status' ('sadly', 'definitely and unfortunately mother-tongue status'); two mention being part of a network ('who you know').

The responses around **perceptions of undervalued or overvalued knowledge and skills** show a somewhat divided field of practitioners. It was very difficult to find any sort of consensus, and the data provided a series of contradicting statements: 'Research is overvalued'; 'Research is undervalued'. Dispositions such as hard work and resilience, teaching skills, creativity and pastoral care are represented as undervalued. Overall, there was a perception that 'knowledge, theoretical knowledge of language, the knowledge-base, scholarship' are undervalued and that teaching skills, 'being a good teacher' (one mocked the legitimacy of 'Being pragmatic or hard working [...] in managerial eulogising') and '(outdated)TESOL/TEFL-tastic learning theories such as CLT, independent learning' are overvalued:

> I would add that I don't think the knowledge base is particularly valued and there is a lack of people in decision-making positions who really have any judgement in this area.

Teaching skills are to a degree still being construed through grammatical choices in opposition to academic or research skills (in bold below). These dichotomies occlude persisting assumptions. In the first quote below, scholarship is construed as needing to result in better practice, with its impact being easily measured. The second quote emphasizes the persisting belief that EAP teachers are necessarily better teachers than academics who tend to 'talk at' students and that 'talking' to students is necessarily not engaging:

> Scholarship or an interest in carrying out research [is overvalued] – it is a useful insight/development of skills **but it doesn't necessarily** result in better practical teaching.
>
> The ability to actually engage with students and help develop their learning **rather than** talk **at** them [is undervalued].

Overall, it is clear that these views reflect an ill-defined field, with varied entrance points, trajectories, qualifications and practitioner habitus (Ding and Bruce, 2017). In this case, and as practitioners mentioned, these struggles are very context dependent, linked to individual centres' culture. In many of the responses, it is management who does the undervaluing, rather than colleagues, students or subject lecturers/scholars. It is also clear that many assumptions about language, teaching and the knowledge base remain pervasive (Mittelmeier and Zhang, 2022).

Contributions to students and to subject lecturers

Another way to explore identity and values in practitioners was to enquire about what **defines their specific contribution to their students and to subject lecturers**. With this question, practitioners presented a more homogeneous profile.

The large majority of practitioners prioritize their knowledge of academic discourse and genre, academic norms and conventions (referencing, integrating sources) as their main contribution, their area of expertise. This forms the bulk of the responses. Among these, a few emphasize knowledge of language as empowering: 'empowering students to become discourse analysts' and 'to critique academic convention', 'to make choices according to communicative contexts'. Only one respondent mentioned accuracy and clarity. There are also a few broader responses around academic practices such as conducting scholarship and academic 'honesty'.

About 20 per cent of the responses concerned items related to study skills, such as *organizational skills, autonomy, motivation, self-management, thought process and critical thinking* or familiarity with *learner-centred approaches*.

Th question related to practitioners' contribution to subject lecturers was not applicable to all, but those who responded agreed that their contribution to subject lecturers is first related to their knowledge of language and academic genres (31 per cent), their knowledge of pedagogical and assessment practices (21 per cent) and their familiarity with intercultural communication and international students' specific needs (12 per cent). Other responses included specific communication skills (presentation) and EdTech skills.

I think I bring an ability to look at a text or a task as an object – I have the metalanguage to identify and describe abstract things that discipline tutors ask students to do, such as 'critical thinking'. Also, I think I'm able to look at tasks and break them down into stages, seeing the linguistic requirements for each stage and possible roadblocks, and then discuss this with disciplinary tutors, so they can get a linguistic perspective on what has become automatic for them.

Ethics

Participants were asked to explain what a code of ethics for EAP might contain so as to understand what they particularly value and see as potentially lacking in the field. About twenty per cent did not answer or wrote they did not know, and two were slightly puzzled as to why EAP needed a specific code, other than the university code or 'the same as anything in life'. Participants understood ethics quite differently and oriented it to their concerns. We classify the responses below into three main areas: general ethics of the field around the key terms of inclusivity, social justice and integrity; ethical needs around the practitioner's working conditions and well-being; and finally ethics around students. So, ethics is viewed as mostly related to the treatment of people in practitioners' responses. Beyond allusions to teaching practices in relation to student-centredness, there was no mention of curriculum content.

Participants mostly mention **general ethical concerns** around a series of key words. They call for increased attention to *social justice, integrity, reflexivity, dignity for all, transparency, lack of bias* and *empathy, collegiality* and *intellectual love, inclusivity of diverse representation, viewpoints and practices, inclusivity* or *inclusion*, notably around the notion of native speakerism as shown here:

> Definitely no more preferential treatment for 'native speakers', more people from the global south doing plenaries, more representation in publishing for women and scholars from poor countries. Some sort of sensible acceptance of varieties of English that might not be exactly how 'we' would do it.

The second most common concern relates to **practitioner working conditions** with a call for institutions to *improve recognition, cancel zero-hour contracts* and *commit to full-time employment*. Some participants also ask for *more respect from management* (for example to be given more agency over types of courses taught) and *support for development and mentorship*. Others mention the need for *consistent and fair hiring practices*.

Many place **students** at the heart of their ethical concerns calling for a refusal to see the '*student as consumer*', for students to be respected and international students' rights met. '*Rationale for our teaching and testing practices should be visible for the benefit of students*.' Occasionally, dichotomies are built which raise questions about practitioners' conception of students' needs:

The students and their needs must be central **rather than** the technical linguistic content.

The practitioners' concerns then focus on political issues such as employment, international students' rights and the consequences of the internationalization of the commodification of higher education. Along with the expressed concern about the lack of scholarly representation from outside of the United Kingdom, the United States, Canada or Australia, these are all indications that the field is undergoing a shift.

There are a few caveats: first, the reading influences shared by the participants (above) did not reflect an impact of 'Global South' scholarship on practitioners. Once again, what is not mentioned is worth noting: ethical considerations do not seem to be connected with the knowledge base or pedagogical practices; instead they relate mostly to people's behaviour. Moreover, ethics seem to be projected out through demands on others rather than on the practitioners themselves. In this section there is perhaps a sense of a lack of reflexivity, a difficulty to acknowledge that, as agents in the field, we are enmeshed in its ethics, and we have some agency to implement some changes. For example, for inclusive and genuine representation to occur, we need to read scholars from outside our usual knowledge base and acknowledge them as influences or cite them in our own scholarship.

Final remarks

In this chapter we have covered a lot of ground already. We have established that the lives of practitioners have been, for a long period in the history of EAP, of only fleeting and marginal concern in the ideational domain. A growing and much more recent body of work focussing on the practitioner has emerged which we have signalled as representing *professional disarticulation* in the field. From this idea of disarticulation, we have suggested that this *anomie* can be better understood as *hysteresis* and, as such, we argued that employing Bourdieu's concepts and tools, especially that of socio-analysis, enables a collective and reflexive account of the field of EAP to become effective by allowing practitioners to understand the forces that shape and distort the field of EAP. By doing so, we hope to equip practitioners and ourselves to resist, contain and overcome injustices in the field of EAP. Moreover, we operationalized socio-analysis through a combination of a survey administered to practitioners and by drawing on a wide range of documents. Our research explored background, class, qualifications, scholarship, funding and editorial roles. Our historical analysis identified the high priests, missionaries and diplomats of the field and those who are erased in accounts of the field. We established a fracture or rupture between EAP as a discipline and EAP as a field of practice. Who is significant in each of these fields is not or is no longer synonymous. What is valued and not valued in the field by practitioners emerged as contested, and the field's ethics remains remarkably unreflexive, focussing on the behaviour of others rather than a sensitivity to what practitioners, as agents, might be able to enact/embody. Ethics was also disconnected from what practitioners perceive as their potential contributions to the field. These contributions read as highly orthodox and focussed on a knowledge of language which, while moving away from prescriptivist form and accuracy, still seems limited in terms of connection with its social and political context and still portrays EAP as limited in terms of the range of semiotic systems it encompasses. Above all, we have tried to write and think about EAP anew, taking seriously the notion, practice and promise of metanoia.

Despite covering a lot of ground, there is still much more to be said. In the remainder of this chapter, we point to some areas, neglected here, where we need to focus further attention to deepen our understanding of the field of EAP and offer a more complete socio-analysis.

> To think in terms of field is to think relationally, one must see that the real is relational. (Bourdieu and Wacquant, 1992: 96–7)

Firstly, we have to acknowledge that incorporating the idea of relations in our analysis was limited. We focussed mainly but not uniquely on relations *within the field*. But a fuller understanding of the field of EAP would require establishing relations *beyond* EAP including with the more general 'position of the field in relation to the field of power' (Bourdieu and Wacquant, 1992: 104–5). Adjacent and potentially conflicting and encroaching fields, including cognate disciplines and fields and higher education, need specific attention especially as EAP is very much a dominated field lacking in autonomy within higher education (see Ding, 2022). Given that EAP is a porous, opaque and ill-defined field, identifying legitimate agents (and agents can include institutions such as private providers, companies, publishers and exam boards as well as librarians, learning developers, testing experts and others staking a claim and place in EAP) and which agents wield power and shape the field is highly complex. That complexity needs further elucidation with a greater focus on analysing the effects of economic capital in the field and the investments made in EAP by agents who encroach within the field.

Secondly, further consideration needs to account for the social capital of agents in the field. This could be achieved with the data sources we have used in this chapter perhaps supplemented with ethnographic studies. Various recent critical studies have been published on the role of associations in the ideational domain (especially BALEAP), on how norms and doxas are enforced through fellowship criteria (Ding and Campion, 2016), on how BALEAP has been and remains largely inward-facing and ineffective in the more outward-facing political arena (Ding and Bruce, 2017), and on how association identity and agency are shaped by gender, location and power (Ding, Bond and Bruce, 2022). However, none of these studies looks closely at the social capital of those who run associations, what enables them to hold positions of power, what makes them legitimate in positions of power and what they do with that power. Furthermore, accounting for, for example, who is invited to give keynotes, plenaries or sit on editorial boards may seem to be a simple case of assessing these agents as having enough cultural capital and ultimately symbolic capital to warrant these rewards and recognition. However, the opaqueness of social capital, of relations and networks, needs exploration as this is also significant in the attribution of rewards and recognition in the field: it is also about who you know. A cursory look at the editorial boards of leading EAP journals reveals that very few members are practitioners (and even practitioners who do sit on these boards have not contributed significantly to scholarship in the field), and many seem to have little or a very tangential relationship to EAP as a field of practice (or even in some cases as researchers). Identifying the social capital that led to them sitting on editorial boards would be revealing. It would also act as a warning that editorial board members, role holders in associations and plenary speakers are all potential gatekeepers of orthodoxy and, as such, their social capital (and their overall configuration of capitals) needs to be very critically explored. If agents are to influence the field, we need to know how they get to harness their social capital and what they then do in positions of power.

Similarly, further exploration of EAP directors could focus on their social capital, how they become directors and what capital they have that appeals to those who appoint them. It is not EAP practitioners who appoint directors, it is those with greater capitals from outside the field who make these appointments, and they have expectations perhaps of loyalty and political orientation, and so the question of how and why directors are appointed and what values, attributes and dispositions they have (their habitus) that appeal to those beyond the field merits further investigation. This is especially true in that the microcosms of EAP unit directors exert considerable power over the lives of practitioners and directors are often at the apex of this microcosm and micro-politics.

In a footnote we alluded to 'social surface', as far as we know a one-off comment made by Bourdieu (2000b) in a relatively obscure publication, hinting at the collection of positions occupied at a given moment by the empirical individual which enables the individual to participate (efficiently) in different fields. This aside by Bourdieu allows us to see that his focus across his many studies is overwhelmingly on the field and the epistemological *agents* within it and *not* the empirical individual – the 'person'. Field analysis does not allow the social surface of individuals to be central to his analysis. Reducing the individual to an *agent* is essential for undertaking field analysis effectively, but accounting for social surface reminds us that practitioners can operate in multiple fields, seek recognition and rewards in different fields and will contend with different field *illusio* at the same time. It also suggests that some agents in the field of EAP may have more significant investments elsewhere, where they perceive a greater alignment between habitus and field and the potential for greater rewards and recognition. This can be seen, for example, when practitioners shift their investments and interests into an adjacent (sub-) field or micro-context, such as higher education or the university, where they might actively engage in promoting 'sustainability', 'belonging', 'decolonization' or any number of initiatives directed and encouraged within and most often by the neoliberal university and its leaders. Anecdotally, investments in other fields do not necessary result in greater rewards or recognition *within EAP* and, indeed, there may be penalties as well as rewards attached to being drawn to the *illusio* of other fields. This leads us to another point; because agents occupy multiple fields, they will have to gauge how much they can (or must) invest in any given field which may entail a trade-off between competing investments and opportunities as well as between conflicting obligations and constraints. It is quite possible that some practitioners are only minimally engaged in EAP while having to dedicate a significant amount of time and resources to another field (one can imagine the 'family' field for example). Investigating how practitioners navigate multiple fields would be of great interest as would a longitudinal study investigating the ways in which agents' investment in a field varies over time and the consequences for agents' configuration and quantity of capitals and their changing position in the field. This is a reminder that one can accrue capitals, but, importantly, they can also wane in one or more fields. The dominant can become the dominated and vice versa.

Our final remark concerns our experience of undertaking a socio-analysis of the field of EAP. In aiming to render the field reflexive with promises of greater objectivity and promises of a deeper understanding of the forces that shape a field, along with promises of revealing the taken for granted (the epistemological unconscious), exposing the doxas and *illusio* and arming ourselves with a metanoia capable of allowing us to see the field afresh and resist injustices, we have come to the conclusion that in objectifying the field (as best we can) this work is also deeply personal. It is as much an auto-analysis as socio-analysis, as much a questioning of our own doxas and *illusio*, our own capitals and positions within the field and our own complicated enmeshments in misrecognition, legitimation struggles and the nebulous ethics of the field. It was a discomforting experience but necessary to take a step away from a sense of crisis to begin to foresee a remedy. We hope to have achieved at least two things: the first,

> If people at least come away with the feeling that it is complicated, that's already a good lesson to have learnt. (Bourdieu, 1990: 52)

And secondly, through a socio-analysis of the field we have:

> a small chance of knowing what game we play and of minimizing the ways in which we are manipulated by the forces of the field in which we evolve . . . [Sociology] allows us to discern the sites where we do indeed enjoy a degree of freedom and those where we do not. (Bourdieu and Wacquant, 1992: 198–9)

Notes

1 Perhaps counter-intuitively 'the true object of social science is not individuals' (Wacquant, 1989: 6–7); rather than individuals, socio-analysis is only interested in agents in the field and as agents in that 'they possess the necessary properties to be effective, to produce effects, in this field' (Wacquant, 1989: 6–7). We are not concerned

with the social surface: 'The collection of positions simultaneously occupied at a given moment in time by a biological individual' (Bourdieu, 2000b: 302, 303n8) nor with an 'efficient agent in different fields and acting as a sociologically rigorous conceptualisation of what most people would refer to as a "personality"' (2000b: 302, 303n8). Atkinson (2020: 181) notes that Bourdieu operates with two types of individuals: empirical (or biological) individuals operating in multiple fields (social surface) and epistemic individuals (where agents exist and have properties which are only related to a specific field). It is only the epistemic individual or field agent that is of interest to us in this chapter, reductive as that might seem, although we will return to this question at the end of the chapter.

2   It may be appropriate to speak of *ethical capital*: through displays of virtue, agents attempt to improve their position and increase their power within a field. This evokes questions of the cynicism or sincerity of agents (and whether and why this matters and how it matters).

3   In some significant ways, this chapter is a very personal piece of writing for both of us and, as such, probably reveals more about us than we intended. This is one of the risks/benefits of undertaking a socio-analysis, it is also a form of *auto-analysis*.

References

Abbott, G. and B. Jordan (2001), *English All Over the Place: Experiences While Teaching Abroad*, London: Starhaven.

Atkinson, W. (2020), *Bourdieu and After: A Guide to Relational Phenomenology*, Abingdon: Routledge.

Bartlett, T. (2014), *Analysing Power in Language: A Practical Guide*, London: Routledge.

Bednarek, M. and J. R. Martin (2010), *New Discourse on Language: Functional Perspectives on Multimodality, Identity, and Affiliation*, London: Continuum.

Belcher, D. (2013), 'The Future of ESP Research: Resources and Access and Choice', in B. Paltridge and S. Starfield (eds), *Handbook of English for Specific Purposes*, 535–51, Boston: Blackwell.

Bell, D. E. (2016), 'Practitioners, Pedagogies and Professionalism in English for Academic Purposes (EAP): The Development of a Contested Field', PhD thesis, University of Nottingham.

Bell, D. E. (2021), 'Accounting for the Troubled Status of English Language Teachers in Higher Education', *Teaching in Higher Education*, 1–16. https://doi.org/10.1080/13562517.2021.1935848

Benesch, S. (2001), *Critical English for Academic Purposes: Theory, Politics, and Practice*, Mahwah: Lawrence Erlbaum Associates Inc.

Bhopal, K. and M. Myers (2023), *Elite Universities and the Making of Privilege: Exploring Race and Class in Global Educational Economies*, Abingdon: Taylor & Francis.

Bourdieu, P. (1984), *Distinction: A Social Critique of the Judgement of Taste*, Abingdon: Routledge.

Bourdieu, P. (1988), *Homo Academicus*, Cambridge: Polity Press.

Bourdieu, P. (1989), 'Social Space and Symbolic Power', *Sociological Theory*, 7 (1): 14–25.

Bourdieu, P. (1990), *The Logic of Practice*, Cambridge: Polity Press.

Bourdieu, P. (1991), *Language and Symbolic Power*, Cambridge, MA: Harvard University Press.

Bourdieu, P. (1996), *The Rules of Art*, Cambridge: Polity Press.
Bourdieu, P. (1998), *Practical Reason*, Cambridge: Polity Press.
Bourdieu, P. (2000a), *Pascalian Meditations*, Cambridge: Polity Press.
Bourdieu, P. (2000b), 'The Biographical Illusion', in P. du Gay, J. Evans and P. Redman (eds), *Identity*, 297–303, New Delhi: Sage.
Bourdieu, P. (2007), *Sketch for a Self-analysis*, Cambridge: Polity Press.
Bourdieu, P. (2008), *Sketch for a Self-analysis*, Chicago: University of Chicago Press.
Bourdieu, P. (2022), *Microcosmes. Théorie des Champs*, Paris: Raisons d'agir.
Bourdieu P. and J. C. Passeron (1977), *Reproduction in Education, Society and Culture*, London: Sage.
Bourdieu, P. and L. Wacquant (1992), *An Invitation to Reflexive Sociology*, Cambridge: Polity Press.
Braine, G. (1999), *Non-native Educators in English Language Teaching*, Mahwah: Lawrence Erlbaum Associates.
Bruce, I. (2021), 'Towards an EAP without Borders: Developing Knowledge, Practitioners, and Communities', *International Journal of English for Academic Purposes: Research and Practice*, Spring Issue, 23–36.
Bruce, I. and B. Bond, eds (2022), *Contextualizing English for Academic Purposes in Higher Education: Politics, Policies and Practices*, London: Bloomsbury Publishing.
Campion, G. C. (2016), '"The Learning Never Ends": Exploring Teachers Views on the Transition from General English to EAP', *Journal of English for Academic Purposes*, 23: 59–70.
Canagarajah, A. S. (1999), *Resisting Linguistic Imperialism in English Teaching*, Oxford: Oxford University Press.
Cheng, A. (2019), 'Examining the "Applied Aspirations" in the ESP Genre Analysis of Published Journal Articles', *Journal of English for Academic Purposes*, 38: 36–47.
Cowley-Haselden, S. and L. Monbec (2019), 'Emancipating Ourselves from Mental Slavery: Affording Knowledge in Our Practice', in M. Gillway (ed.), *Proceedings of the 2017 BALEAP Conference. Addressing the State of the Union: Working Together = Learning Together*, 39–46, Reading: Garnet.
Crew, T. (2020), *Higher Education and Working-Class Academics*, Cham: Springer International Publishing.
Davis, M. (2019), 'Publishing Research as an EAP Practitioner: Opportunities and Threats', *Journal of English for Academic Purposes*, 39: 72–86.
Ding, A. (2019), 'EAP Practitioner Identity', in K. Hyland and L. L. C. Wong (eds), *Specialised English: New Directions in ESP and EAP Research and Practice*, 63–76, London: Routledge.
Ding, A. (2022), 'Bourdieu and Field Analysis: EAP and its Practitioners', in A. Ding and M. Evans (eds), *Social Theory for English for Academic Purposes: Foundations and Perspectives*, 155–76, London: Bloomsbury.
Ding, A., B. Bond and I. Bruce (2022), '"Clearly You Have Nothing Better to Do with Your Time than This": A Critical Historical Exploration of Contributions to the BALEAP Discussion List', *Journal of English for Academic Purposes*, 58: 101109.
Ding, A. and I. Bruce (2017), *The English for Academic Purposes Practitioner: Operating on the Edge of Academia*, Cham, Switzerland: Palgrave Macmillan.
Ding, A. and G. Campion (2016), 'EAP Teacher Development', in K. Hyland and K. Shaw (eds), *The Routledge Handbook of English for Academic Purposes*, 547–59, London: Routledge.

Ding, A. and M. Evans, eds (2022), *Social Theory for English for Academic Purposes: Foundations and Perspectives*, London: Bloomsbury.

Dudley-Evans, T. and M. J. St-John (1998), *Developments in English for Specific Purposes*, Cambridge: Cambridge University Press.

Elsted, F. J. (2012), 'An Investigation into the Attitudes and Attributes that can Support Teachers in their Transition from General English to English For Academic Purposes', Unpublished Master's Thesis, The University of Essex, UK.

Errey, L. and M. A. Ansell (2001), 'The MA in EAP and ESP', *BALEAP PIM Reports*, 7. http://www.uefap.com/baleap/pimreports/2001/bath/errey_ansel.htm

Ewer, J. R. (1983), 'Teacher Training for EST: Problems and Methods', *The ESP Journal*, 2: 9–31.

Fairclough, N. (1995), *Critical Discourse Analysis: The Critical Study of Language*, New York: Longman.

Flowerdew, J. (2019), 'Power in English for Academic Purposes', in K. Hyland and L. L. C. Wong (eds), *Specialised English: New Directions in ESP and EAP Research and Practice*, 50–62, London: Routledge.

Frangie, S. (2009), 'Bourdieu's Reflexive Politics: Socio-Analysis, Biography and Self-Creation', *European Journal of Social Theory*, 12 (2): 213–29.

Grenfell, M (2023), *Bourdieu's Metanoia: Seeing the Social World Anew*, Abingdon: Routledge.

Hadley, G. (2015), *English for Academic Purposes in Neoliberal Universities: A Critical Grounded Theory*, Heidelberg: Springer.

Halliday, M. A. K. (1985), *An Introduction to Functional Grammar*, London: Edward Arnold.

Hasan, R. (1998), 'The Disempowerment Game: Bourdieu and Language in Literacy', *Linguistics and Education*, 10 (1): 25–87.

Hodge, B. (2017), 'Discourse Analysis', in T. Bartlett and G. O'Grady (eds), *The Routledge Handbook of Systemic Functional Linguistics*, 544–56, London: Routledge.

Hutchinson, T. and A. Waters (1987), *English for Specific Purposes*, Cambridge: Cambridge University Press.

Hyland, K. (2012), '"The Past is the Future with the Lights On": Reflections on AELFE's 20th Birthday', *Ibérica, Revista de la Asociación Europea de Lenguas para Fines Específicos*, 24: 29–42.

Hyland, K. and L. Hamp-Lyons (2002), 'EAP: Issues and Directions', *Journal of English for Academic Purposes*, 1 (1): 1–12.

Hyland, K. and F. K. Jiang (2020), 'A Bibliometric Study of EAP Research: Who is Doing What, Where and When?', *Journal of English for Academic Purposes*, 49. https://doi.org/10.1016/j.jeap.2020.100929

Jansen, J. D. (2019), 'On the Politics of Decolonisation: Knowledge, Authority and the Settled Curriculum', in J. D. Jansen (ed.), *Decolonisation in Universities: The Politics of Knowledge*, 50–78, Johannesburg: Wits University Press.

Johns, T. F. (1981), 'Some Problems of a World-wide Profession', in *The ESP Teacher: Role, Development and Prospects*, 16–22, London: British Council English (Teaching Information Centre. ELT Document 112).

Johnson, C. D. (1971), 'Presentation to the Beirut Conference on Adult English for National Development', in *Proceedings of Conference on Adult English for National Development*, 63–73, Beirut: Center for English Language Research and Teaching, the American University of Beirut (ERIC Document Reproduction Service No. ED 130 525).

Jordan, R. R. (1997), *English for Academic Purposes: A Guide and Resource Book for Teachers*, Cambridge: Cambridge University Press.

Kirkpatrick, A. (2002), *Englishes in Asia: Communication, Identity, Power and Education*, Melbourne: Language Australia Ltd. http://languageaustralia.com.au/

Krzanowski, M. (2001), 'S/He Holds the Trinity/UCLES Dip: Are they Ready to Teach EAP', *BALEAP PIM Reports*. http://www.uefap.com/baleap/pimreports/2001/bath/krzanowski.htm

Kubota, R. (2015), 'Questioning Language Myths in English Language Teaching: Toward Border-crossing Communication', in *Selected Papers from the Twenty-Fourth International Symposium on English Teaching*, 44–57, English Teachers' Association-Republic of China (ETA-ROC).

Lukin, A. (2019), *War and Its Ideologies*, Singapore: Springer.

MacDonald, J. (2016), 'The Margins as Third Space: EAP Teacher Professionalism in Canadian Universities', *TESL Canada Journal*, 34 (1): 106–16.

Martin, J. R. and P. R. White (2005), *The Language of Evaluation: Appraisal in English*, Basingstoke: Palgrave Macmillan.

Martin, O. (2017), *L'analyse Quantitative des Données*, Malakoff: Armand Colin.

Martin, P. (2014), 'Teachers in Transition: The Road to EAP', in P. Breen (ed.), *Cases on Teacher Identity, Diversity, and Cognition in Higher Education*, 287–316, Hershey: Information Science Reference.

Maton, K. (2005), 'The Sacred and the Profane: The Arbitrary Legacy of Pierre Bourdieu', *European Journal of Cultural Studies*, 8 (1): 101–12.

Mittelmeier, J. and B. Zhang (2022), 'The Ideologies and Practices of Internationalization within Universities', in I. Bruce and B. Bond (eds), *Contextualizing English for Academic Purposes in Higher Education: Politics, Policies and Practices*, 27–44, London: Bloomsbury Academic.

Monbec, L. (June 2022), 'Systemic Functional Linguistics for the Self-Taught, Part 2', *BALEAP Research and Publications* (blog). https://research.baleap.org/2022/06/29/systemic-functional-linguistics-for-the-self-taught-part-2/

Ndebele, N. S. (1987), 'The English Language and Social Change in South Africa', *The English Academy Review*, 4 (1): 1–16.

O'Regan, J. P. (2021), *Global English and Political Economy*, Abingdon: Routledge.

Pascal, B. ([1670] 2016), *Pensées*, Paris: Éditions du Seuil.

Pellandini-Simányi, L. (2014), 'Bourdieu, Ethics and Symbolic Power', *The Sociological Review*, 62 (4): 651–74.

Pennycook, A. (1994), *The Cultural Politics of English as an International Language*, London and New York: Longman.

Pennycook, A. (2002), *English and the Discourses of Colonialism*, London: Routledge.

Pennycook, A. (2021), *Critical Applied Linguistics: A Critical Introduction*, London: Routledge.

Phillipson, R. (1986), 'English Rules: A Study of Language Pedagogy and Imperialism', in R. Phillipson and T. Skutnabb-Kangas (eds), *Linguicism Rules in Education*, 124–343, Denmark: Roskilde University Centre.

Phillipson, R. (1988), 'Linguicism: Structures and Ideologies in Linguistic Imperialism', in J. Cummins and T. Skutnabb-Kangas (eds), *Minority Education: From Shame to Struggle*, 339–58, Avon: Multilingual Matters.

Phillipson, R. (1992), *Linguistic Imperialism*, Oxford: Oxford University Press.

Post, D. (2010), 'The Transition from Teaching General English to English for Academic Purposes: An Investigation into the Challenges Encountered by Teachers', Unpublished Masters diss., University of Bath.

Raimes, A. (1991), 'Instructional Balance: From Theories to Practices in the Teaching of Writing', in J. Alatis (ed.), *Georgetown University Round Table on Language and Linguistics*, 239–49, Washington, DC: Georgetown University Press.

Reisigl, M. and R. Wodak (2016), 'The Discourse-historical Approach (DHA)', in R. Wodak and M. Meyer (eds), *Methods of Critical Discourse Analysis*, 3rd edn, 24–61, London: Sage.

Renandya, W. A., T. T. M. Nguyen and G. M. Jacobs (2023), 'Learning to Unlearn Faulty Beliefs and Practices in English Language Teaching', *Studies in English Language and Education*, 10 (1): 1–15. https://doi.org/10.24815/siele.v10i1.26009

Roberts, P. (2001), 'Teacher Training for EAP', *BALEAP PIM Reports*, vol. 7. http://www.uefap.com/baleap/pimreports/2001/bath/roberts.htm

Robinson, P. C. (1991), *ESP Today: A Practitioner's Guide*, Hemel Hempstead: Prentice Hall.

Salö, L. (2017), *The Sociolinguistics of Academic Publishing: Language and the Practices of Homo Academicus*, London: Palgrave Macmillan.

Savolainen, J., P. J. Casey, J. P. McBrayer and P. N. Schwerdtle (2023), 'Positionality and its Problems: Questioning the Value of Reflexivity Statements in Research', *Perspectives on Psychological Science*. https://doi.org/10.1177/17456916221144988. PMID: 36780607

Singleton, D. and C. Muñoz (2011), 'Around and Beyond the Critical Period Hypothesis', in E. Hinkle (ed.), *Handbook of Research in Second Language Teaching and Learning*, 407–25, Abingdon: Routledge.

Stibbe, A. (2020), *Ecolinguistics: Language, Ecology and The Stories We Live By*, Abingdon: Routledge.

Strevens, P. (1988), 'The Learner and Teacher of ESP', in D. Chamberlain and R. J. Baumgardner (eds), *ESP in the Classroom: Practice and Evaluation*, 91–119, London: Modern English Publications in association with the British Council. ELT Document 128.

Swales, J. (1977), 'ESP in the Middle East', in S. Holden (ed.), *English for Specific Purposes*, 36–8, London: Modern English Publications.

Swales, J. (1990), *Genre Analysis: English in Academic and Research Settings*, Cambridge: Cambridge University Press.

Swales, J. (1997), 'English as Tyrannosaurus Rex', *World Englishes*, 16: 373–82.

Swales, J. (2019), 'The Futures of EAP Genre Studies: A Personal Viewpoint', *Journal of English for Academic Purposes*, 38: 75–82.

Swartz, D. L. (2013), *Symbolic Power, Politics, and Intellectuals: The Political Sociology of Pierre Bourdieu*, Chicago: Chicago University Press.

Táíwò, O. O. (2022), *Elite Capture: How the Powerful took over Identity Politics (and Everything Else)*, Chicago: Haymarket Books.

Tupas, R. and W. A. Renandya (2021), 'Unequal Englishes: Re-envisioning the Teaching of English in Linguistically Diverse Classrooms', in B. Spolsky and H. Lee (eds), *Localizing Global English: Asian Perspectives and Practices*, 47–62, Abingdon: Routledge.

Turner, J. (2004), 'Language as Academic Purpose', *Journal of English for Academic Purposes*, 3: 95–109.

Van Leeuwen, T. (2008), *Discourse and Practice: New Tools for Critical Discourse Analysis*, Oxford: Oxford University Press.

Venkataraman, N. (2018), 'What's not in a Frame? Analysis of Media Representations of the Environmental Refugee', in M. Schröter and C. Taylor (eds), *Exploring Silence and Absence in Discourse: Empirical Approaches*, 241–79, London: Palgrave Macmillan.

Wacquant, L. J. D. (1989), 'For a Socio-Analysis of Intellectuals: On "Homo Academicus"', *Berkeley Journal of Sociology*, 34: 1–29.

Webster, S. (2022), 'The Transition of EAP Practitioners into Scholarship Writing', *Journal of English for Academic Purposes*, 57: 101091.
Wong, J. O. (2014), *The Culture of Singapore English*, Cambridge: Cambridge University Press.
Yenn, T. Y. (2022), *This is What Inequality Looks Like*, Singapore: Ethos Books.

Chapter 2

AN EXPLORATION OF THE ETHICS OF SCHOLARSHIP IN EAP

COLLEGIAL CONNECTIONS AND ETHICAL ENTANGLEMENTS

Bee Bond

Introduction: Mapping the chapter

As with most scholarship work, the motivation behind, the origins of and most of the ideas discussed in this chapter have become increasingly complex and enmeshed with the work, experiences and ideas of many other colleagues. In a single-authored chapter that focusses on ethics in practitioner scholarship, this is an uncomfortable place to begin. It is also, however, the driving conundrum that has led to my belief that there is a need for greater consideration of ethics within the work of English for academic purposes (EAP) scholars and practitioners. As McNamee suggests in the introduction to a special edition of the *Journal of Philosophy of Education*, 'little attention is paid to the philosophical character of the nature of problems encountered in the process of educational research' (2001: 309). It has already been claimed that this is also the case for EAP in general: 'The ethics of EAP remains for the field and its practitioners a source of disquiet and concern' and requires a 'more concerted discussion' (Ding, 2022: xv). Here I suggest this is even more the case for EAP scholarship. Unanswered ethical questions about the ideological underpinnings of EAP, its role in supporting problematic university structures and inequalities relating to access and stable employment as well as its as yet uncertain knowledge base are all areas that require further investigation. Who has the interest, opportunity, knowledge and skill-set to investigate these questions opens up further ethical problems. Therefore, in this chapter I focus specifically on the ethics of scholarship in EAP and consider what a focus on ethics can tell us about the identity and agency of EAP practitioners.

This involves an exploration of the ethical reflexivity required when the practices and people under investigation in our scholarship are tightly woven into the professional life and identity of the practitioner. Consideration is made of power dynamics and of differing perceptions of power and identity within an EAP unit, across a higher education (HE) institution and within the field. Essentially, though, this chapter poses a series of questions for consideration rather than providing answers or frameworks to follow. The aim is to connect theoretical considerations with the reality of EAP scholarship and practice. The hope is that the chapter will help to prepare those practitioners who wish to embark on their own scholarship projects with an understanding of some of the complex questions they may need to ask themselves, not only at the beginning of a project in order to gain formal ethical approval, but throughout their scholarship journey, as contexts, people and events unfold and lead to further and ongoing ethical considerations.

To address these questions, it is also necessary to ethically consider the purpose in writing this chapter as a non-expert and that of the audience in reading it, the position and capital of the writer within the community that makes up the audience, 'and . . . and . . . and . . .' (Deleuze and Guattari, 2000: 25).

The tracings of a theory: A Thousand Plateaus

Throughout this chapter I borrow concepts from the work of Deleuze and Guattari (2000). I do not pretend to be an expert on posthumanism, nor am I fully committed to this theory, but I have found the concepts to be useful to 'think with' (Kinchin and Gravett, 2020).

Posthumanism challenges the idea that only humans have agency in the moral world, arguing for a new epistemology that moves away from the anthropocentrism of, specifically, European/Cartesian philosophical thought. A posthuman ethics, then, requires us to think beyond our own human interests and to consider our interconnectedness with technology (and how it can mediate experiences of the world) and with the natural world in its entirety. It requires us to place equal value on the interests and rights of all. It is 'an ethics of joy or affirmation' and 'is a pragmatic engagement with the present in order to collectively construct conditions that transform" (Braidotti, 2018: 223 in Braidotti and Hlavajova, 2018). How this is done, what is emphasized from this broad philosophy, depends on the focus of your work and thinking. In education, for example, posthumanism suggests 'locating oneself politically vis-à-vis one's knowledge construction activities – which includes teaching' (Strom and Lupinacci, 2019: 104)

Deleuze and Guattari's seminal *A Thousand Plateaus: Capitalism and Schizophrenia* (2000) is a foundational posthumanist text. It is not an easy read. It is full of complex metaphors; it is purposefully non-linear and provides very few definitions, leaving the reader to interpret and draw their own conclusions. I have taken comfort from other scholars who have both struggled with the work of Deleuze and Guattari and also found value in it, who have drawn on their work without necessarily claiming to understand or accept all they wrote (Hertz, 2016; Strom, 2018). What *A Thousand Plateaus* does do is argue for multiplicity, defining a plateau as 'any multiplicity connected to other multiplicities by superficial underground stems in such a way as to form or extend a rhizome' (2000: 22). It is this multiplicity, the idea of continuous change, or the 'and . . . and . . . and . . .' (2000: 25) of posthumanist thought, that sits well with an ethics that requires constant reflexivity around understanding, knowledge and behaviours. *A Thousand Plateaus* also provides an eclectic range of concepts that have since been further developed and theorized, providing a loose framework for posthuman thinking (see Braidotti and Hlavajova, 2018, for a glossary of posthuman terms). I have found that the permission to 'pick and mix' from this conceptual framework and to see posthuman thinking as 'a navigational tool through which to read the world' (Braidotti, 2012) works well for my own EAP practice. One ethical decision for EAP practitioner scholarship is whether to delve deeply into one specific aspect and become a true expert in that area, or to take this more pick-and-mix approach to the range of knowledge bases available. Posthumanism argues, in fact, for the creation of an 'assemblage', which looks at how networks or 'rhizomes' (of people, of 'things', of structures – human and non-human) connect in different ways, at different times and for different purposes, to have powerful impacts.

In their writing, Deleuze and Guattari suggest that mapping and tracing can enable us to focus in on particular areas that are of most concern to us at any particular moment; the map 'fosters connections between fields' (2000: 12). These concepts of mapping and tracing stem from the idea that there are multiple, limitless connections between 'things' (people, objects, ideas, etc.), each with an equal position on a flat plane. By mapping and tracing certain connections, based on our own preoccupations, we highlight and add differential weight and consequence for ourselves and possibly others at a particular point in time. This mapping process creates one of many other possible routes through a nomadic journey of constant learning and 'becoming'.

The route this chapter takes through the complex and interwoven ethics of scholarship is, therefore, just one of many possibilities. I hope it is easy to follow. It has been a difficult one to map out; you may decide to follow your own path.

The route

I chose to begin with an overview of the scholarship of learning and teaching (SoTL) and its place and practice in the context of EAP. Here I position EAP scholarship within a wider SoTL movement in higher education because the nature of the ethical considerations is more closely aligned than those required for EAP *research on texts*. I argue that, while there is frequent mention of ethics in the literature around SoTL, and there are guidelines to help scholars meet the requirements of ethical approval boards, there is little in the literature that goes beyond these tick-box type exercises. I then attempt to identify some of the hidden ethical issues that arise while undertaking scholarship projects, drawing on a case study that exemplifies the ethical reflexivity required when scholarship is undertaken within the context of the scholars' own working context. In doing so I aim to help others imagine how these issues might be encountered and addressed. Having described how ethical concerns can arise in practice, I attempt to develop a heuristic for future ethical EAP scholarship, following Braidotti's suggestion of a need for 'affirmative ethics' (2006, 2019). This cannot be an easy-to-follow framework, but a list of areas for consideration, requiring dynamic ethical questioning.

Scholarship in EAP: An assemblage of practices

The turn towards scholarship of learning and teaching, or SoTL, in, with and for EAP educational practices, as opposed to research **on** English as it is used to communicate for academic purposes, has not happened in isolation. It is part of a wider movement within higher education to focus on the quality of teaching and learning and to develop an evidence-based approach to this, with clear knowledge and practice foundations. Ding (2016) and Ding et al. (2018) provide a detailed consideration of SoTL, especially in relation to language teaching and EAP. In 'Challenging Scholarship' (2016), Ding provides an overview of the historical development of SoTL, highlighting the uncomfortable (unethical?) role it can sometimes play in perpetuating the neoliberal agendas of universities, feeding into metrics around excellence and student satisfaction. He also suggests ways in which scholarship can be used to counter this and can be used to inform, engage and hopefully transform education and educators in positive ways. 'Engaging in scholarship contributes to greater professional autonomy, enabling new professional identities to emerge; it allows for development and transformation of praxis. Most of all, we believe that scholarship has the potential to enable language educators to actively shape their educational contexts rather than be shaped by circumstance, others and powerful ideologies and structures' (Ding et al., 2018). Here, as well as in other work (cf. Ding and Bruce, 2017; Ding, 2019), a direct link is made between engaging in scholarship and increased practitioner agency and the development of a clearer identity for the field.

However, it is clear from the literature that there is no one way to 'do SoTL'. There is no one definition. Healey et al. (2013) assert that the concept of SoTL remains fluid, although they do state that scholarly teaching is the foundation of SoTL. Others make a clearer distinction between scholarly teaching (seen as an imperative for all who teach) and SoTL (viewed not as compulsory but ethically necessary if our students 'deserve the best knowledge and understanding we can muster' (Ding et al., 2018; Ding, 2017)). SoTL is, in posthuman terms, an 'assemblage' of practices, where assemblage is taken to be an aggregate of elements, 'multiplicities, or heterogenous collectives that function together in a contextually unique manner to produce something, to create new ways of functioning' (Strom, 2018: 108). The 'something' that is produced is more powerful and has a different identity to the separate parts from which it is assembled.

Just as there are many ways to 'do' SoTL, there are also many routes into and through SoTL and it is undertaken by academic educators across all disciplines. This is one way in which it can be distinguished from educational research. SoTL is done by those who are involved in education within their own context rather than by researchers who come from outside. Therefore, some of the ethical considerations are also different.

Those engaged in SoTL are not necessarily trained in educational research; they will bring their own disciplinary epistemologies to their work and may not consider investigations they conduct around student education to require the same rigorous ethical processes as are required within their disciplinary research. Equally, the disciplinary ethical approval boards that they submit their scholarship proposals to may also not have the necessary understanding and expertise to ensure they ask the right questions and are able to provide clear guidance. The purpose of these boards is to focus on key concerns, but these often relate to research in the discipline rather than working within the educational practices of the discipline. The posthuman concept of rhizomatic tracings can help to explain the issue here. Rhizomes are 'heterogeneous multiplicities. They are acentered – that is, they are without a unifying entity – and characterized by connection and expansion, constantly becoming different in nature as they add dimensions' (Strom, 2018: 106). Disciplinary ethical approval, based on disciplinary epistemologies and ontologies, highlights and maps different parts of an ethical rhizome to those we might consider in SoTL; it also attempts to create a complete map that 'has to do with performance' (Deleuze and Guattari, 2000: 12), aiming to 'root' and 'aborify' the rhizome, thus causing obstruction and fossilization, imposing the verb 'to be' rather than encouraging continued questioning and exploration of ethics beyond the form-filling process. As others have posited, 'formal codes of ethics are not the best way of addressing ethical issues arising in educational research' (Small, 2001: 387), and it is 'not the job of the ethics committee to take over ethical responsibility' (Small, 2001: 391).

However, it is the specific difficulty of gaining ethical approval for SoTL that has, to date, occupied most space in the SoTL literature around ethics. Chick (2019) provides a clear list of bullet points for consideration, many of which draw on Martin (2013) who discusses how SoTL scholars can navigate the North American Institutional Review Board (IRB). Healey et al. (2013) go slightly further and draw on a range of key Western ethical traditions:

- Teleological or pragmatic – considering the potential positive or negative consequences for stakeholders.
- External – what impact does it have externally?
- Deontological – demonstrating respect for person, autonomy and choice.

They do so in order to develop an ethical scholar matrix (taking students and the institutional community, the teaching community and the research community as the three 'stakeholders'), the aim of which is to provide ethical possibilities that are 'immediate and practical, without overwhelming readers' (2013: 28).

Beyond this, SoTL literature has continued to draw largely on, and refer readers to, the ethics of educational research as outlined in documents such as the British Educational Research Association's (BERA) *Ethical Guidelines for Educational Research* (2018). This is also largely practical in nature – a list of questions to ask of the research or project you are undertaking in order to ensure you are working within the boundaries of agreed ethical guidelines.

To date, then, it seems that the ethics of SoTL has focussed on practicalities and processes and remains undertheorized.

The ethical lacuna

The broader SoTL field's focus on what constitutes 'coded' ethics, that is, the need for institutional ethical approval rather than the more philosophical concerns of positionality, ethos and moral values, is problematic. There also remains a lack of clarity over when normal educational practices shift into practice under investigation with the parallel requirements of ethical approval and processes.

To address this, much, but not all, can again be drawn from the ethics of educational research. Brooks, te Riele and Maguire 'argue for the situated nature of ethical decision making' (2015: 2) and draw on different theories of ethics as a way of moving beyond the tick-box approach to completing ethical approval forms. However, their focus remains on ethics in relation to the subjects of educational research, with these subjects being viewed as 'other' to the researcher, being subjected to the research, which is done on, for or about them, rather than with, in collaboration and within the same working context as the researcher themselves. It is the contextual nature of (EAP) scholarship that adds further complexity and difference to the required continuous, rhizomatic ethical considerations. These cannot be addressed at the outset of a project and then put aside. Ethics in scholarship should be an ongoing and iterative concern.

It is therefore hardly surprising that there is also a lacuna in the understanding of ethics among EAP practitioners, working in marginalized positions (Ding and Bruce, 2017), often in precarity and with unclear routes into and through the profession (Campion, 2016; Ding and Campion, 2016), and often with little training, time or support to develop their understanding of research processes.

There is not yet much literature focussing on EAP practitioner research or scholarship, despite it being a core requirement in the BALEAP TEAP competency framework (2022). In the 2022 version of the TEAP scheme, scholarship is defined as becoming 'aware of new developments in discourse processing and its implications for academic literacy' (2022: 14), while research is positioned as something that most practitioners will not have the time or opportunity to engage in. The only mention of ethics in the whole document is in relation to knowledge of ethical academic practices or academic integrity.

Writing that focusses explicitly on EAP scholarship, similar to the wider literature of SoTL, assumes ethics as integral to scholarship but does not explore it in much depth (e.g. Ding et al., 2018). Literature that positions this kind of work as research, or practitioner research, barely seems to consider the role of ethics at all. For example, Blaj-Ward's *Researching Contexts, Practices and Pedagogies in English for Academic Purposes* provides an overview of a range of possible areas of inquiry for practitioners interested in conducting research. In one chapter, she discusses the importance of 'positionality', suggesting the need to consider the question: 'How do *my position and the role(s) I am taking* in this interaction shape what I am being told and what I am hearing?' (2014: 139) as well as considering the setting and the timing of any interactions that are part of your research. This is, however, the only nod she makes towards *ethical* research practices. Davis (2019) in 'Publishing Research as an EAP Practitioner: Opportunities and

Threats' considers what could be viewed as the unethical lack of support of EAP centre managers for those who wish to engage in practitioner research but also claims that 'the majority of EAP practitioners are not researchers'. Throughout the article, a range of ethical issues are hinted at: lack of expertise around how to conduct research; the ethics of EAP as a business and how this impacts research opportunities; practitioners prioritizing teaching over research rather than viewing them as interconnected; and lack of support from both the workplace and the wider profession, but these remain unexamined. Webster's (2022) 'The Transition of EAP Practitioners into Scholarship Writing' also ignores the question of ethics.

Finally, Hanks (2022) in 'De-Mystifying the Nimbus of Research: Reigniting Practitioners' Interest in Exploring EAP' argues that exploratory practice is widely used as a form of EAP practitioner research. Exploratory practice (EP) operates under seven principles, which work to create an ethical discourse as they point to the importance of 'quality of life', the inclusion of all stakeholders who work continuously together to understand classroom life and learning, positioning students and teachers as equals in the investigative process and leading to mutual benefit. EP should also be integrated into, rather than take place outside, usual curricula practices. However, this framework also remains undertheorized and does not really define or fully explore, for example, the ethics of the *requirement* that 'everybody needs to be involved in the work for understanding' (Allwright and Hanks, 2009: 149–53). There is, for example, little exploration of the ethics around the unequal power dynamics that exist in a classroom environment, despite much of the work of EP claiming to draw on the work of Freire. Furthermore, the extent to which EP is and can be seen as a form of scholarship that leads to the public sharing of developed understandings in EAP remains unclear. If EP is integrated into classroom practices (i.e. not planned as research with ethical approval), any understandings gained cannot be ethically publicly shared with others and cannot, therefore, be anything more than a pedagogical tool. This may explain why, as Hanks's article (2022) bemoans, there are scant citations drawing on exploratory practice research within the EAP literature.

This ongoing lacuna in our understanding and exploration of the ethics of (EAP) scholarship makes the importance of taking an ethical approach to our scholarship work even more vital. This includes being clear about ethical boundaries and knowing the set of rules or codes we need to work under, but also being able to apply ethical reflexivity throughout. It requires an 'ethics of sustainability, based on . . . interconnections . . . This transformative ethics includes a critical or reactive and an affirmative or active phase' (Braidotti, 2006: 8); it also requires a critique of tradition, with movement away from 'inert repetition of established habits of thought or self-representation', instead cultivating 'the political desire for change or transformation' (Braidotti, 2006: 8). In the next section of this chapter, I explore how this iterative critical and active questioning could be intertwined into a scholarship project by providing a case study example.

A case study

EAP teaching is highly contextual. It is built around the needs of specific students in specific contexts. It therefore follows that any scholarship focussing on that teaching will be influenced and impacted by that context. The contextual nature of this scholarship also has important ethical implications – the extent to which it can be relevant beyond the context, but also the extent to which data, findings and conclusions can be used while protecting those people and institutions who are involved in the project. By presenting a case study as an example of collaborative and multi-layered scholarship work, I hope it is possible to draw parallels and learn lessons that can be applied elsewhere, while acknowledging that the context in which I work provides affordances for scholarship, decision-making and collaborative working practices that may not be available to others. Essentially, the aim is to open conversations around the ethics of scholarship in EAP, following the argument that 'Working with an ethical code is learning to use language successfully in real social situations . . . socially in conversational communities, not in isolation' (Brooks, te Riele and Maguire, 2015: 2).

This social, collective and collaborative development of understanding – of our practices, principles, ethics and impact – was the underpinning ethos for the scholarship project I present here as a case study.

The project: A rhizomatic mapping of ethics

The case study project had the working title: 'Evaluating the Impact of Embedded Insessional Academic Language and Literacies Provision across the Disciplines'. Those of us working on insessional provision were becoming increasingly conscious of the need to be able to provide evidence of the value and impact of the work we were doing in this area. As our provision expanded and diversified, as director of the provision I also wanted to find a way to encourage and support colleagues who were new to scholarship so that they felt able to investigate their practice and collaborate with the schools they were connected to with more academic confidence. The project was therefore purposefully broad, hopefully enabling individuals to make autonomous decisions as to how they would investigate impact within their own insessional work.

My own focus in the umbrella project was not on the impact of insessional work on students or the disciplines we worked with, but on EAP tutors themselves. With colleagues increasingly dispersed across campus, I was hoping that the project would provide a means to reconnect with Language Centre colleagues in a purposeful manner and engender a sharing of experiences, ideas and development.

I do not consider the results of this investigation here (for more information about the work we are still doing around this project, see (The Language Centre, 2023) https://insessional.leeds.ac.uk/). Rather, I draw attention to the different ethical questions that arose at different stages of the project. These will have been different for different colleagues at different times, so each of us will have 'rhizomatically mapped' these differently. I can only provide my own tracing or perspective. I have categorized these under four separate themes: thinking about ethics; collegiality and trust; power and scholarship as a continuous endeavour.

The ethics of thinking about ethics

The obvious starting point for mapping the range of ethical dilemmas this project has raised is the formal ethical approval form.

The completion of this form has been highlighted as a potential barrier to undertaking SoTL projects (Martin, 2013; Chick, 2019). Within my own context, colleagues have often questioned the lack of transparency around the process as well as its onerous and tick-box nature. It seemed that the form itself was becoming a barrier to the professional development of colleagues, to our developing an understanding of our work and to being able to share any understanding with others. By requesting umbrella approval, I was hoping to enable colleagues to take steps towards engagement with scholarship in their teaching context by removing an administrative barrier. There was an ethical position here, using my own previous experience and position in my workplace to support and encourage others to meet 'the core values of professional communities [which] revolve around the expectations that we do not keep secrets, whether of discovery or of grounded doubt' (Schulman, 2000: 50).

However, it could be argued that in doing this, agency around the process was removed. A removal of agency can lead to an abdication or denial of responsibility and therefore reduce the focus on the ethics of the work being undertaken. By not having gone through the process of planning out and completing the form, did I both deny others the opportunity to develop their own thinking and agency and also undermine the ethics of the project by not pushing others to think them through via the form?

I have previously touched on concerns around the current ethical approval process for scholarship projects (Bond, 2020). Whereas Martin's (2013) work was around enabling SoTL practitioners to navigate the process, my concern is that the current process does not ask the right questions of us and does not, therefore, ensure we have fully considered the implications and impact of our work on those involved before we embark on it. While it is not the form that makes you think, by completing the form you are forced to take the time to do so. For those new to scholarship, often working with little support or training, the potential impact of their work may not always be obvious until too far into the project. If the form is limited, and the focus on ethics is only built in at the starting point, it is possible that thinking deeply about ethics will also be limited to these questions and this point.

In order to address these concerns, while completing the form myself, I repeatedly drew attention to the ethics of the work we were doing during meetings and through our online discussions via our Teams channel. I had been concerned that colleagues had paid scant attention to the ethical processes. This was not the case. Some questions we discussed in relation to the form were largely technical, for example, did the approval extend to this form of data collection, to speaking to those outside our institution? Other, more interesting ethical discussions extended beyond the form and demonstrate again how interconnected scholarship is with our EAP teaching practice.

Brooks et al. point out that 'The use of consent forms can also lull a researcher into believing they have fully informed the participants, even though this is impossible within a short form provided in advance; and even though in practice many participants may not fully read or understand the information on the form' (2015: 16). As a group we had many concerns around informed consent and around our participants feeling free and comfortable to express themselves and how this related to our own positions and the use of both academic legalese in the consent forms and of English in general when working with our EAP students.

One example of this was around the use of end-of-module feedback. While we agreed that it was possible to use quantitative data from this as evidence (e.g. 80 per cent of respondents agreed teaching was effective), we felt it was unethical to use student comments without informed consent. However, once one colleague added extra information about the wider potential use of student feedback for scholarship purposes to her module survey, the number of students who responded drastically reduced. This then impacted on her ability to evaluate the module and share this with colleagues in the school she was connected to.

We also discussed the ethics of using comments made via Teams channels. Particularly during the 2020 COVID pandemic and UK lockdown, this provided a rich source of potential data, with students directly contacting tutors with comments about the impact their classes had had on their understanding. For my own investigation, looking at how EAP teachers developed through insessional work, our staff insessional Teams channel was also a tempting source of information. Collectively, we considered the ethics of using this data – whether Teams comments can be seen as public documents and available to all, or whether they should be viewed as private correspondence. One colleague did contact her insessional school's ethics advisor to get guidance on this. Following this and our collective discussions we concluded that we should not use these conversations as we had not requested prior consent. We also concluded that requesting consent for future use would constrain and limit free discussion in those spaces.

My own ethical conundrum now is that I cannot unsee the 'data' I have had access to through my staff Teams channel. Although I will not use any of it directly in any future publications, it has all added to a picture of the ongoing development of insessional EAP practice and knowledge. I need to ask myself the extent to which I can/should morally present this background understanding. My response is to continue discussing this with my colleagues and to share anything I produce with them before I share with others.

By taking this 'community of practice' approach to thinking about ethics (Brooks, te Riele and Maguire, 2015: 21), we did not reject the forms and processes but went beyond them to share, discuss and attempt to apply the principles 'intelligently or wisely in the light of particular features of a situation'.

The ethics around collegiality and trust

One distinguishing feature of SoTL, particularly EAP SoTL, is its focus on collaborative work. As it relates to teaching and learning, even small-scale SoTL investigations need to include some interaction with others – whether that be a small group of students or other educators. Often it is both. Within ethical review forms, this is outlined as *'research on or with human participants'*. This phrasing is rather clinical and suggests an objective distance from those participants, whereas I would suggest that in SoTL we need to consider *all* those we are working with (whether as participants or investigators – and maybe as both) as *colleagues*. Taking this view alters our perspective and again raises several ethical questions, some of which can be exemplified through my case study.

EAP teaching, in this case specifically insessional EAP teaching that takes place within schools or disciplines, requires close collaboration with educators within that discipline. This EAP teaching should then become specific to the discipline – building in a knowledge of the context, cultures and ways of being and knowing that are required for students to be able to gain access and study successfully. Developing knowledge and understanding of this requires developing strong and trusting relationships with colleague-educators in the discipline. By acting as a bridge to their discipline, EAP teachers also generally seem to gain high levels of trust from their students.

One of the ethical questions we continue to consider as we work through our investigations into the impact of insessional teaching is the importance of kindness, trust and relationships with others (see, for example, Clegg and Rowland, 2010; Gravett, Taylor and Fairchild , 2021; Rowland, 2008).

When conducting interviews or questionnaires or employing other methods of data collection, it is well established that the building of trust will result in more open and honest responses, providing more reliable data. Bourdieu suggests that 'Social proximity and familiarity in effect provide two of the social conditions of "non-violent" communication' (1996: 20). For research, and for SoTL, this is surely a desired outcome. However, there are times when this information, provided in unguarded and relaxed conversation (even though informed consent has been provided and the participant/colleague is aware of the SoTL purpose of the conversation), needs to be carefully, ethically, handled. When reporting on one specific institution, on one specific discipline, it is much more difficult to maintain true anonymity. We have constantly and reflexively needed to revisit a range of 'what if' questions, for example:

- What if data we get from students seems to suggest criticism of individual teachers or vice versa?
- What if data we get from colleagues (staff and students) indicates prejudice based on protected characteristics (e.g. race, gender)?
- What if data we get indicates poor student education practices?

SoTL is supposed to loop (back) into practice, but in collecting data from and around the practice of others, based on trusting, collegial relationships, we can unearth issues that go beyond our own practices. Ethically, then, we need to ask ourselves what, where, how and when we can and should work to change the practice of others. If a key aspect of scholarship is that we make our investigations public, how can we do this while protecting the identities, careers and academic futures of our colleagues? And at what point should we not? Where do we draw lines in terms of confidentiality and anonymity? I would suggest that the ethical considerations around scholarship and interwoven relationships – with colleagues and our institutions – are even more complex and entangled for EAP scholars.

The ethics around power

There are many forms of power and many ways it can be wielded, perceived, developed, described and defined. Here I focus mainly on power as a form of capital and specifically a form of cultural capital which provides 'weight' in a particular field (Bourdieu, 2001).

This is, in part, an extension of the issues considered around collegiality and trust, which is more connected to social capital. For SoTL, power most obviously needs to be acknowledged when involving students in an investigation. It is important to consider why a student might participate or not, whether their agreement is given freely or because of fear of consequences (in relation to assessment outcomes/ treatment in class/withdrawal of support) if they do not.

However, this is not the only situation where power relationships need to be considered. To explore this further, I take my own investigation within the wider insessional case study as an example of how 'power shifts and changes throughout the process of research (so that ethical decisions need to be made not just at the start but on an ongoing basis). Moreover, power is not just a negative phenomenon, it can also be productive' (Brookes et al., 2015: 4).

At the outset of the project, there were around fifteen colleagues who were teaching insessional classes in a range of schools across campus. As a member of our Language Centre's leadership team and direct line manager for some, but not all, of the insessional teachers, I was, in some obvious ways, in a position of 'power'. Furthermore, I have worked at my institution for over twenty years and recently completed a highly visible, institutionally sponsored scholarship project. This kind of cultural capital is explained by Bourdieu (2001) as: 'the space of possibles [. . .] realized in individuals exercising an "attraction" or "repulsion" that depends on their "weight" in the field, in other words their visibility, and also on the more or less great affinity of habitus, which leads one to find their thought and action "sympathetic" or "antipathetic".'

In instigating a collaborative scholarship project, I/we have needed to constantly question why and how others have chosen to be involved (or not). There are a range of possible reasons. This is a non-exhaustive list of the questions I/we reflected on throughout the project:

- Did they feel unable to say no to someone who makes decisions about their workload/someone who is their teacher?

- Did they feel coerced into it in some way? Did peer pressure play a part in their decision?
- Were they genuinely interested in the project and felt they would learn something about themselves?
- Did they agree without really thinking about/understanding it (and then maybe regret their decision)?
- Did they decline the offer because they were concerned about the complexity and power involved in this particular researcher/participant relationship? And what impact has this decision had on the group and the individual?
- (How) have I behaved differently with those who have agreed to participate in the project?
- To what extent am I appropriating the ideas and knowledge of my colleagues/ students when I speak publicly about our work, and to what extent am I supporting their development? Can I really interpret their thoughts?
- (How) have my other (non-researcher) relationships with participants impacted on my understanding of the data?

I carefully worded requests and consent forms, frequently reminding colleagues of their right to withdraw. The development of insessional teaching in our institution has been a collective enterprise; the capital that comes with the title 'director' requires an ethical navigation of the boundaries of recognition; as we work together to develop our understanding of what our work requires and start to move towards increasing consensus, it is difficult to remember where ideas originated. I need to always remember I am in a position that gives me greater access to the wider institution and, to some extent, the wider EAP community, and I therefore need to be more careful to point out the collaborative and collegial nature of our developing work and not claim ownership. I have attempted to do this through, for example, the development of a website to showcase the range of our work which includes case studies written by all colleagues.

Ethically, then, I understand that I have a responsibility to acknowledge the power and capital I have and aim to use it with care and for the benefit of others. This requires conscious choices and actions and stems from a personal ethos in relation to professional behaviour and leadership as well as around how to undertake scholarship. This ethos connects with Braidotti's (2019) 'affirmative ethics' as well as the feminist ethics of responsibility (Lindermann, 2019). The ethics of responsibility is positioned as a way of applying and '*doing* ethics' and necessitates reflexivity and an emphasis on the importance of relationships. 'Here morality is depicted as practices of responsibility that may be thrust upon one, contested, accepted, delegated, deflected, and so on, and that are often epistemically rigged in favour of those in positions of power' (Lindermann, 2019).

To exemplify, I had an understanding of how to navigate the ethical approval process and so worked to support colleagues through this. I was aware that individuals working in different schools were feeling isolated, so I worked to build reasons for the collaboration and sharing of practice that would counter this and also have useful outcomes. The focus of my own scholarship question – around the identity development of insessional teachers – resulted from my ethical imperative in my own role to ensure that colleagues were supported and had opportunities to develop that were useful and impactful.

I was also in a position that enabled me to know and see where other colleagues were building their own 'power' – through strong relationships in the disciplines, through external professional networks, through formal qualifications or through engagement and success with scholarship – and worked to support and highlight this. This all required extra work on my part and an acceptance of greater responsibility, which I felt ethically or morally obliged to take on to practice affirmative, sympathetic and productive, and so ethical, leadership and scholarship. The same ethos was evident in my colleagues' approach to their scholarship as well. Engaging in scholarship required extra work and effort beyond their usual teaching practices, but those who did also clearly developed a form of 'productive power' that enhanced their practice and enabled them to speak with confidence to others about the needs of their students and the value of their work in meeting these. Their work became more confident and affirmative for themselves, their students and their colleagues.

There are also other types of power that need to be considered beyond those of individual cultural and/or social capital. The institutional context we work in, as well as broader higher education structures and systems, all exert power on the direction any scholarship might take. This includes institutional culture around, for example, the extent to which SoTL is valued and supported. The case study I am describing took place in an institution and a centre which, broadly, values SoTL work. This places those of us who work there in a position of privilege that other EAP practitioners may not hold. The extent to which we make use of this privilege, how we can use it to either focus on the development of our students, our own careers and reputations and our own centre or to find ways to support and become a voice for others in the discipline, is also an ethical question. When we are given real opportunities to engage in scholarship, what do we choose to focus on and to what end? Who is going to benefit from the support and resources we are given?

One of the key resources that enables us to engage more deeply with scholarship is time. The capital that time allocation within workloads affords cannot be underestimated. Each of us involved in this broad project had twenty per cent of our overall workload allocated to scholarship. However, the productive use of this time also requires ethical reflexivity. If working within a personal–professional ethics of responsibility, that includes a responsibility towards the multitude of other requirements that our roles and lives entail. Decisions around how to spend and make time – during busy teaching periods, when faced with personal crisis, when asked to support the career development of others through mentoring, checking promotion applications, when other interesting projects arise, when students need extra support – each of these exert a power over us and demand us to question where our own values lie, and who or what we are able to give our time to. Sometimes we have agency that allows us to make these decisions; at other times global events, institutional decisions or the structures in which we work remove this agency. We are, however, still able to make moral choices; they will simply map out differently.

Furthermore, there may be times when our scholarship leads us into questioning the power held by the institutions that employ us or the structures we work in. In our group scholarship, for example, there have been moments when we have encountered problematic attitudes towards 'international students', much of which is intertwined with neoliberal structures and a flawed understanding of language and language development. We have had many conversations around the ethics of working with these opinions to educate for change or whether we should be more immediately forceful in our responses. There is not one simple answer to this question as each encounter is unique, so again ethically aware reflexivity and support from others are required.

Therefore, by acknowledging where power lies, understanding this power and working to harness it through an affirmative ethics of responsibility, I suggest it should be possible to develop a shared sense of empowerment and of what Rowland terms 'intellectual love' (2008). It is here that the ethics of scholarship weave around and through the ethics of leadership, becoming a rhizomatic personal ethos.

Scholarship requires and entails an entanglement of (power/ful) relationships, practices and purposes. There is not one fixed ethical route through these rhizomatic interconnections; a tick-box list of questions to consider will not provide a full map. An ethos of principled reflexivity is important; however, 'The reflexivity which I recommend is not an end in itself' (Bourdieu, 1996: 47). This echoes the posthuman/Deleuzian perspective that 'There are no beginning and endpoints, just a middle in perpetual transformation or *becoming*' (Strom, 2018: 108). It is necessary not only to examine our own feelings, intentions and reactions but also those of others and those of the structures and institutions within which we operate and to understand that each of these is ever-changing, in a process of *becoming* that all *things* are playing a part in.

The ethical imperative for becoming continuously scholarly

I have already stated that one of the defining features of SoTL is that it develops out of and feeds into practice. However, I am also clear that this is not the same as (continuous) professional development (CPD), which is a form of training (how to) and learning from others (about something) rather than an independent investigation into/through/with.

One of the ethical imperatives within scholarship is to make our work public and in doing so to add to the knowledge base of others – in this way our own scholarship becomes a form of professional development for others and contributes to the development of a coherent identity for a profession. I would also argue that once you embark on scholarship, to use Deleuzeguattarian concepts, you are more likely to move away from 'aborescent' thought, which is 'essentialized or universalist, hierarchical and linear, dichotomous, reductionist, and fixed/static ... Because it only reproduces itself, this type of thought closes down any creative, as-yet-unthought possibilities' (Strom, 2018: 106), into thinking rhizomatically, more aware of (inter)connections and the multiplicity of possibilities and able to 'appreciate the complexity of the system for what it is' (Braidotti, 2019: 8). In other words, scholarship takes you in multiple directions. I would also suggest that, through scholarship, your practice becomes more ethical. For EAP practitioners, scholarship should be woven through all areas of practice – teaching, syllabus design, leadership and the professional development of yourself and others. This scholarship requires a critique of tradition or experience, away from 'inert repetition of established habits of thought or self-representation', cultivating 'the political desire for change or transformation' (Braidotti, 2006: 8). It is an ethical obligation to engage in scholarship in order to maintain and develop expertise as a practitioner.

Within the case study I have presented here, the umbrella scholarship project provided a natural route into and through some of the more pressing development issues we were collectively facing. Not everyone chose to be involved in the scholarship project; as demand for insessional teaching grew, others joined the team and needed support in their transition but were also not part of the scholarship project. I grappled with the ethics around the exclusion of these colleagues from my own project as it was already underway. However, all had access to frequent (in) formal meetings and participated in almost daily use of our Microsoft Teams chat around the scholarship project, our teaching and our departmental relationships. Interwoven in all of this was an exploration of ethical questions and conundrums.

In this way, the different lens each of us brought to our scholarship and the different questions we were asking within our specific teaching context also became a form of professional development for others involved in the conversation. It aimed to include as many as possible and work collectively to question our past habits, which Braidotti describes as 'inertia' or as bestowing an exaggerated authority to past experiences (2006: 9). In a very posthuman sense, the affordances of technology (our Teams channels and latterly the development of our website) enabled us to connect, interact, share, develop through collective and individual scholarship projects and become more aware of ourselves, our practices and our shared knowledge, as well as our vulnerabilities, and to challenge our past habits. 'The transformation of habits represents exactly what Deleuze calls *becoming*; that is, a transfer to a new mode of existence characterized by "new percepts and new affects" (Deleuze, 1995: 164) as some new ways of thinking, feeling and perceiving' (Semetsky, 2004: 321).

Ethical scholarship should work to support the '*becoming*' (i.e. not necessarily the development, the transformation or the improvement) of all who are in some way interconnected with our scholarship and our teaching and learning practices. As *becoming* is a continuous process, with no end, there is therefore a continued imperative to engage with scholarship, with this questioning of habits and practices helping us to describe and define who we are other than through the inertia of past habits. 'Deleuze's conceptualization of *becoming* asserts a self-*becoming*-autonomous' (Semetzky, 2004: 324). And this autonomy is 'not given but contingent on the act of shared communication embedded within the experiential situation ... The ethics of care emphasizes moral interdependence and 'rejects the notion of a truly autonomous moral agent ... As teachers, we are as dependent on our students as they are on us' (Noddings, 1998: 196). In this sense, then, scholarship is reflexive and acknowledges the interconnectivity of all actors and the dependency we have on others. It thus includes a sharing of responsibility through the continuous process of *becoming*.

Theorizing ethics, agency and identity in EAP scholarship

So far, I have attempted to explore some of the ethical considerations that I suggest it is necessary to return to iteratively and reflexively throughout any scholarship journey. Within this I have included some of the questions I/we asked ourselves throughout our own projects but have also attempted to provide four broader categories within which I feel it is necessary to scrutinize our own and others' intentions and actions. These may be used as a heuristic guide for your own ethical journey and are summarized in Table 2.1.

Table 2.1 Iterative ethical questions

Ethical considerations	Suggested guiding questions
Thinking about ethics	What is my own ethos? What are my boundaries? Who/what do I place most value on? Do my ethics align with those of my institution, the technology I use, colleagues and students, my profession? What might I do if they don't align? When do I consider ethics? Who with? Why? How do I act upon my ethical questioning? Have/can/will my personal ethics and intentions change over time? Why (not)? What/who influences my ethical choices?
Collegiality and trust	Who are my colleagues? Who deserves my trust and should be able to trust my own ethics and choices? What are the consequences if that trust is broken? How are collegial, trusting relationships built? At what cost? If my ethics don't align with the actions of colleagues, what are my choices? How much responsibility do I have towards the multiple others I interact with?
Ethics and power	Where does my own power lie? Is power attributed to me by others? Do others perceive power in the same places that I do? How does that impact my choices and the responsibilities I have? Where does power shift and change in different relationships? Do I recognize the capital I have and understand it? (How) can I use this productively? Can I use it to speak up for those with less power or capital? And who are these people? What powers am I fighting/opposing/supporting with my work? Is this within my own ethical code? Who/what do I value? Do I have the power of time? How am I using the time I have available to me responsibly? Who and what am I responsible to?
Ethics and the purpose of scholarship	Why am I undertaking this project? (Is it instrumental, developmental, externally driven?) What and who will gain from my scholarship? Who is included and who is excluded? Who can I collaborate with? Who do I have the right to speak for?

This is not a finite list of questions or issues, simply the ones that are currently foremost in my own context and in relation to the case study I have described.

I hope I have presented a view that the ethics of scholarship is less a list of criteria to be met to gain the approval of a committee and more of a personal and/or collectively considered ethos. This ethics is not fixed but interacts with contexts, structures, technology and others (human and non-human) and so requires but also develops autonomy and agency as we question, reflect and reconsider the impact of our work in relation to these 'others'. Taking a posthuman perspective, we are in a constant state of 'becoming' a scholar, a researcher, a practitioner. Scholarship and the ethics of scholarship are rhizomatic, heterogenous multiplicities.

Conclusion: The ethical aporia

Ultimately, ethics is about 'doing the right thing' or, at least, doing no harm. The conundrum is not knowing for certain what the impact of actions, questions, scholarship and consequent publications might be – in the present and in the future. This is why ethical guidelines such as those produced by BERA are both helpful yet dangerous. They provide an important framework for asking the right kinds of questions but are dangerous if taken as being answerable and even more dangerous if answered at the beginning of a project and not revisited throughout.

Our 'Manifesto for the Scholarship of Language Teaching and Learning' (Ding et al., 2018) argues: 'We promote **scholarship that is governed and driven by ethics**. More specifically, a scholarship ethics of humility, fallibility, care, curiosity, inclusiveness and truthfulness . . . An ethics of rigour must govern all approaches, genres and perspectives.' The challenge remains how this can be achieved while there are so many (contradictory) perspectives, ideological commitments and purposes to consider.

At the outset of this chapter, I stated the aim of making a first attempt to develop a heuristic for future ethical scholarship. Table 2.1 provides one such attempt. However, the approach to ethics I suggest is in itself its own heuristic, where the ethics of positions held, actions made and motivations behind them remain a constant question throughout the scholarship, with all of us learning from this questioning and discovering new ways of thinking, being and doing through this questioning. Posthuman concepts of mapping and tracing, rhizomatic connections and of being in a constant state of becoming provide ways of thinking through the multiplicity of ethical encounters that will emerge. I argue that we all have an ethical responsibility to go beyond reflexivity and to consider collectively and interconnectedly what we might do and what we might become as a profession through our scholarship endeavours.

References

Allwright, D. and J. Hanks (2009), *The Developing Language Learner: An Introduction to Exploratory Practice*, London: Palgrave Macmillan.

BALEAP (2022), 'BALEAP TEAP Individual Accreditation Scheme 2022 Handbook'. https://www.baleap.org/wp-content/uploads/2022/04/BALEAP-TEAP-Handbook-2022-edition.pdf (accessed 02 February 2023).

Blaj-Ward, L. (2014), *Researching Contexts, Practices and Pedagogies in English for Academic Purposes*, London: Palgrave Macmillan.

Bond, B. (2020), *Making Language Visible in the University. English for Academic Purposes and Internationalisation*, Bristol: Multilingual Matters.

Bourdieu, P. (1996), 'Understanding', *Theory, Culture and Society*, 13 (2): 17–37.

Bourdieu, P (2001), *Sketch for a Self-Analysis*, Chicago: The University of Chicago Press.

Braidotti, R. (2006), *Transpositions. On Nomadic Ethics*, Cambridge: Wiley.

Braidotti, R. (2012), *Nomadic Theory: The Portable Rosi Braidotti*, New York: Columbia University Press.

Braidotti, R. (2018), 'Ethics of Joy', in R. Braidotti and M. Hlavajova (eds), *Posthuman Glossary*, London: Bloomsbury Academic, an imprint of Bloomsbury Publishing Plc.

Braidotti, R. (2019), 'A Theoretical Framework for the Critical Posthumanities', *Theory, Culture & Society Special Issue: Transversal Posthumanities*, 36 (6): 31–61.

Braidotti, R. and M. Hlavajova (2018), *Posthuman Glossary*, ed. R. Braidotti and M. Hlavajova, London: Bloomsbury Academic, an imprint of Bloomsbury Publishing Plc.

British Educational Research Association [BERA] (2018), *Ethical Guidelines for Educational Research*, fourth edition, London. https://www.bera.ac.uk/researchers-resources/publications/ethicalguidelines-for-educational-research-2018

Brooks, R., K. te Riele and M. Maguire (2015), 'Ethical Theories, Principles and Guidelines', in R. Brooks (ed.), *Ethics and Education Research*, London: SAGE Publications Ltd. https://dx.doi.org/10.4135/9781473909762

Campion, G. C. (2016), 'The Learning Never Ends': Exploring Teachers' Views on the Transition from General English to EAP', *Journal of English for Academic Purposes*, 23: 59–70.

Chick, N. (2019), 'Strategies for Ethical SoTL Practice', *The National Teaching and Learning Forum*, 28 (6): 7–10.

Clegg, S. and S. Rowland (2010), 'Kindness in Pedagogical Practice and Academic Life', *British Journal of Sociology of Education*, 31 (6): 719–35. https://dx.doi.org/10.1080/01425692.2010.515102

Davis, M. (2019), 'Publishing Research as an EAP Practitioner: Opportunities and Threats', *Journal of English for Academic Purposes*, 39: 72–86.

Deleuze, G. (1995), *Negotiations 1972–1990*, trans. M. Joughin, New York: Columbia University Press.

Deleuze, G. and F. Guattari (2000), *A Thousand Plateaus: Capitalism and Schizophrenia*, London: Continuum.

Ding, A. (2016), 'Challenging Scholarship: A Thought Piece', *The Language Scholar* 0: 6–19.

Ding, A. (2019), 'EAP Practitioner Identity', in K. Hyland and L. L. C. Wong (eds), *Specialised English. New Directions in ESP and EAP Research and Practice*, 69–77, London: Routledge.

Ding, A. (2022), 'Series Editors' Foreword', in I. Bruce and B. Bond, *Contextualising English for Academic Purposes in Higher Education. Politics, Policies and Practices*, London: Bloomsbury.

Ding, A., J. Boden-Galvez, B. Bond, K. Morimoto, V. Ragni, N. Rust and R. Soliman (2018), 'Manifesto for the Scholarship of Language Teaching and Learning', *The Language Scholar*, 3: 58–60.

Ding, A. and I. Bruce (2017), *The English for Academic Purposes Practitioner: Operating on the Edge of Academia*, London: Palgrave Macmillan.

Ding, A. and G. Campion (2016), 'EAP Teacher Development', in K. Hyland and P. Shaw (eds), *The Routledge Handbook of English for Academic Purposes*, 571–83, London: Routledge.

Gravett, K., C. A. Taylor and N. Fairchild (2021), 'Pedagogies of Mattering: Re-conceptualising Relational Pedagogies in Higher Education', *Teaching in Higher Education*. https://doi.org/10.1080/13562517.2021.1989580.

Hanks, D. J. (2022), 'De-mystifying the Nimbus of Research: Re-igniting Practitioners' Interest in Exploring EAP', *Journal of English for Academic Purposes*. https://doi.org/10.1016/j.jeap.2022.101176.

Healey, R. L., T. Bass, J. Caulfield, A. Hoffman, M. K. McGinn, J. Miller-Young and M. Haigh (2013), 'Being Ethically Minded: Practising the Scholarship of Teaching and Learning in an Ethical Manner', *Teaching & Learning Inquiry: The ISSOTL Journal*, 1 (20): 23–32. JSTOR. https://doi.org/10.2979/teachlearninqu.1.2.23 (accessed 14 September 2022).

Hertz, E. (2016), 'Pimp My Fluff: A Thousand Plateaus and Other Theoretical Extravaganzas', *Anthropological Theory*, 16 (2–3): 146–59.

Kinchin, I. M. and K. Gravett (2020), 'Concept Mapping in the Age of Deleuze: Fresh Perspectives and New Challenges', *Education Sciences*, 10 (82): 2–13.

The Language Centre (2023). https://insessional.leeds.ac.uk/ (accessed 24 February 2023).

Lindermann, H. (2019), *An Invitation to Feminist Ethics*, Oxford Scholarship Online.

Martin, R. C. (2013), 'Navigating the IRB: The Ethics of SoTL', *New Directions for Teaching and Learning*, 136: 59–71.

McNamee, M. (2001), 'Introduction: Whose Ethics, which Research?' *Journal of Philosophy of Education*, 35 (3): 309–27.

Noddings, N. (1998), *Philosophy of Education*, Boulder: Westview Press.

Rowland, S. (2008), 'Collegiality and Intellectual Love', *British Journal of Sociology of Education*, 29 (3): 353–60.

Semetsky, I. (2004), 'Becoming-Language/Becoming-Other: Whence Ethics?' *Educational Philosophy and Theory*, 36 (3): 313–25. https://doi.org/10.1111/j.1469-5812.2004.00070.x

Shulman, L. S. (2000), 'From Minsk to Pinsk: Why a Scholarship of Teaching and Learning?' *The Journal of Scholarship of Teaching and Learning*, 1: 48–52.

Small, R. (2001), 'Codes Are not Enough: What Philosophy can Contribute to the Ethics of Educational Research', *Journal of Philosophy of Education*, 35 (3): 387–406.

Strom, K. J. (2018), '"That's Not Very Deleuzian": Thoughts on Interrupting the Exclusionary Nature of "High Theory"', *Educational Philosophy and Theory*, 50 (1): 104–13. https://doi.org/10.1080/00131857.2017.1339340

Strom, K. J. and J. Lupinacci (2019), 'Putting Posthuman Theories to Work in Educational Leadership Programmes', in C. A. Taylor and A. Bayley (eds), *Posthumanism and Higher Education: Reimagining Pedagogy, Practice and Research*, 103–21. Cham, Switzerland: Palgrave Macmillan.

Webster, S. (2022), 'The Transition of EAP Practitioners into Scholarship Writing', *Journal of English for Academic Purposes*, 57: 101091.

Chapter 3

EAP PRACTITIONERS IN THE GLOBAL SOUTH

PARTICIPATION, POSITIONING AND AGENCY IN THE CONTEXT OF 'PERIPHERAL' SCHOLARS AND SCHOLARSHIP

Namala Lakshmi Tilakaratna

Introduction

The fact that academic research, publications and discussions about academic identity are dominated by studies produced in 'western', 'global north', 'hegemonic', 'inner circle', 'centre', 'first world' and 'developed countries' is well documented (Mittelmeier and Zhang, 2023; Hyland and Feng, 2020). As expected, this means that research contributions and discussions about practitioner experiences from non-Western, 'global south', 'marginalized, 'outer circle', 'peripheral', 'third world' and 'developing countries' are often rendered invisible on a global stage (Tight, 2021). This is especially evident in studies such as bibliometric investigations of EAP scholarship which show that citations in leading journals can predominantly be attributed to white male authors working in Western contexts (Hyland and Feng, 2020; Mehdi, Ghanbar and Fazel, 2020). Peripheral scholars are also limited to contributing contextualized (rather than 'universal') knowledge, context-specific (rather than 'general') results of studies (Pennycook and Makoni, 2020) that focus on the application of frameworks from the centre to peripheral contexts (e.g. Chen, 2016; Kohnke, 2022; Liyanage and Walker, 2014). More problematically, peripheral scholars have also been the object of study themselves, being represented rather than self-representing (Canagarajah, 2002). Often this 'representation' or exploration of peripheral scholars' identities comes in the form of 'tales of woe' with practitioners seen as excluded from academia, lacking resources and funding and being silenced or marginalized by the 'centre' (Canagarajah, 2002). Additionally, in the context of EAP provision, the language centre is often marginalized within academia , functioning as a support service or a 'remedial safe-house staffed by demoralized and inexperienced staff where EAP is relegated to a minor support role' (Hyland, 2016: 20).It seems that the only position available to 'Global South' scholars is an even further marginalized role within a marginalized profession in higher education.

This study attempts to challenge some of these dominant discussions about EAP provision and EAP practitioner identity by engaging in conversations about issues of access, agency and recognition through interviews with scholars working in Singapore. As the discussions below will show, participants in this chapter represent a more empowered perspective on their role within the university by challenging their classification, their positioning and their perceived lack of agency by redefining their roles and functions within their institutions and within the 'field of EAP' (Bruce and Ding, 2017). By sharing their perspectives, this study also aims to show how the field can be enriched through engagement with a deeper and more nuanced understanding of issues of agency and identity that are determined by the challenges afforded to scholars who study, work and research in contexts other than the 'hegemonic West'. By allowing participants to self-represent, the study aims to shine light on their capacity to thrive despite the institutional, professional and identity-based barriers that they might encounter as EAP practitioners and will provide opportunities for the Global North to learn from experiences of others within the field.

The chapter also argues that while existing research in the field has provided eloquent and important critiques of EAP scholarship in the West and raises questions about how and why scholars from the 'Global South' are excluded from academic publishing and research, these studies can be critiqued for 'knowledge blindness' (Maton, 2014a) or a lack of systematic engagement with knowledge practices. This makes it difficult to uncover the kinds of knowledge and knowers peripheral scholars engage with and how this contributes to their practice, identity and struggle for legitimacy within the field of EAP. The study draws on the dimension of Specialization from Legitimation Code Theory (a sociological framework) which 'begins from the premise that every practice is oriented towards something or by someone' (Maton, 2014a; Maton and Chen, 2020). In attempting to uncover the underlying principles of knowledge practices, a distinction is made between *epistemic relations* (hereafter ER) or relations between practices and their object or focus (that part of the world towards which they are oriented) and *social relations* (hereafter SR) or relations between practices and their subject, author or actor (who is enacting the practices). This chapter aims to show that accounting for how knowledge and knowers are construed in interview data from 'periphery' EAP practitioners will present an important opportunity to examine how these practitioners engage with the theory/practitioner dichotomy in EAP and enrich the understanding of what constitutes a larger EAP practitioner identity.

EAP practitioner identity: The author

The chapter begins then with an account of my own journey as an EAP practitioner to show how I am invested in questions related to EAP identity and agency in the Global South.

My career began initially in TESOL because in the context of Sri Lanka, where I am 'originally' from, English is a language of economic power and social class (Raheem and Devendra, 2006). While teaching English courses focussing on canonical literature in local universities, I also took the certificate in teaching English to speakers of other languages (CELTA) at the British Council in Sri Lanka and started to teach English as a Second Language. If anything, my experience in the British Council was my first introduction to racism in the profession (there were many more experiences to come). I was considered and classified as a 'non-native' speaker, which surprised me because I was in fact bilingual and had been proficient in English my whole life. It was the first moment I realized that looking South Asian meant somehow already being considered peripheral or outer circle to native speakers in English, making me the 'wrong' kind of knower. Luckily, at the British Council library, I picked up my first copy of Pennycook's *The Cultural Politics of English as an International Language* (1994) and was excited to discover an entire field of research that focussed on uncovering issues of race and hegemony in TESOL and applied linguistics. I decided immediately that I needed to focus on English Language Teaching and develop my skills in linguistics.

The next few years consisted of a master's and a PhD in linguistics and applied linguistics in Australia. While studying, I had the privilege of working at an excellent writing centre at my university where I was able to experience how Hallidayan linguistics was translated into genre pedagogy and first encountered the field of English for Academic Purposes. To a great extent, my time as a practitioner in TESOL was about developing my identity and my position as a 'knower', about negotiating the social relations which governed the field of TESOL and showed where I was positioned because of my race. The second half of my experience was related to developing knowledge in applied linguistics, genre pedagogy, Systemic Functional Linguistics and Legitimation Code Theory. This chapter then is an attempt to reconcile these two halves – the epistemic relations that constitute my knowledge practices as an SFL-trained linguist and the social relations of my racial identity as a South Asian EAP practitioner who is very aware of the racial politics that define my agency in the field of EAP. The chapter does this by drawing on the experience of other Global South EAP practitioners through discussions of how they negotiate the epistemic and social relations that constitute their practice and how this shapes their professional practitioner identities.

The one piece of the puzzle that I have omitted from my narrative perhaps is that of social class. Certainly, in terms of privilege and access, I come from the elite upper classes of English-speaking bilingual Sri Lankans, from the majority ethnic group (Sinhala-Buddhist) (Kandiah, 1984; Raheem and Devendra, 2006; Raheem and Ratwatte, 2004). This means that to a certain extent my story doesn't take into account how class distinctions determine or are determined by a profession that is not as valued as others within the landscape of higher education institutions and practice. In Sri Lanka, English Language Teaching and learning are mired in class conflict, but my role as a practitioner in 'Western' contexts (which I acknowledge I was only able to access because of my class privileges) placed me in a different category of exclusion that was determined entirely by race. As one of the participants in the study states, we are 'third class citizens' excluded because of race in the context of Singapore as non-white, non-majoritarian Chinese and instead representing the minority of South Asians. In my field, as a student and then later as a practitioner, I was always the only South Asian in the classroom and one of the few in the conferences I attended, and I quickly realized that while the fields of STEM and many fields in the humanities were dominated by Asian and South Asian scholars, EAP, linguistics and applied linguistics and higher education research was not.

This chapter then starts with the premise that my social and epistemic relations have given me a particular vested interest in exploring the status of EAP practitioners who are considered as 'peripheral' or constituting the Global South. This chapter then attempts to capture the range of issues that confront the EAP lecturer practising within the neoliberal university who is also confronted by race-based (Asian, South Asian and South East Asian) identity in the field of EAP and in the larger landscape of the global university. As many of the terms used in this chapter are contested, the chapter will focus on elucidating them by drawing on the interview data and using the participants' perspectives to understand how many of the terms that are used to define the participants and their practice can be challenged and reframed particularly when explored in relation to how they are associated with knowledge and knowers within the field of EAP. To begin with, I will introduce the complex identities of the EAP practitioners who have generously given their time to this study followed by an overview of the context of the study.

EAP practitioner identity: The participants

Three participants agreed to participate in one-on-one interviews each lasting between sixty and ninety minutes. The study has been approved by Institutional Review Board (IRB) at the National University of Singapore, and each of the participants was asked for consent to record the interviews. Certain details about the individuals in the study have been changed in order to preserve anonymity.

One of the challenges in accounting for EAP practitioner identity is attempting to identify a coherent common identity for EAP practitioners and EAP as a discipline or an academic field. This includes attempting to identify what kinds of knowledge practices EAP practitioners draw on. Many EAP practitioners, such as those involved in this study, have a broader set of skills that encompass what Hyland and Hamp-Lyons (2002: 2) refer to as

> language research and instruction that focuses on the specific communicative needs and practices of particular groups in academic contexts. It means grounding instruction in an understanding of the cognitive, social and linguistic demands of specific academic disciplines.

Yet unlike sustained study in a specific discipline, participants share that many of these skills have been developed through experience in the classroom, through their own adaptation and recontextualizing of their humanities and social sciences knowledge to the EAP and discipline-specific context. Each of the participants' specific knowledge and experiences in teaching are briefly introduced below.

The first participant, Participant A, is Singaporean Chinese with a PhD from a leading Western university in a humanities-related field. In terms of Singapore identity, this means that she represents the hegemonic and politically powerful group of Chinese Singaporeans who constitute the majority race and identity of the country (see for instance Chua, 1997; Hong and Huang, 2008). She is currently in a polytechnic institution where she teaches composition and rhetoric to students in technical STEM fields. She defines her institution as one which is primarily concerned with the application of knowledge and aligns itself with industry rather than a research-intensive higher education institution. While her position is within the humanities department, her primary function is one of a support service in that she teaches a subject that is different to the core disciplinary units students will take within the institution. As the institute is focussed on applied fields, it is also less focussed on research. She therefore notes that she is not expected to publish or research in pedagogy or in her own field of humanities which is unrelated to applied linguistics, TESOL or any other field related to writing and communication. Her focus is on excellent teaching and her impact as a teacher. When she does publish, she publishes in her own field where she has growing expertise as a South East Asian scholar.

The second participant is of South Asian origin with a PhD in linguistics from a leading Singaporean university. She has lived and worked in Singapore for several decades and is often associated with the minority identity of Singaporean Indian in the context of Singapore (Kathiravelu, 2019). She teaches in a language centre in a leading research-intensive university. The centre provides a range of EAP services including a number of core first-year undergraduate units and embedded 'communication skills' within other disciplinary areas. As with Participant A, the primary function of Participant B is to provide support services in English for academic purposes to students across the university. The centre is focussed on teaching, and pedagogical research is highly encouraged. Participant B publishes research in discourse analysis in her field of expertise. Her knowledge of higher education and teaching and learning is something she has acquired through teaching experience and, therefore, she does not publish pedagogical research.

Participant C is of South Asian origin and has a PhD in English literature from a leading Singaporean university. As with Participant B she has lived and worked in higher education for two decades in the context of Singapore. She currently teaches at a major research-intensive university in which she is part of a non-research-based language centre that provides support services in English for academic purposes to students. Her primary function is one of support services where EAP, research skills and 'communication' are considered important academic skills for students but not central to their main areas of study such as STEM or the social sciences and humanities. The centre for language teaching that she works at is one that supports research, particularly pedagogical research in EAP. However, similar to the previous participants, she chooses to publish in fields related to the humanities rather than in EAP. Her expertise in EAP, as with the other participants, has emerged through her experience as a practitioner and through her engagement with course materials and readings that she has encountered while teaching English language communication at various higher education institutions.

The higher education context of the study

An important aspect of this study is the context in which it is conducted. Unlike many Asian countries that are often, almost unproblematically, defined as part of the 'developing world', Singapore is an Asian country that has experienced rapid economic growth following fifty-six years of independence from the British to become one of the world's highest-income countries. It remains one of the most competitive countries in terms of educational achievement, frequently topping global rankings for literacy and numeracy. Recently, the National University of Singapore, the top-ranked university, which has consistently ranked in the world's top thirty universities, was ranked nineteenth globally by Times Higher Education World University Rankings (THE)[1] and eleventh by QS rankings. The second most highly ranked university, Nanyang Technological University (NTU), reached thirty-sixth in the THE world rankings indicating the global impact that the two universities are having in terms of 'a global approach to education, research and entrepreneurship, with a focus on Asian perspectives and expertise' (THE, 2022). Singapore in terms of research capacity on a global scale then has reached the status of the hegemonic West in that it has a considerable impact on the world's knowledge production.

A further element that is of significance in the context of Singapore's political landscape is that it has been headed by a one-party dominant government since the 1968 general elections (Chua, 1997). Along with strict censorship laws and laws controlling public protest, the government is heavily invested in the nationalization of education and oversight to maintain control over what is taught. The National University of Singapore, for instance, was involved in controversy over teaching content that was in conflict with the country's strict laws on protest and dissent, resulting in a debate over the censorship of specific subjects and materials in parliament.[2] This means that liberal arts, critical thinking and argumentation are limited to distribution in elite schools (Lim, 2016), with the overall focus in education being on future-orientedness, technology and innovation and creativity in particular in relation to STEM subjects.

Below, the theoretical framework, Legitimation Code Theory (LCT), that is used to analyse the interview data and a proposed theory for EAP identity (Ding, 2016) that is used to thematically explore participant responses are briefly introduced.

LCT dimensions for revealing knowledge practices in EAP in the Global South

Legitimation Code Theory is a sociological framework drawing on the work of Bourdieu and Bernstein that has been widely used in education to reveal the 'rules of the game' or knowledge practices in different disciplines. LCT provides a conceptual toolkit for analysing knowledge practices consisting of four dimensions: Specialization, Semantics, Autonomy and Temporality.

This study draws on the dimension of Specialization which begins from the premise that every practice is about or oriented towards *something* or *someone* (Maton, 2014a). A distinction is made between practices and the part of the world towards which they are oriented (*epistemic relations* between knowledge and its proclaimed object of study) and practices and whomever is enacting those practices (*social relations* between knowledge and its authors or subjects). These distinctions highlight what constitutes legitimate knowledge and legitimate knowers in a field. Specialization is useful when exploring knowledge practices such as EAP because it reveals what kinds of knowledge and knowers are valued and to what degree. LCT makes a distinction not only between epistemic and social relations but also the strength of these relations independently, for example, stronger (+) or weaker (−) epistemic relations and social relations, and when in relation to each other in generating specialization codes (ER+/−, SR+/−). Specialization codes can be mapped on a cartesian plane with four principal modalities (see Figure 1.1):

- *Knowledge codes* (ER+, SR−), where possession of specialized knowledge, principles or procedures concerning specific objects of study is emphasized as the basis of achievement, and the attributes of actors are downplayed.
- *Knower codes* (ER−, SR+), where specialized knowledge and objects are downplayed and the attributes of actors are emphasized as measures of achievement, whether viewed as born (e.g. 'natural talent'), cultivated (e.g. 'taste') or social (e.g. feminist standpoint theory).
- *Élite codes* (ER+, SR+), where legitimacy is based on both possessing specialist knowledge and being the right kind of knower.
- *Relativist codes* (ER−, SR−), where legitimacy is determined by neither specialist knowledge nor knower attributes – 'anything goes'.

In the field of EAP, Specialization has been used by Monbec (2018) to explore the concept of the 'transfer' of EAP knowledge to other fields of study that university students are engaged in. She argues that strengthening epistemic relations in EAP provision and making knowledge visible and explicit will enable students to transfer concepts from EAP to their fields of study. Specialization has also been used to reveal EAP practitioners' dispositions towards theory and visible knowledge (Cowley-Haselden and Monbec, 2019). Cowley-Haselden and Monbec show that dispositions towards theory in EAP practitioners surveyed include a recognition that practitioners should be theoretically informed, that a range of theories are enacted in EAP and that the EAP practitioners they interviewed revealed an uneasy relationship with theory.

A positive theory of identity for EAP

In addition to LCT specialization, this chapter attempts to explore EAP identity in relation to Ding's 'positive theory of identity for EAP' by attempting to:

1. Provide a link from identity to agency.
2. Have explanatory powers to articulate the relationship between structure and agency and specifically account for morphostatis and morphogenesis, that is, to account for how agents are shaped by structural forces and how agents change structure over time.
3. Account for, at least theoretically, how professional identity is shaped. What are the discourses, knowledge bases, practices and social material contexts and forces that intersect to influence professional identity?
4. How does personal identity relate to social identity (or which one aspect is professional identity)? How do our personal concerns and commitments manifest themselves in the social sphere?
5. What connects or affiliates one practitioner to another? Is there such thing as a profession? Is there an essence to EAP? Something that binds all practitioners?
6. How do we account for recognition, distinction, social stratification and boundaries in defining a practitioner? Who makes these distinctions? And how do we change them?
7. How do neoliberal values impose themselves in universities, and how do these values transform practitioner identity?

The scope of the chapter is limited to exploring the EAP practitioners within the context of Singapore. As a result, the fifth point about a larger EAP identity is excluded from the discussion or is only referred to marginally by participants. What is most discussed as a theme in the interview data below is how the individual practitioners related identity to agency and explored how their agency is linked to structural forces such as the institution they practice within and the national context that defines the values and culture of the institution.

In conducting interviews with the participants, a number of issues emerged regarding the definition of terms and classifications in the chapter title such as 'Global South' and 'peripheral' due to the fact that Singapore and its higher education institutions are economically no longer classified as belonging to a 'developing' context. Some of the questions that emerge include definitions of EAP practitioners (who counts as an EAP practitioner?), the Global South (what is the 'Global South'? How is Singapore positioned in relation to the dichotomy of the Global South and Global North?), participation (what counts as participation in research and practice in EAP?), positioning (how are scholars in Singapore positioned and by whom?) and agency (how is agency defined, understood and practiced in the context of EAP in Singapore?). As many of these classifications appear to overlap with larger concerns of EAP practitioner identity in the field, these issues will be discussed in relation to research in the field in the results sections.

The above points can be more broadly classified as related to social and epistemic relations depending on their focus. For instance, in the interview data below, participants might discuss epistemic relations in referring to their knowledge bases whether these are in academic literacy, linguistics and applied linguistics or in other fields in the humanities such as theatre studies, gender studies, political science and so on, or participants might chose to focus on social relations by discussing their dispositions and values as a researcher (e.g. critical discourse analysis, critical race theory or expertise based on context such as South East Asian or South Asian theatre studies) or how they are positioned in relation to racial or ethnic categorization as being the right (or wrong) kind of 'knower' who is or isn't valued by the institution or the discipline of EAP. Notably, there is a clear distinction in the data between how participants are externally valued, by their individual language centres or by students, for instance, and how they value themselves and their contributions as practitioners.

In the interviews, a number of themes emerged about Singaporean EAP practitioners that can be broadly categorized as (i) *classifying EAP practitioners*, (ii) *institutions and the EAP practitioner* and finally (iii) *knowledge practices in EAP*.

The first theme, *classifying EAP practitioners*, overlaps with questions 3 and 4 in Ding's framework for a 'positive theory of EAP identity' on professional and personal identities by exploring how academics classify their practice and research in relation to discussions about Global South teaching and scholarship. This theme also explores how practitioners view their own function as EAP practitioners (as opposed to how they are institutionally positioned as is discussed in the second theme). Participants are given an opportunity to discuss how they perceive their role and function as practitioners, how they enhance student learning and how they engage with the 'macro' social relations that are enacted such as their classification in relation to race and ethnicity. Participants were not explicitly asked to engage with identity in the interview questions, but often these issues emerged in the data as practitioners voiced the challenges they face in reconciling their personal and professional identities.

The second theme which focusses on the intersection between the institution and practitioner explores questions 6 and 7 in Ding's proposed framework by focussing on the kind of university that the practitioner functions within and how this shapes the EAP practitioner's identity and their value within the institution. This second theme of *institutions and the EAP practitioner* also necessarily engages with the concepts of structure and how practitioners are institutionally positioned as for instance a 'support service' providing students with communication skills that are transferrable to their core disciplines. Notably these themes overlap with institutional concerns and how institutions position EAP as either a support function or a core disciplinary function. This then raises questions about identity and positioning and the intersection of these identities with agency. Does being relegated to the role of support function limit/restrain or increase and enable the agency of the EAP practitioners?

The third and final theme that emerges in the data is in relation to *knowledge practices in EAP*. This includes discussions about what kinds of knowledge EAP practitioners bring to their role (whether these are more closely aligned with epistemic or social relations) and how they use, engage with and contribute to these bodies of knowledge and epistemic and social relations as practitioners.

The three themes are discussed in great detail below.

Classifying EAP practitioners: The 'Global South' and 'periphery' and the EAP practitioner

While in TESOL, ESL, EFL, discourse analysis and other fields similar to EAP, inquiries into practitioner identity have yielded a lot of research and insights, EAP practitioner identity has, Ding argues, 'no discourses which have erased or promoted specific aspects of identity'. The attempt to identify what constitutes EAP practitioner identity and to rectify the glaring gap in identity research in our field of practice is being led by practitioners in the Global North. Their research reveals that EAP practitioners are often marginalized, relegated to support services and rarely given the same privileges as other academics (Ding and Bruce, 2017). However, while research on identity in TESOL and other sub-fields of linguistics like Critical Discourse Analysis has engaged with discussions about race and exclusion, EAP explorations of identity focus more on the intersection between the practitioner and the institution (e.g. Campion, 2016; Ding and Bruce, 2017; Martin, 2014). One of the challenges in accounting for EAP identity then is in writing the social relations of race and ethnicity and experiences determined by geographical contexts back into the narrative of the EAP practitioner.

One of the inevitable issues that arises in trying to identify what is experienced by practitioners working in different contexts or contexts other than the Global North is in defining the context of practice itself. For the purposes of this chapter, I selected the recent term 'Global South' to classify Singaporean scholars. However, if we take Pennycook and Makoni's definition of the Global South (2019) as referring to 'people, places, and ideas that have been left out of the grand narrative of modernity' and to 'broader histories of exclusion and disenfranchisement' such as indigenous communities or the urban poor in the 'Global North', then Singapore, as the interview participants point out, sits between the Global South and North. Many of the issues that emerged for Global North EAP practitioners in terms of their institutional positioning also confronted Singaporean EAP practitioners such as marginalization by the university who valued other core disciplines (such as STEM or Social Sciences and Humanities). One of the interview questions focussed on identifying where contextually Singapore was located and included conversations about whether within this context EAP practitioners experience 'exclusion' and/or marginalization.

Participant B contests the classification of the Global South precisely because it feeds into a narrative about marginalization, disempowerment and exclusion that doesn't define her sense of identity or agency as an EAP scholar in the context of Singapore. She notes that she doesn't want to classify herself as a 'Global South' scholar because:

> I wouldn't call myself a Global South scholar. I would say that I'm the fulcrum of my discipline ... The moment I make my division, it means that I am accepting a sort of labelling that they see as one up and we down.
>
> I don't want myself to be seen as better off or less better than. I see myself as I am a scholar, I contribute and I am a fulcrum.

Participant C also critiques the dichotomy that emerges in the definition of Global South and Global North by noting it's a 'controversial term':

> It seems to be another term for underdeveloped, developing and now it's the Global South ... it's to give a post-post colonial divide ... I think it's very useful terms to use when you are trying to segregate scholarship ... the words you use like the centre and periphery ... that balance has been disturbed by the way we teach ... the case studies we use the examples we give.

Participant C notes that teaching and higher education practices have evolved in the context of Singapore, even though teaching and learning scholarship is dominated by research in the Global North. She notes that it is problematic to transfer teaching practices from one context to another without having the capacity to understand the students, their specific needs, their cultural backgrounds and other factors which necessarily shift the way in which the 'Global South' practitioner engages with students in the classroom.

Participant A notes that classification is a complex issue and proposes that the practitioner constitutes an 'assemblage' of identities following Deleuze and Guattari (1987), rather than the notions of centre/margins or Global South and Global North:

> I would say maybe it's because I'm not trying to position myself in any field its not something that I'm so stressed out about. I've always been quite deliberate in not falling into Asian scholar, Singaporean scholar, for me the bigger space that I find myself being contextualized within would be the South East Asian trope ... than the Global South. The South East Asia context has diverse and complex voices. I wouldn't say there's a straightforward answer.

By contesting the term Global South, the participants were also choosing to disassociate and disalign with the social relations that were used to differentiate between participant identities in EAP. They refuse the Global South label because it is a dichotomy created by the North which does nothing but highlight a supposed deficiency in their capacity to participate fully as EAP practitioners who contribute to the larger landscape of higher education teaching and learning.

Choosing not to be defined as Global South scholars meant that the participants were also able to discuss their agency as EAP lecturers in terms of their engagement with and their positioning by the university aligning with the institutional positioning that functions as a common experience to EAP practitioners globally. Agency and identity for these participants, as with Global North research, intersect with the agendas set by their neoliberal institutions which focus on financialization (Bruce and Ding, 2017); this frames the discussion of the second theme on the institutional and the EAP practitioner below.

The section below explores how social and epistemic relations are determined by the institutional setting in which the participants practice and how practitioners are shaped by the institution and how the institution is shaped by the practitioner, by exploring how the practitioners see themselves as positioned within the universities and how they practice their agency within certain institutional confines.

Theme 2: The institution and the EAP practitioner: Institutional positioning and agency

Discussions about the institution and the EAP practitioner raise a number of questions such as how EAP practitioners are positioned in relation to the neoliberal university and whether the institutions value social or epistemic relations in EAP practitioners. In a number of Global North contexts, the neoliberal university has relegated EAP to 'support services' or the 'butler' (Raimes, 1991) of the university often serving a liminal position of preparing students for their degrees rather than being essential knowledge for their growth as professionals (Bruce and Ding, 2017). All the participants in this study, however, differentiated their contribution from the way in which universities positioned them as external to 'core' disciplinary faculty while being aware of the way in which their institutions relegate them to support services. Practitioners chose to carve out their own space for their practice by representing themselves and their roles within the university in an empowered manner through reference to epistemic relations and by identifying EAP as indispensable knowledge in the context of higher education. For example, Participant B shared that

> I don't see myself as support or the mainframe, I see myself as part of an ecosystem that basically is *required* by the university, is valued by the university, it's just that *the university doesn't know* it. (emphasis added)

Two of the participants linked the EAPs relegation to 'support services' to issues related to epistemic relations and how they are practised in relation to the profession. For instance, both Participants A and C note that many EAP practitioners focus on the transfer of a specific set of skills such as study skills, language skills (for example, reading skills such as skimming and scanning; listening skills such as note-taking) and process writing (brainstorming, outlining, revising a draft) as well as sourcing and citing skills such as paraphrasing and summarizing (Jordan 1997). They note that these types of 'generic' research skills are becoming less relevant in higher education. Participant C for instance notes the focus on 'interdisciplinarity' at her university and states that making the EAP content relevant to the discipline that it is being applied to (such as engineering or architecture) makes EAP provision an opportunity for 'value adding' for the student and the institution and not the standard 'existing yellow pages' approach to teaching a generic set of skills that dominates typical EAP contexts. She notes that the focus on epistemic relations that are discipline-specific separates her style of EAP provision from a repetition of similar skills-based concepts, making her style one that is steeped in the discipline and that can provide students with insights into how to communicate in their own disciplinary fields. Importantly this positions the EAP practitioner as situated within the knowledge code, downplaying who they are in favour of focussing on what they teach and how they teach it.

All of the participants demonstrate that they feel confident in their understanding of EAP knowledge practices and how to tailor these practices to disciplinary content and therefore make changes to generic EAP provisional materials to benefit their students. This echoes the dominant view in the field that EAP provision has to meet the needs of students in order to be successful (e.g. Hyland, 2002; Sloane and Porter, 2010). Participant A notes that she, for instance, realized that her STEM students wouldn't benefit from research skills or writing an academic essay and therefore she tailor-makes content to suit the kinds of epistemic relations that students are engaging with while focussing on how students can use EAP knowledge to better communicate these skills. All three participants note that an essential function of their work within the institution is to provide students with the linguistic or more broadly 'communication' tools that they need to communicate their specific disciplines to a broader audience of stakeholders, investors, grants institutions or potential employers. In order to downplay the classification as EAP as support services all three participants emphasize epistemic relations and their contribution to student learning as crucial for defining and providing value to their position as practitioners within the higher education landscape.

Finally, Participant A brings in an additional insight into the less privileged role of the EAP practitioner in the context of the Singaporean university. She notes that role of EAP and its centrality to the university is also determined by the national focus of Singapore as a nation that is invested in research on STEM:

> I think when it comes to geopolitical classifications of scholarships and people I find it a little bit problematic... because there are two things going on here – the economic growth of a space (where you suggest Singapore is now)... then we have the other part of the tension where EAP doesn't seem to be moving with the same rigor in the Global North... the oxymoron of strong economic growth but at the same time a lack of attention to what should be important... EAP programs. It makes sense why EAP doesn't matter here (in Singapore). The work

of EAP takes too long to materialize, the effects of EAP on students cannot be quantified or qualified in the same way that you can with economic growth and skillsets that can translate to market value . . . the attention in Singapore will not be on EAP . . . it is hard to measure in economic success.

What is interesting here is the national classification of subjects from STEM disciplines as constituting 'knowledge' whereas EAP appears to be classified as a less valued form of knowledge or a set of 'skills' that are somehow external to disciplinary knowledge. This means that the marginalization of EAP as support services is underpinned by a national narrative that emphasizes in LCT terms 'knower blindness' (Maton, 2014a: 14) with an overfocus 'on explicit structures of knowledge at the expense of practices more concerned with developing knowers' by valuing 'knowledge most easily seen explicit, abstract, condensed, hierarchical forms that visibly announce themselves' and failing to see 'less explicit' knowledge that is 'more concrete, context-dependent, embodied and axiological'.

In summary, the institutional positioning of the EAP practitioner as a support service is challenged by Singaporean practitioners who share that they feel that their function within the university is essential. They all reveal that institutions don't value the epistemic relations that they align with and that support services are marginalized by these institutions by making a distinction between core disciplinary knowledge and 'communication skills'. Despite this lack of recognition of the value of EAP provision, all of the practitioners still feel a sense of agency within the system. This comes from the premise that all of the EAP practitioners interviewed were confident about the knowledge practices that they align with, their disciplinary expertise, its relevance to academic literacy provision in the context of higher education and their capacity as practitioners. Notably, what counts to them as professionals is their epistemic relations and not their social relations as they each refer back to their fields of expertise as the basis on which they draw in teaching EAP as explored in Theme 3 below.

Theme 3: Knowledge practices and the EAP practitioner

The third theme that emerges in the interview data is that of *knowledge practices* and what kinds of knowledge EAP practitioners bring to their role and how they use, engage with and contribute to these bodies of knowledge as practitioners. One of the challenges in engaging with Global South scholarship in the field of EAP is that, while a number of studies call for the inclusion of peripheral perspectives, they often do so in a limited way. In TESOL, for instance, peripheral scholar identity is relegated to experiential participation through autoethnographic studies (Canagarajah, 2002). In applied linguistics, there are calls for alternative forms of knowledge even if these forms of knowledge are not associated with the power and access afforded by engagement with mainstream. For example, there is a call for 'scholarship about the Global South' that 'presents a critical mode of intervention that seeks to decolonize the geopolitics of knowledge generation, by challenging the hegemony of Northern-centricity, in favour of new and diverse ways of learning and practicing our intellectual craft' (Lazar, 2020: 7). The section below explores how participants position themselves in relation to the epistemic relations that constitute the field of EAP and EAP as a discipline.

One of the challenges which emerged in interviewing the participants, or even identifying participants to be interviewed, was identifying what constitutes knowledge in EAP. The three participants interviewed were all experts in their disciplines of humanities and social sciences. However, they were not trained in EAP and therefore didn't consider themselves EAP 'experts'. All of the participants emphasized that they learnt how to teach while doing their PhDs and, while they taught core disciplinary content, they also taught academic 'writing and communication skills'. This echoes Cowley-Haselden and Monbec's (2018) study in which explicit theory was somehow downplayed by survey participants. However, in the case of these participants, they focussed more on the fact that they didn't have all of the necessary knowledge and less on whether that knowledge was a necessary core function or not. Each of them for instance mentions learning new disciplinary content that emerged as a result of teaching 'English for Specific Academic Purposes' and yet didn't feel comfortable to, for instance, publish in EAP journals or present at EAP conferences. However, this doesn't signal an absence of knowledge, with all of the participants saying that they have expertise in other fields despite the fact that their journeys into EAP, writing studies or communication skills were more recent and informed by practice rather than expertise. Participant C for instance notes that she draws on her expertise in teaching literature:

> I know I'm supposed to teach them how to talk to an audience that is clever but doesn't know the tech[nical] aspects. So then I begin to think of ways and means to do it wherein I can use my own expertise of creative writing and connotations of words and then we push it a bit more we say culturally . . . the words you use and the gestures you make they are also culturally specific and sensitive . . . we are value adding in our own way. We are not teaching from established ideas and templates. If we can value add beyond that then I feel we are doing a bit more.

To add to this knowledge of communicative needs in the context of academic disciplines, each of the participants notes that they chose to adapt, change and develop material to further suit the needs of their specific students and the disciplinary communicative competencies that students need depending on whether their core disciplines and degrees are in STEM or in social sciences and humanities. Their approach then accounts for the 'discipline-specific variation' proposed by Hyland (2016: 21) and the need for students to be apprenticed into an understanding of the different ways in which different disciplines communicate. In discussing how they teach and use their knowledge in EAP classrooms, Participant C notes the importance of 'appropriating' knowledge from the centre and recontextualizing knowledge to the context of Singapore:

If we say that we are writing from the periphery then we are writing back to the centre so I'm not taking on what the centre is giving me and teaching it as it is but I've taken what the centre has given me and using the language to change what we teach because now it has been appropriated and being used in a very different context. That's what I mean by culturally appropriating certain subject matters and presenting . . . the component of communication skills from a very South point of view (if you want to use that term) . . . where does the periphery meet the centre what is the west giving to us . . . what about the theories that emerged within the marginalized countries and the colonized lands . . . what was the post-colonial consciousness about what was brought from the west?

The discussion about the appropriation of concepts or even the emergence of new approaches to education in Global South contexts is arguably constrained by Global North academia in a number of ways. For example, Global South scholars need to have training in and mastery of Global North knowledge in order to engage in the intellectual fields that they may set out to 'challenge'. This often means that access to these forms of cultural capital is limited to Global South scholars with access to privileged universities in the North (or globally ranked Global South universities) and the economic capital to be able to fund the kinds of scholarship that are valued in EAP. As many scholars have pointed out in relation to their research, publishing in top-ranking journals in the field requires engaging with the kinds of northern-centric academic knowledge that is often only accessible through Northern universities, access to journal subscriptions and conference participation. Canagarajah critiqued this position and the access of 'native speakers' to privileged English language journals almost two decades ago (Canagarajah, 2005). Yet access and impact have remained almost negligible since the inequalities in academic research and publishing were brought to the forefront. In the context of Singapore, the participants all note that they believe they have a legitimate contribution to make to higher education and EAP learning and teaching research but are reluctant to enter the conversation because it is extremely time-consuming, requiring them to learn a new field of research and publish in fields that are adjacent to their own (e.g. learning and teaching communication skills in disciplines as opposed to specific expertise in communicating environmental science).

In the field of EAP, the slow and extremely minimal impact of the Global South (or any non-Northern scholarship) is evident in all of the major journals published in the field. In the year that one of my publications was accepted to a leading journal in EAP, I was one of two scholars from outside a Global North context and a second author. The lack of visibility of GS scholars in impactful journals in the field has a number of implications for understanding scholarship, academic research and exclusion. Notably, countries beyond the Global North have started to make an impact in terms of research productivity; Hyland and Jiang's (2020) bibliometric study shows the impact of economic prosperity on the capacity to publish in the field with China emerging as the third most productive country in publications from 2001 to 2020. Unsurprisingly, a number of GS countries (Iran, Malaysia, Turkey and Singapore) round up the bottom half of the table that ranks fifteen countries according to their productivity in producing publications in the field of EAP.

In the context of this study, the fact that the participants are primarily experts in fields outside of traditional EAP knowledge or even higher education pedagogy means that their contribution to Global North scholarship in EAP is minimal. Two of the participants whose core knowledge was in the humanities and social sciences and not in EAP, for instance, state that publishing in the field requires the acquisition of new knowledge. Participant A notes that much of her pedagogical approaches are 'intuitive'. She elaborates that publishing in EAP:

> would mean for me having to give a part of my research energy now to something else when I already have limited resources . . . there's really no support for the research I do . . . our job is to teach.

Participant B adds to her idea of constituting the 'fulcrum' of scholarship and practice that was discussed in relation to the classification of scholars as constituting the Global South by stating:

> If I say I'm the fulcrum then I'm the centre and you decide where you are in the network. I believe that I'm a fulcrum scholar, I am the scholar . . . in the middle.

In the interviews, Participant 1, who works for a polytechnic, mentioned the institutional agenda which attempts to align with the national agenda which privileges STEM research and the 'smart nation' initiative by the Singaporean government. She notes that the focus on STEM and the focus on applied disciplines means that the institution is not research based. As such she finds herself in a unique position in that her research in core humanities is not supported by the institution. At the same time, she reports that she doesn't feel compelled to publish in research on EAP that is outside her domain of expertise. She notes that the lack of research orientation in the institution gives her a unique position of being able to publish in her field:

> that's also the beauty of being in a space like that [e.g. a non-research-oriented tertiary institution] where you can research anything you want but at the same time you don't have to . . . so I find that it is a good place for me because if I was in writing centre or language centre then I would have to write pedagogically interested topics which is not what I would do. So I would say at this point it is a good place that I don't have to research and that I can write about things that are part of a conversation I would rather be a part of.

Language centres then are not necessarily places of exclusion but also ones of opportunity for enriching the field of EAP. In the current higher education landscape in which graduates struggle to find jobs in their areas of specialization, EAP provision allows them to teach while researching in their own areas of interest. An exploration of the divergence and variation of knowledge in EAP, from linguistics and literacy to encompassing broader skills that are more related to academic inquiry and scholarship, is better suited to exploration with other LCT concepts that are beyond the scope of this chapter. In terms of knowledge practices, however, it is evident that knowledge does exist in the context explored in this paper and the practitioner is able, through their capacity to adapt to their specific contexts, through the disciplinary requirements particular to each specific subject and through the recontextualization of their humanities knowledge, to occupy an elite code space of being the right kind of knower (a PhD in humanities with an expertise in communication) who possesses the right kind of knowledge (scholarship and inquiry and EAP provision). What is significant is that all of the participants in this study are determined to veer away from the social relations of classification according to context, race and ethnicity along pre-colonial lines (as Global South or 'periphery'). This then presents a position of the agentive redefining of 'tales of woe' to tales of success and opportunity in the context of the neoliberal institution and EAP provision.

Conclusion

EAP research has, as with many educational theories, been associated with knowledge blindness – the lack of theoretical frameworks which underpin EAP practice and the dominance of 'practice' over theory (Maton, 2014a, 2014b). In calling for theory to be included in EAP, a number of scholars are moving towards legitimizing EAP practice, underlining its centrality to the university and advocating for more recognition and prestige for the EAP practitioner (e.g. Bruce and Ding, 2017). However, when explored in relation to theories of representation, this approach is in danger of subscribing to 'knower blindness' (Maton, 2014a) by moving the focus away from the subject, the author or actor or who is legitimate in practice.

Knower blindness occurs as EAP and discussions of practitioner identity shift from focussing on native speakerism and racial identities that dominate identity discussions in relation to ESL, EFL and TESOL practice, to aligning with applied linguistics and linguistics where there is an increasing *invisibility* of social relations or 'knowledge myopia' (Maton, 2014a). Similar to applied linguistics and linguistics, in the pursuit of epistemic relations, there is a tendency to valorize epistemic relations over social relations. Maton (2014a: 14) defines 'knower blindness' as 'overfocusing on explicit structures of knowledge at the expense of practices more concerned with developing knowers' by valuing 'knowledge most easily seen explicit, abstract, condensed, hierarchical forms that visibly announce themselves' and failing to see knowledge that is 'less explicit' 'more concrete, context-dependant, embodied and axiological.' While emphasizing knowledge and calling for EAP 'practitioners . . . to develop an academic identity – one that is congruent with the expertise, experience, and knowledge that practitioners can, potentially, bring to higher education – through scholarship and research',[3] the danger emerges of forgetting that ultimately there is a dichotomization of the discipline according to social relations into those working in the 'centre' who have access to knowledge and powerful and valued scholarship and those working on the 'periphery' or margins. This means that scholars in the margins have their contributions to practice and knowledge rendered invisible because of their exclusion from publication and dissemination even if they are engaging with diverse and exciting approaches to teaching and learning in contexts that have the potential to challenge and change the understanding of EAP practitioner identity in general.

What was perhaps most inspiring in engaging with these practitioners during the interviews was that they demonstrated that they were able to overcome marginalization and exercise their agency by choosing not to be easily classified or to fall neatly into the many dichotomies which emerge in the field. They defined their own identities as complex; they defined their own institutional positioning as empowering them to engage with their areas of interest and scholarship while contributing to EAP knowledge through their expertise in the humanities in their contexts of practice. They didn't allow their institutions, global academia or discussions of EAP practitioner identity to define who they are, how they practice and how they positively impact their students' learning and development. As one participant put it, in Shakespeare's Caliban's words '[y]ou taught me language, and my profit on't is I know how to curse'. Of course the participants in this chapter are more than capable of using the language to their profit, to move beyond the limitations of cursing to mastering its use across a range of disciplines and fields. This chapter has, I hope, shown how capable participants are of moving beyond the prescribed practices of EAP in the Global North and of making EAP scholarship and identity theory aware that the periphery is redefining itself as the 'fulcrum', as capable of participating fully and, rather than subscribing to the 'survival' mode that EAP often takes in relation to the university's core functions, choosing to thrive.

Acknowledgements

I would like to thank Professor Karl Maton for his suggestion on the chapter title and for suggesting that the chapter should present a positive perspective on practitioner identity in a marginalized field. I would also like to thank the participants who read early drafts of this chapter and made comments so that the chapter reflected their self-representation rather than my interpretation of their perspectives on EAP practitioner identity.

Notes

1. https://www.timeshighereducation.com/world-university-rankings/national-university-singapore
2. https://www.washingtonpost.com/world/asia_pacific/at-yales-singapore-college-a-canceled-course-on-dissent-prompts-censorship-claims/2019/09/26/692c9736-d946-11e9-a1a5-162b8a9c9ca2_story.html

3 https://teachingeap.wordpress.com/2021/12/18/eap-practitioners-and-a-collective-sociological-imagination/

References

Campion, G. C. (2016), 'The Learning Never Ends': Exploring Teachers' Views on the Transition from General English to EAP', *Journal of English for Academic Purposes*, 23: 59–70.

Canagarajah, A. S. (2002), *A Geopolitics of Academic Writing*, Pittsburg: University of Pittsburgh Press.

Canagarajah, A. S. (2005), *Reclaiming the Local in Language Policy and Practice*, 3–24, Mahwah: Lawrence Erlbaum Associates Publishers.

Chen, A. (2016), 'EAP at the Tertiary Level in China: Challenges and Possibilities', in K. Hyland and P. Shaw (eds), *The Routledge Handbook of English for Academic Purposes*, 17–29, London: Routledge.

Chua, B. H. (1997), *Communitarian Ideology and Democracy in Singapore*, London and New York: Routledge.

Cowley-Haselden, S. and L. Monbec (2019), 'Emancipating Ourselves from Mental Slavery: Affording Knowledge in Our Practice', *BALEAP 2017 Conference Proceedings*.

Deleuze, G. and F. Guattari (1987), *A Thousand Plateaus: Capitalism and Schizophrenia*, Minneapolis and London: University of Minnesota Press.

Ding, A. (2016), 'The Limits of Identity Theory'. https://teachingeap.wordpress.com/2016/09/03/the-limits-of-identity-theory/ (accessed 20 November 2022).

Ding, A. and I. Bruce (2017), *The English for Academic Purposes Practitioner: Operating on the Edge of Academica*, Switzerland: Springer International.

Hong, L. and J. Huang (2008), *The Scripting of a National History: Singapore and Its Pasts*, Singapore and Hong Kong: NUS Press and Hong Kong University Press.

Hyland, K. (2002), 'Specificity Revisited: How Far Should We Go Now?' *English for Specific Purposes*, 21 (4): 385–95.

Hyland, K. (2016), 'General and Specific EAP', in K. Hyland and P. Shaw, *The Routledge Handbook of English for Academic Purposes*, 17–29, London: Routledge.

Hyland, K. and J. Feng (2020), 'A Bibliometric Study of EAP Research: Who Is Doing What, Where and When?' *Journal of English for Academic Purposes*, 49. https://doi.org/10.1016/\j.jeap.2020.100929

Hyland, K. and L. Hamp-Lyons (2002), 'EAP: Issues and Directions', *Journal of English for Academic Purposes*, 1 (1): 1–12.

Jordan, R. (1997), *English for Academic Purposes: A Guide and Resource Book for Teachers*, Cambridge: Cambridge University Press.

Kandiah, T. (1984), '"Kaduva": Power and the English Language Weapon in Sri Lanka', in P. Colin-Thome and A. Halpe (eds), *Honouring EFC Ludowyk*, 36–65, Colombo: Tisara Prasakayo.

Kathiravelu, L. (2019), '"What Kind of Indian Are You?" Frictions and Fractures between Singaporean Indians and Foreign-born NRIs', in T. Chong (ed.), *Navigating Differences: Integration in Singapore*, 110–28, Singapore: ISEAS Publishing.

Kohnke, L., ed. (2022), *Cases on Teaching English for Academic Purposes (EAP) During COVID-19: Insights From Around the World*, Hershey: IGI Global.

Lazar, M. (2020), 'Politics of the "South": Discourses and Praxis', *Discourse & Society*, 31 (1): 5–18.

Lim, L. (2016), *Knowledge, Control and Critical Thinking in Singapore: State Ideology and the Politics of Pedagogic Recontextualization*, New York: Routledge.

Liyanage, I. and T. Walker, eds (2014), *English for Academic Purposes (EAP) in Asia: Negotiating Appropriate Practices in a Global Context*, Rotterdam, Boston and Taipei: Sense Publishers.

Martin, P. (2014), 'Teachers in Transition: The Road to EAP', in P. Breen (ed.), *Cases on Teacher Identity, Diversity, and Cognition in Higher Education*, 287–316, Hershey: IGI Global.

Maton, K. (2014a), *Knowledge and Knower: Toward a Realist Sociology of Education*, London: Routledge.

Maton, K. (2014b), 'A TALL Order? Legitimation Code Theory for Academic Language and Learning', *Journal of Academic Language and Learning*, 8 (3): 34–48.

Maton, K. and R. T. H. Chen (2020), 'Specialization Codes: Knowledge, Knowers and Student Success', in J. R. Martin, K. Maton and Y. J. Doran (eds), *Accessing Academic Discourse: Systemic functional linguistics and Legitimation Code Theory*, 35–58, London: Routledge.

Mehdi Riazi, A., H. Ghanbar and I. Fazel (2020), 'The Contexts, Theoretical and Methodological Orientation of EAP Research: Evidence from Empirical Articles Published in the Journal of English for Academic Purposes', *Journal of English for Academic Purposes*, 48: 1–17.

Mittelmeier, J. and B. Zhang (2023), 'The Ideologies and Practices of Internationalization within Universities', in I. Bruce and B. Bond (eds), *Contextualizing English for Academic Purposes in Higher Education: Politics, Policies and Practices*, 27–44, London: Bloomsbury Academic.

Monbec, L. (2018), 'Designing an EAP Curriculum for Transfer: A Focus on Knowledge', *Journal of Academic Language and Learning*, 12 (2). http://journal.aall.org.au/index.php/jall/article/view/509/435435440

Pennycook, A. (1994), *The Cultural Politics of English as an International Language*, London: Pearson Education Limited.

Pennnycook, A. and S. Makoni (2019), *Innovations and Challenges in Applied Linguistics from the Global South*, London: Routledge.

Pennycook, A. and S. Makoni (2020), *Innovations and Challenges in Applied Linguistics from the Global South*, London: Routledge.

Raheem, R. and D. Devendra (2006), 'Changing Times, Changing Attitudes: The History of English Education in Sri Lanka', in S. Fernando, M. Gunesekara and A. Parakrama (eds), *English In Sri Lanka: Ceylon English, Lankan English and Sri Lankan English*, 162–80, Colombo: Sri Lanka English Language Teachers' Association.

Raheem, R. and H. Ratwatte (2004), 'Visible Strategies, Invisible Results: Language Policy and Planning in Sri Lanka', in S. M. A. T. S. Mansoor (ed.), *Language Policy, Planning and Practice – A South Asian Perspective*, 91–105, Karachi: Oxford University Press.

Raimes, A. (1991), 'Instructional Balance: From Theories to Practices in the Teaching of Writing', in J. Alatis (ed.), *Georgetown University Roundtable on Language and Linguistics*, 238–49, Washington, DC: Georgetown University Press.

Sloane, D. and E. Porter (2010), 'Changing International Student and Business Staff Perceptions of Insessional EAP: Using the CEM Model', *Journal of English for Academic Purposes*, 9 (3): 198–210.

Tight, M. (2021), 'Globalization and Internationalization as Frameworks for Higher Education Research', *Research Papers in Education*, 36 (1): 52–74.

Part II

MICROCOSMS

Chapter 4

EAP PRACTITIONERS' AGENCY AND IDENTITY IN PAKISTAN

FROM SOCIAL CLASS TO SOCIAL CAPITAL

Tanzeela Anbreen and Samina Ayub

Introduction

The current chapter focusses on the impact of social class on the agency and identity of EAP practitioners in Pakistan. EAP practitioners' social class in the context of Pakistan is important as it contributes to inculcating various characteristics among the class members. These same characteristics impact practitioners' understanding of who they are. Researchers (e.g. Weiss, 1998) have highlighted the significant role of social classes in Pakistan from economic, gender, caste and ideological perspectives; the current study views the social class of EAP practitioners from the perspective of the type of schools they attended, such as English-medium and Urdu-medium schools.

EAP itself is a demanding field due to stakeholders' (e.g. Higher Education Commission, university authorities and students) competing needs. Practitioners' day-to-day work is challenging in the local Pakistani context for several reasons; for example, EAP is a relatively recent and less established field which needs attention from the Higher Education Commission (HEC) and university authorities in terms of devising fair policies related to EAP practitioners' issues, such as the allocation of fair teaching workload and the delegation of other duties and equal opportunities for training, development, scholarship and promotions. In the absence of clear policies, practitioners face a variety of challenges in their day-to-day work, for example, discrimination from the departmental and university administration based on their social and academic background. However, practitioners' challenges from a social class perspective in Pakistan's higher education context have not been researched. Thus, it is important to understand the mechanisms which position the practitioners differently in the EAP field in Pakistan and, in particular, how social class origin and educational background affect a practitioner's trajectory. To explore this situation, Bourdieu's concepts of field, habitus and capital will be used to analyse the data. This study's overarching question is: how does EAP practitioners' social class shape their professional lives?

Working in the English department

English language teaching has a privileged place in Pakistani universities due to the HEC ruling to make English a medium of instruction (Mansur and Shrestha, 2015) at the university level as well as to conduct all examinations in English, except a few subjects in the humanities. English is a compulsory subject to get an undergraduate degree. Due to the HEC's promotion of the English language at university level, English language teaching and learning is a lucrative industry. More English language teaching means more language teaching jobs, and universities have recruited a large number of EAP teachers. In Pakistan, middle-class people enter this field as it provides them with a living and raises their social status because English is considered the language of the elite class and a ladder to upward social mobility (Mansoor, 2003; Rahman, 2002; Coleman, 2011). English-medium schooling is considered a prerequisite to English language proficiency which is widely needed to progress. Employers in business, private- and public-sector organizations prefer to recruit graduates fluent in English. Important civil and military service exams are also conducted in English medium (Anbreen, 2015).

To become a university lecturer in English, candidates must have at least an MS/MPhil in English linguistics or literature. However, despite similar higher education qualifications and working in the same institution, EAP practitioners' school and educational backgrounds play an important role in practitioners' professional life because of an absence of clear policies, particularly about the fair distribution of work, class size, research and development training, scholarships and promotions. In this paper we will call EAP practitioners who attended English-medium schools 'elite' and those who attended Urdu-medium schools 'middle class', and we will show that the university administration, in its day-to-day decisions, advantages elite over middle-class practitioners. Thus, it is important to explore how EAP practitioners from both social classes operate in this environment while working in the same institution and how social class provides agency as well as impacting their identity.

University administration starts from the heads of the department and the upper-level administrative body; they include deans, the registrar, the vice-chancellor and other administrative offices from the university. The officials and the departmental and university administration members are directly and indirectly responsible for the recruitment and allocation of duties to the EAP practitioners, handling their promotion-related matters and making policies and decisions about career-related matters. How EAP practitioners operate in this hierarchy-based working environment is important for understanding the role of practitioners' social class.

The English department includes lecturers, assistant professors, associate professors and professors who themselves are not part of the administration but follow the instructions and decisions of the administration. Importantly, EAP practitioners mainly perform a support role. The term support role refers to duties which are not directly related to teaching, for example, doing clerical jobs at admissions, examination paper printing and invigilation help or discipline maintenance during events. These jobs are considered lower in prestige in the local context. Most EAP classes are allocated to lecturers who are the junior staff in the departmental hierarchy and teach maximum workloads; workload decreases with promotion to the upper ranks in the hierarchy.

The organizational structure of universities places EAP teaching as the responsibility of the English department which also offers degrees in English literature and linguistics. The teaching of English linguistics and literature is allocated to the senior staff (with only limited teaching of EAP modules). It is important to note that the class size in the English literature and linguistics major is smaller, unlike the large class size of EAP (which may reach up to eighty students in one group/section); also, it is seen as more prestigious in the local academic context. However, promotion to senior positions in the department is tricky and challenging because it is subject to strict criteria. The promotion criteria are a combination of requirements, for example, a PhD in the relevant field, a specific number of publications in the HEC's recognized research journals and a number of service years in HEC-recognized institutions. These HEC criteria are the same across all university disciplines, though minimal funding is allocated for language research.

Key concepts

This study explores the impact of social class in shaping EAP practitioners' professional lives. To analyse this, we decided to use Bourdieu's key concepts of field, habitus and capital, which are widely used to explain the characteristics of people from different social classes. Bourdieu's (1986) perspectives on field, capital and habitus (dispositions) are important concepts in his theoretical toolkit and can account for EAP practitioners' traits, positioning and handling of day-to-day working in their workplace in this study. This section describes field, habitus and capital in some detail and the way they relate to this study, followed by how they are linked with social class.

Field

In *The Rules of Art* (1996/92), Bourdieu used 'field' as a term to refer to a specific context, and he defined a field as a 'configuration of relations between positions objectively defined, in their existence and in the determinations they impose upon the occupants, agents or institutions' (1996: 72–3).

A field is a structured space in which individuals acquire different positions based on habitus. Bourdieu (2005) considered a field an important site where various social phenomena, such as interactions among people, occur. The current study uses the term 'field' in Bourdieusian terms and refers to the EAP practitioners' workplace, that is, a renowned university in Pakistan. As EAP practitioners mainly perform a support role in the university, their position is weaker than other subjects' faculty members from STEM and social sciences. Furthermore, in the absence of clear policies and a strong hierarchical model existing in the university administration and the English department, practitioners constantly face challenges in the field. So, understanding a field is mandatory to explain the positioning of the practitioners. This study agrees that EAP in our chosen university context is

> a social field with the distribution of power and its monopolies, its struggles and strategies, interests and profits. (Bourdieu, 1975: 19)

A field has agents, for example, people who dominate and who are dominated (Ding, 2022). In this study, these agents include a range of employees working there, for example, the teaching faculty (EAP practitioners) of the English department, a head of the department (HoD) who is responsible for administering the department's day-to-day affairs, registrar office staff, deans of the faculties and the vice-chancellor (VC). The way these agents promote one social class over the others in the chosen context is of interest; their role in relation to impacting EAP practitioners' position in the field is of critical importance. Based on the authority and power according to the agents' designation, they dominate or are dominated (Ding, 2022). Bourdieu (1994) also highlighted that a field is a permanent relationship of inequality where agents struggle to either change or preserve the field; all agents harness their powers in this struggle, and power defines agents' positions in the field and their strategies. An important question arising here is what traits lead some agents to a dominant position, whereas some others are dominated. Similarly, what tussles or traits make a field a site for struggle where relationships are unequal? This study will explore such questions, that is, the characteristics of agents and how they are valued within the university's hierarchy, using Bourdieu's concept of 'field'.

In every field, agents face and cope with different struggles in their own way. In our investigation, different social class-specific traits of the agents (from the elite and middle class) emerge, which make one group dominant over the other; in this case, the social classes of practitioners contribute to the power of the agents.

Capital

Capital is one of Bourdieu's (1986) important theoretical tools and will be used in this study to explore the process of the accumulation of knowledge and skills reproduced by the agents in their specific field. He defines capital as 'accumulated labor (in its materialized form or its "incorporated," embodied form) which, when appropriated on a private, that is, exclusive, basis by agents or groups of agents, enables them to appropriate social energy in the form of reified or living labor' (Bourdieu, 1986: 15). A social group's (e.g. elite-class or middle-class groups) values, tastes and lifestyles are common characteristics or dispositions that depend on their position in society (Moore, 2014). We understand that the dispositions of both the elite class and middle class are distinctive to their social group and are a valuable resource that Bourdieu (2000) called capital. In the current context, practitioners' capital likely impacts their identity, that is, their understanding of who they are. Importantly, Bourdieu extended his concept from monetary capital (e.g. property, money, bonds or any form of financial assets) to other forms of capital, such as cultural capital, social capital and symbolic capital. This section briefly discusses these types of capital here and will be used to analyse the data. In this study, social capital refers to

> the sum of active or potential resources that are connected through the possession of a network of permanent relations of mutual acquaintance and mutual recognition . . . also tied by bonds that are useful and permanent. (Bourdieu, 1994: 90)

Cultural capital refers to

> the distinctive forms of knowledge and ability that students acquire – whether at home, at school, or in the relations between the two – from their training in the cultural disciplines. (Bourdieu, 1984: 20)

Cultural capital is 'convertible' into economic capital under certain conditions (Bourdieu, 1986: 242), for example, some educational qualifications may result in getting employment. Bourdieu's (1986) cultural capital exists in three major forms: (i) the embodied form, which refers to the 'long-lasting dispositions of the mind and the body' (Bourdieu, 1986: 243), (ii) the institutionalized form which refers to degrees, certificates and diplomas which stamp the value of embodied cultural capital and (iii) the objectified form which refers to cultural goods, such as pictures, books, music, dictionaries and so on. In this study we compare and contrast middle-class and elite-class EAP practitioners' capital, which they most likely use in the workplace to identify themselves and handle challenges. However, there is limited research evidence showing practitioners' capital and the way it impacts their identity. The current study will begin to address this research gap. In addition, it will also show how far the elite class uses their capital to legitimize their 'authority to define situations' (Ding, 2022: 160). Ding's (2022) point is valid for the context of Pakistan in that

> EAP practitioners enter the field with little cultural capital in terms of both intellectual and academic capital. This positions them in a highly dominated position within the larger HE field, impacting their power, agency and symbolic capital. (Ding, 2022: 162)

EAP practitioners in the context of Pakistan try to overcome their low cultural capital and weaker position in the field by building their capital in various ways (e.g. by obtaining an additional degree, receiving training and certification from English-speaking countries or, for example, enhancing social ties with the university and department's top leadership using social class values).

Based on our experience, we understand that social class dispositions, for example, values, tastes, ties and lifestyles, are often used as capital by practitioners. We also realize that elite-class practitioners dominate the field; however, this process needs to be explored. Thus, we use the concept of 'capital' to understand how EAP practitioners' dispositions, learnt through their social class habitus, perform an important role in addressing day-to-day matters in the field (university). We will explore which capital is valued more and how the practitioners' field (university) allows one type of capital to be converted into another form of capital, for example, how fluent foreign language proficiency or scholarship may help achieve rewards such as promotions.

In our particular field, we expect that elite-class practitioners draw power from their stronger social ties with the university's top hierarchy as well as from the recognized objectified, embodied and institutionalized capitals (e.g. fluency in spoken English, access to global cultures, books, schooling type, training and certifications).

Habitus

Bourdieu (2000) named the dispositions and characteristics of agents' 'habitus' and refers to it in various ways depending on the situation(s), for example, as a 'product of history, a system of continuous and transferable predispositions and past which survives in the present and is perpetuated in the future' (Bourdieu, 1994: 63; Bourdieu, 2000: 21–2, 158). A habitus may be an individual's own history or a collective history of a social group (class) (Bourdieu, 2000, 2002). Thus, a relationship exists between an individual and a class habitus (Mounier, 2001).

Practitioners embody habitus at their workplace as it is an 'outcome of repetition and conservation' (Bourdieu, 2000: 159; Corcuff, 2007) and also because 'the responses habitus generates without calculation appear as adapted, coherent and immediately intelligible' within a field (Bourdieu, 2000). Thus, EAP practitioners' habitus is a product of their individual and their group history (social class), which is an outcome of their experiences. This study considers that habitus concerns all sorts of behaviours and ways of being/thinking, including the propensity for docility in relation to cultural traditions and norms.

Practitioners' schooling, economic background and social experiences play an important role in shaping their habitus (dispositions) in the local context of Pakistan. Bourdieu (1984) considers agents' home background and formal education important sites for learning the culture. Agents' culture learnt in this process of home training and schooling reflects their tastes which act as markers of their class. This study is interested in exploring what dispositions, tastes and practices are peculiar to the elite-class and middle-class practitioners and how they shape their professional lives.

In this study, we consider EAP practitioners as agents in the field (their university) who acquire habitus (various dispositions) through their upbringing, as members of economically rich or middle-class social groups. Their habitus determines their agency at their workplace (field). The current study uses habitus and dispositions interchangeably. This study will carefully analyse data to identify middle-class and elite-class practitioners' prominent habitus (dispositions) and how they use them in handling day-to-day challenges in their field.

Research methodology

To address the key research question, 'How does practitioners' social class shape their professional lives?', we adopted a mixed-method qualitative approach to collect and analyse the data.

Participants

Various individuals may hold similar volumes of capital and capital configurations (i.e. share material conditions) in conjunction with others, and they would constitute a homogeneous and identifiable group (Grenfell, 2012). In this study, we divided EAP practitioners into two identifiable groups (elite class and middle class) as they each have similar capital and also share a somewhat similar position in the social space's (university's) overall structure. Members of each group share similar habitus and consequent dispositional characteristics.

Twenty practitioners participated in this study; ten practitioners were educated in English-medium schools in the local Pakistani context (called the elite class in this study), and another ten practitioners attended Urdu-medium schools (called the middle class). They all worked in a renowned public-funded university. We explained to them the purpose of the current study and what we wanted from them. Also, it was explained that their participation was voluntary and that they could withdraw at any time if they wished to. Their names and data would be kept anonymous at all stages. All of them consented to participate.

Data collection

As this study aimed to understand how EAP practitioners' social class impacts their agency and identity, it was important to understand their workplace challenges and how they handled them. So, we decided to employ a qualitative approach for data collection using the following methods: semi-structured interviews, a WhatsApp group chat and shadowing two participants from each group.

Semi-structured interviews

To get an in-depth understanding of the challenges practitioners face in their day-to-day work and how they handle them, we conducted semi-structured interviews with the participants. Interviews were conducted three times over six months, with approximately two months in between. This two-month gap after each interview was maintained intentionally to understand the variety of challenges they face over time. In our local context, challenges vary each term, for example, the first term comes with pressure related to admissions and settling the students, whereas subsequent terms are heavy in teaching and co-curricular activities. The interview questions mainly focussed on (i) practitioners' day-to-day routines, (ii) the challenges they encounter in their institutions and (iii) the skills/ways they handle these issues.

WhatsApp chat

In the local EAP context of Pakistan, WhatsApp is a mandatory way to connect with colleagues. EAP practitioners tend to reply to WhatsApp messages as soon as they receive them. A departmental WhatsApp group existed already; the researchers decided to observe the group chat to get an in-depth understanding of the practitioners' challenges. The researchers obtained consent from the WhatsApp members and were included in the group. WhatsApp chat proved a useful, non-intrusive way of collecting data in a natural setting. We particularly looked participants' conversations/comments about various duties, appreciations and acknowledgements. Sometimes chats had participants' personal views, which reflected their identity and agency, such as in Figure 4.1.

Shadowing

We shadowed two members from each group throughout their working day to get an understanding of their work. The researcher followed the participants in their classrooms, the admin and HoD offices, the library, the cafeteria and the department. Important observations were noted in a diary, including the moods and gestures of the practitioners and the people they interacted with, for example, students, deputy registrar, cafeteria owner. We particularly noticed situations of disagreement, argument and agreement.

Data analysis

To answer the key research question, 'How does EAP practitioners' social class shape their professional lives?', we found it necessary to focus on two levels:

1. The capital they used to handle their day-to-day life challenges in the field (university).
2. The habitus (i.e. dispositions/characteristics) they displayed in the field.

All data was qualitative. Participants' WhatsApp chat was already in written form, whereas semi-structured interviews were transcribed and checked by another expert for accuracy; the other expert was also a bilingual Urdu and English speaker who was teaching EAP. Observations after shadowing also existed in written form. We analysed all written data using thematic analysis (Braun and Clark, 2006); in this process, we took the following steps:

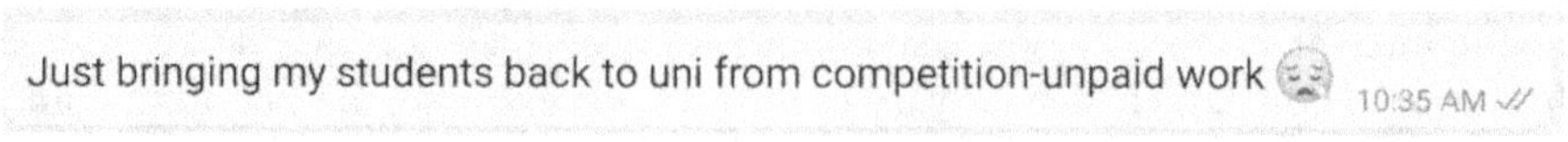

Just bringing my students back to uni from competition-unpaid work 😒 10:35 AM ✓✓

Figure 4.1 WhatsApp message.

Step 1: Familiarization with all of the data.
Step 2: Development of initial codes.
We carefully looked for the ideas (themes) in all datasets and noted how and where they occurred. Also, we gave labels to similar ideas.
Step 3: Extraction and refining of themes.
We carefully repeated this process and analysed the data by merging similar themes and refining their labels accordingly. We found the following themes: (i) English-medium (EM) schooling and English level, (ii) familiarity with global cultures, (iii) foreign degrees/qualifications, (iv) access to the powerful elite class and (v) spending money vs. social responsibilities. These themes clearly showed the types of capital and dispositions which were used to shape practitioners' professional lives and are briefly described below.

English-medium (EM) schooling and fluency in English level

Participants often referred to their English 'level' or EM schooling as an important capital. While elite practitioners tended to see this as a positive element in their identity, middle-class participants hinted that the lack of this capital was damaging.

Familiarity with global cultures

Participants often mentioned that their knowledge of the English culture was an important capital. Elite practitioners accessed it through reading popular English literary texts at EM schools and physical trips to anglophone countries; they acknowledged this capital as a positive element in their identity. In contrast, middle-class practitioners pointed out the lack of this capital, which negatively impacted their identity.

Foreign degrees and qualifications

Participants agreed on the value associated with foreign degrees and qualifications, especially from English universities. Elite practitioners often possessed this highly valued asset. Middle-class practitioners only rarely had this capital due to their limited finances, and they mentioned lacking foreign degrees and qualifications as a disadvantage that had an impact on their identity; they considered themselves less skilled and less proficient than elite-class practitioners.

Access to the powerful elite class

Participants expressed the benefits of developing social networks and having access to the powerful elite class. Elite practitioners reported having strong ties with the senior officials as they shared similar EM schooling backgrounds, and they considered it to be valuable capital. Middle-class practitioners were lacking in this capital and were distant from the senior officials at the workplace.

Spending money vs. social responsibilities

Participants reported that spending money (e.g. offering expensive gifts to senior officials) is valuable capital to maintain a pleasant work life. Elite practitioners' affluence helps them spend money on gifts for higher officials and get concessions in duties in return. Middle-class practitioners cannot afford to do so; instead, they perform more duties, taking them as a social responsibility (e.g. cover teaching or discipline duty).

Results

The analysis described above allowed us to map the very different capitals that practitioners from different social classes rely on and the impact these have on their professional lives. Practitioners perceived that they mainly acquired this capital through EM or Urdu-medium schooling. All such aspects represented their membership in a particular social class – elite class and middle class. Elite practitioners had more valued capital than middle-class practitioners, such as familiarity with global cultures, which they used from time to time in handling their professional life. Table 4.1 presents both social classes' capitals, followed by a discussion of how this capital impacted the practitioners.

The results suggested that the dispositions of both of the participating groups developed differently owing to the capital they owned and the outlook their social class capital inculcated in them; these differences in capital, in fact, impact their day-to-day working, which is discussed below.

Impact on status and standing

First, we found that EAP teaching is mainly allocated to lecturers (junior staff). In contrast, the teaching of linguistics and literature is allocated to the senior staff, along with some limited teaching of EAP. We found that all of the HoDs in the English department in the last decade belonged to the elite social class. Our data suggested that the HoD and the senior university officials recognize all forms of the elite class's cultural capital (embodied, objectified and institutional forms) more than that of the middle class. Recognition in the local context means that their capital is acknowledged and rewarded, for example, they will be promoted sooner than middle-class practitioners, sent as university representatives abroad and chosen to perform key responsibilities. Elite-class practitioners would be encouraged to take prominent roles, such as conducting the annual graduation ceremony, hosting annual debates and declamation and holding roles as directors of academics. They are considered the soft face of the university. In contrast, middle-class practitioners are recognized as good for support roles. In short, they perform physically and mentally tougher jobs but are less visible publicly.

Table 4.1 Different types of capital possessed by elite-class and middle-class EAP practitioners

Cultural capital	
Elite-class practitioners	**Middle-class practitioners**
i. Embodied: Presenting familiarity with diverse/ global cultures and world views. Training in social manners, (e.g. meet and greet). More financial ability to throw parties, buy expensive brands to exchange as gifts, participate in occasions and celebrations. Higher fluency in spoken English and therefore valuable linguistic capital.	**i. Embodied**: Familiarity with the local culture with limited exposure to other cultures. Limited training in social manners. Limited financial ability to participate in gift exchange. More limited fluency in spoken English and therefore limited linguistic capital.
ii. Objectified: Access to foreign printed books, library resources, trips and invited guest speakers' talks.	**ii. Objectified**: Rare or limited access to foreign printed books, library resources, trips.
Example: 'I studied in the Convent of Jesus and Mary school [*a top English-medium school in Lahore*]. At Convent school, the sisters introduced various English texts such as *She*, *Return of She* and *The Hunchback of Notre Dame*, to name a few. We also read later texts like *The Old Man and the Sea* and *Love Story*, *Take Three*, and others. All this reading developed my language skills and exposed me to English and global cultures. I learned a lot about relationships, manners, and wisdom. You know, such exposure is rare in local medium schools. I am privileged to study there, and it pays a lot to me in my professional life.' (Participant #8)	Example: 'I am victimized due to limited knowledge of English culture. In our department, cultural knowledge is considered important. Teachers from the upper class from DHA, Model Town, and Gulberg [*economically richest areas of the city*] do not face this as they go on foreign visits and have English medium schooling. So they have more benefits in the job.' (Participant #2)
iii. Institutional: Degrees and certification by renowned institutions – attractive to employers.	**iii. Institutional**: Degrees and certification by ordinary institutions – less attractive to employers.
Example: 'My UK-based degree taught me a lot, I have the edge over others owing to this degree. I can perform my job better than my colleagues. After all, I am a foreign degree holder.' (Participant #10)	Example: Congratulations 😊 B.....What a news.....a well deserved promotion. Your achievements especially a PhD from Warwick made it happen. m so happy for you. 17:07 (Participant #3 on congratulating a newly promoted staff member from the elite class)

(Continued)

Table 4.1 (Continued)

Social capital	
Elite-class practitioners	**Middle-class practitioners**
Social capital: Access to powerful elite class (e.g. politicians, civil and military officials, technocrats) who influence the university administration's decisions. **Example**: 'Our VC is an alumna of the same school from where I come from. We have good family relations as well. I may walk into her office when I am needed. She (the VC) is a very kind-hearted lady and takes care of us.' (Participant #10)	**Social capital**: Meagre chances for access to the powerful elite class, personal relationships limited to the middle class who are in less authority. They have less access to university administration. **Example**: "I am unable to get the opportunity to avail myself a scholarship as I do not have social connections with the university management and Head of the Department. They decide whom to grant a scholarship. You know relationships and social links are very very important to be a successful professional here, and this is where I lack.' (Participant #5)
Economic capital	
Elite-class practitioners	**Middle-class practitioners**
Economic capital: Practitioners from the elite class are economically stronger than middle-class practitioners. For example, they own independent cars to drive or even chauffeur-driven cars to travel to/from the university; they can afford expensive gifts to offer senior management. Their outlook is more sophisticated, for example, they wear expensive brands. **Example**: 'You know gifts are a form of compensation from duties and allocated work in our university. We have to do it to make our professional life easier.' (Participant #6)	**Economic capital**: Middle-class practitioners travel on local public transport or in hired vans used by multiple people – locally a symbol of less economic stability. They cannot afford expensive brands and it is visible in their appearance. **Example**: 'Miss . . . was exempted from examination, funfair and escort duties because she spends a lot of money to give presents to the decision-makers.' **Researcher: *What do you mean by decision-makers? Who are they?*** Participant: 'Head of the Department, Dean and his staff, Registrar, and VC office staff all are decision-makers. Once they are obliged by rich staff with expensive gifts, they would be exempt from the duties. People like me do not prefer to do this practice as this is against our middle class social and moral values and I face the music.' (laughter) 'I take social responsibilities more than my rich colleagues. I teach maximum hours among EAP staff in the department. I performed sixteen invigilation duties in eight days last exam. Performed discipline duty during Sports Gala yesterday under the scorching heat for about four hours. Not only this but maintaining respectful behaviour towards senior staff is also sometimes challenging, I marked 50 extra exam scripts in place of Mrs "X" who is a senior teacher in last mid-term exams as she was sick. You know, we are not paid extra money for any such duties.' (Participant #4)

Elite-class practitioners use independent cars to travel to/from the university. Middle-class practitioners use public transport and vans which stop at multiple stops and are frequently late. On arriving late, middle-class practitioners are often reminded of their lateness which impacts their professional reputation negatively. Thus, economic capital makes a difference in professional reputation in several ways.

Impact on workload

The HoD is responsible for the departmental timetable, including allocating the teaching workload and classes to the EAP practitioners. EAP is a compulsory subject across all undergraduate courses, and there are different class sizes in each department, for example, in the journalism department, there may be up to eighty students. A middle-class EAP practitioner will teach and assess such a larger cohort. In contrast, there is a small class size in the fine arts department (thirty or fewer students), and elite-class practitioners will be allocated such smaller classes owing to their stronger social ties with the HoD. Similarly, students from STEM subjects are more advanced in language skills and are easier to teach due to these students' better existing language skills and more engaging attitude towards studies than those from social sciences and humanities subjects. Elite-class practitioners are favoured by being allocated STEM subjects-related groups to teach EAP, and the remaining classes are allocated to middle-class practitioners. Hence, the practitioners' social capital helps them get the classes of their choice. The same is the case with allocating co-curricular and extra-curricular duties (e.g. escorting different teams locally and outside the city) to middle-class practitioners. Thus, the social class of practitioners plays an important role in handling the workload.

Impact on recognition

There is intense competition among the members of the English department for the very limited sponsorship for PhD studies. Because of the stronger capital of the elite-class practitioners, they are most commonly successful in receiving foreign scholarships. Importantly, proof of an English language proficiency test, e.g. International English Language Testing System (IELTS) with required band scores is mandatory for the foreign scholarship application submission. IELTS is a very expensive test locally due to the high exchange rate of PKR and British pound sterling. Elite-class practitioners can easily afford to pay the IELTS test fee and can even afford to repeat if needed to achieve the required/better band score. In contrast, middle-class practitioners cannot afford to invest such money to take the IELTS test, so many drop out at the application submission stage.

Institutional policies and departmental standards reward the elite class's knowledge, skills and conduct. For example, a foreign degree from an English-speaking country is recognized throughout the practitioners' professional careers. The linguistic capital also continues to provide them with the opportunities to gain visibility and prestige within and outside the institution on behalf of the university. An important point here is that the level of recognition is not only at the departmental level but at the university level, for example, in recognition of elite-class practitioners' English-medium schooling and strong economic and social backgrounds, they are often invited to become part of the university policy-making team. In contrast, middle-class practitioners cannot avail themselves of such recognition. At most, it would be acknowledged that they are performing their duties and that this is what they are expected to do, but that, in simple words, they are not going the extra mile. Thus, the acknowledgement of practitioners' skills and their relationship with the top management and decision-makers play an important role in their day-to-day work recognition.

Impact on prospects

In the absence of clear policies, 'who you know' is the most prevalent guideline that impacts practitioners' immediate and future prospects. Elite-class EAP practitioners' capital opens more prospects for them as compared to middle-class practitioners. The university's top officials play a key role in promotion. Since promotion brings professional recognition, increased salary benefits, reduced teaching hours and several other benefits (including switching from compulsory EAP classes to the teaching of English linguistics and English literature major classes), EAP practitioners' social class and the capitals associated with them as discussed earlier come into action.

Discussion

This study reiterated that social class is a fundamental construct in the local Pakistani EAP context. School type is an indicator of EAP practitioners' social class in the local context and has a long-lasting impact. Schools are important sites for developing cultural capital (Bourdieu, 1984).

Though in terms of institutionalized capital, most practitioners (except two from the elite class with foreign degrees) had similar qualifications, their embodied capitals were different, for example, elite-class practitioners' fluency in spoken English, their accent, their familiarity with global cultures and their confidence in conversation in English were more valued than middle-class practitioners and were more appreciated by the dominant agents (e.g. the department and university's senior management) in their field. With the appreciation of their capital, they are prominent and dominant in their field, whereas middle-class practitioners are dominated. Middle-class practitioners are aware of their less valued capital and also that their habituses influence their behaviour (e.g. the notion of hard work or politeness and respect for elders is also linked to class origin), and yet this does not seem to create an agency to push back but rather a painful awareness of the unfair world around them. For example, respecting one's elders in age or seniority is a common aspect of Pakistani society, but in case of an argument or difference of opinion, practitioners from the middle class and elite class handle the situation differently. Following their habitus, a middle-class practitioner will stay quiet when interacting with a senior or elderly person and show agreement with their opinion. In contrast, an elite-class practitioner does not keep quiet to show respect; rather they tend to present their point of view without negating the senior. As this situation prevails, it is accepted by all that there is a power differential between the agents and this situation is tolerated because of the lack of options for middle-class practitioners. While elite-class practitioners and their habituses (dispositions) determine their agency, middle-class practitioners are aware that their habitus does not provide them with an adapted response, but they see this as ineluctable, that is, if they don't act according to 'their social class values' their membership in that class may be questioned or, as one participant said, they 'face the music'.

Elite-class practitioners were found to have important social capital as they were closely linked with the social network of the field's top management (HoD, dean, registrar, VC, etc.). Economic capital allowed them to engage in social practices, for example, spending money on parties and gift exchange, which in turn might allow them to avoid fulfilling academic and professional responsibilities. For example, the elite class might network with the university administration through social activities and get compensated with limited classes and small class size or exemption from duties. This social capital also gives them better access to nominations for PhD scholarships or funding and so on. Thus, elites can subtly blur the boundaries of friendship and professional realms, which is simply a normal practice expected by elite practitioners. In contrast, middle-class practitioners take social responsibilities, for example, more physical and mental work, showing dedication and hard work and respecting others (only limited parties and gift exchange); these are done to compensate for their weak social and economic capital. Agents' habitus or dispositions configure the way these EAP practitioners' groups are positioned and stand in this field or social space. In the context of this study, it seemed difficult for the middle-class practitioners to develop or reach the point where they became equal to the elite class. This study confirms that EAP practitioners from English-medium schools display more acceptable cultural capital in their outlook and activities and are more successful in their field. But gaining embodied capital is not under the individual's control as it is developed over a period of time and cannot be transferred instantaneously (Hampton-Garland, 2015) and so there are limited possibilities for the middle-class practitioners to improve their prospects.

Conclusion

This research explored how social class shapes EAP practitioners' professional lives in the context of a Pakistani university. Two social classes of EAP practitioners, named 'elite-class' and 'middle-class', were compared. Using Bourdieu's theoretical concepts, the study found that practitioners' schooling type impacted their dispositions as well as equipping them with a relatively valued capital in the EAP field, which influenced their prospects and their conditions. We found that this class belonging is directly linked to how agentic practitioners see themselves (regardless of whether they recognize the injustices or not). Urdu-medium schools helped practitioners build middle-class habitus (dispositions), whereas English-medium schools promoted the development of elite-class habitus (dispositions) which shaped their various behaviours and understanding of the field. While an elite-class habitus guaranteed these practitioners better professional outcomes, in comparison, middle-class practitioners were found to be less advantaged. Thus, capital and habituses led to inequality among various social groups. It is hoped that this study can begin discussions on clearer policy-making in Pakistan's university context to benefit EAP practitioners and overcome this inequality.

References

Anbreen, T. (2015), 'The Influence of English Second Language Learning on Pakistani University Students' Identity', *Procedia - Social and Behavioral Sciences*, 192: 379–87. https://doi.org/10.1016/j.sbspro.2015.06.054

Bourdieu, P. (1975), 'The Specificity of the Scientific Field and the Social Conditions of the Progress of Reason', *Social Science Information*, 14 (6): 19–47.

Bourdieu, P. (1984), *Distinction: A Social Critique of the Judgement of Taste*, London: Routledge & Kegan Paul.

Bourdieu, P. (1986), 'The Forms of Capital', in J. Richardson (ed.), *Handbook of Theory and Research for the Sociology of Education*, 241–58, Westport: Greenwood.

Bourdieu, P. (1994), *Texts of Sociology*, Athens: Delfini.

Bourdieu, P. (1996/92), *The Rule of Art*, Cambridge: Polity Press.

Bourdieu, P. (2000), *Pascalian Meditations*, Cambridge: Polity Press.

Bourdieu, P. (2002), 'Symbolic Capital', *Sygxrona Themata*, 80: 18–21.

Bourdieu, P. (2005), *For the Science and Its Social Uses*, Athens: Polytropon.

Braun, V. and V. Clarke (2006), 'Using Thematic Analysis in Psychology', *Qualitative Research in Psychology*, 3 (2): 77–101. https://doi.org/10.1191/1478088706qp063oa

Coleman, H. (2011), *Dreams and Realities: Developing Countries and the English Language* (Hywel Coleman), British Council. https://www.teachingenglish.org.uk/sites/teacheng/files/Z413%20English%20Development%20Book.pdf

Corcuff, P. (2007), *Les Nouvelles Sociologies*, Paris: Armand Colin.

Ding, A. (2022), 'Bourdieu and Field Analysis: EAP and Its Practitioners', in A. Ding and M. Evans (eds), *Social Theory for English for Academic Purposes Foundations and Perspectives*, 155–76, Bloomsbury Academic. https://doi.org/10.5040/9781350229198

Grenfell, M. (2012), *Pierre Bourdieu: Key Concepts*, 2nd edn, Durham: Routledge

Hampton-Garland, P. (2015), *The Influence of Embodied Cultural Capital on the Retention and Matriculation Adults Entering College*, New Prairie Press. https://newprairiepress.org/aerc/2015/roundtables/7/ (accessed 04 October 2022).

Mansoor, S. (2003), 'Language Planning in Higher Education Issues of Access and Equity', *The Lahore Journal of Economics*, 8 (2): 17–42. https://doi.org/10.35536/lje.2003.v8.i2.a2

Mansur, S. B. and P. Shrestha (2015), 'The EAP Course Design Quagmire – Juggling the Stakeholders' Perceived Needs', in P. Shrestha (ed.), *Current Developments in English for Academic and Specific Purposes: Local Innovations and Global Perspectives*, 93–113, Garnet Education.

Moore, R. (2014), 'Capital', in M. Grenfell (ed.), *Pierre Bourdieu Key Concepts*, 2nd edn, 98–113, Abingdon, UK: Routledge.

Mounier, P. (2001), *Pierre Bourdieu, une introduction*, Paris: Agora.

Rahman, T. (2002), *Language, Ideology and Power: Language-Learning among the Muslims of Pakistan and North India*, Karachi, Pakistan: Oxford University Press.

Weiss, A. M. (1998), 'The Gendered Division of Space and Access in Working Class Areas of Lahore', *Contemporary South Asia*, 7 (1): 71–89. https://doi.org/10.1080/09584939808719830

Chapter 5

TRIALS AND TRIBULATIONS OF EAP PRACTITIONERS IN ZIMBABWE

Tambawoga C. Muchena

Introduction

Though a number of studies in Zimbabwe have been done within EAP, the majority have either focussed on the learners or the development of teaching material resulting in the focus on the EAP practitioner being peripheral (Gonye et al., 2012; Kahari and Takavarasha, 2013). It is actually surprising that there is lack of such scholarship on Zimbabwean EAP practitioners given that the identity of EAP practitioners across the world has historically and continues to be a debatable topic, significantly differing from one context to another. For instance, researchers based in the developed world are different from those from the developing world (Lund and Shamsi, 2021). Access to basic resources like internet connectivity, library resources that are not open access and even scholarship funding separates the Global North and the Global South.

While there is rapid growth in the commercialization of EAP services in the UK (Ding and Bruce, 2017), the field is relatively stable in Zimbabwe. In Zimbabwe, the nomenclature English for academic purposes is seldom used; such activity is termed communication skills. Thus, across Zimbabwean higher education, departments or centres that offer English for academic purposes modules or courses are either housed in the English departments, languages departments or are stand-alone communication skills departments or centres. Unlike Fulcher's (2009) findings that most EAP units in the UK that were not standalone departments were housed in administrative departments, the case in Zimbabwe is that those communication skills units that are not standalone departments are housed in academic departments like languages/linguistics. The communication skills modules assist students across the university with academic skills that cover the four language skills: writing, reading, speaking and listening. While the basic communication skills module is compulsory for all first-year first-semester students, there are also other modules that the department can teach to other specified group of students like extended communication skills modules.

The focus of this chapter therefore is to gain a panoramic view of how Zimbabwean EAP practitioners see and position themselves within this landscape, how they are viewed by colleagues from other academic departments, how they negotiate their academic identity and what challenges they face.

Research questions

1. What qualifications do EAP practitioners in Zimbabwe hold?
2. What EAP practitioners' skills are valued in Zimbabwe?
3. How do higher education authorities view the EAP profession?
4. How do fellow lecturers and students view EAP teaching and learning?
5. How do Zimbabwean EAP practitioners view themselves?

Literature review

EAP, a global perspective

In the Global North, some literature has explored the status and professional development of EAP practitioners (Campion, 2016; Ding and Bruce, 2017; Ding, Bond and Bruce, 2022; Ding 2019). Studies beyond the Global North are quite rare. Kaivanpanah et al. (2021) examined Iranian EAP teachers' competences and professional development and also looked at how the teachers perceived their roles, responsibilities and the challenges that they faced in their EAP teaching. The study noted that, despite encouraging research in EAP, a focus on EAP practitioners is still peripheral just as had earlier been noted by Basturkmen (2014, 2019). To Basturkmen (2014), it is not only the needs of the learners that are important but also the needs of the teacher; thus scholarship focus should also be directed at the EAP practitioner. Kohnke and Zou (2021) is one recent study that made an attempt to focus on the EAP teacher through exploring how Hong Kong EAP teachers coped with the transition from traditional face-to-face teaching to online teaching as a result of COVID-19. While this study was a noted shift towards the study of the EAP practitioner, its focus was on the transition, a change that was not just peculiar to EAP practitioners but affected all other university teachers. The lack of preparedness noted on the part of Hong Kong EAP practitioners was also noted in other distant disciplines as a result of COVID-19 restrictions. Ding, Bond and Bruce (2022), besides working on historical issues related to EAP practitioners and their member associations, also focussed on their identity and agency and issues related to their roles within and outside the UK. The study pointed out that there was a need to pay attention to the interest and concerns of EAP practitioners themselves. Just as Bruce (2021) notes, the EAP field is not homogeneous and is also not static but continuously developing; thus focus on the practitioner in different contexts is increasing within scholarship. Generally, 'Professional identity is not a stable entity; it is complex, personal, and shaped by contextual factors' (Clarke, Hyde and Drennan, 2013: 8) What this means is that the realization of what Bruce (2021) calls 'EAP discourse' will be fruitfully realized if the identity, agency and predicament of EAP practitioners in Zimbabwe are scrutinized. This will be in sync with the notion that professional identity formation is heavily influenced by contextual factors (Beijaard, Meijer and Verloop, 2004). It seems in a challenging new economy it is prudent that there is a profound understanding of professional identity and issues that affect its development (Dobrow and Higgins, 2005).

EAP, a Zimbabwean perspective

Literature has shown that very little scholarship focussing on EAP practitioners within the Zimbabwean context has been done; thus the area deserves intellectual scrutiny. A number of studies that have been done within Zimbabwean EAP focus on either the learner or on the learning processes. Gonye et al. (2012) took a case study approach in analysing academic writing weaknesses of first-year undergraduate students at Great Zimbabwe University after concerns about weak academic writing skills among students were raised. Kahari and Takavarasha (2013) analysed the factors that contributed to the attitudes of University of Zimbabwe students towards the learning of communication skills among medical students. The study found out that the communication skills lecturers were viewed as 'outsiders' or foreigners by both medical staff and students. The medical students also thought that the communication skills taught by the linguistics department were too easy. Mhindu and Chindedza (2018) focussed on the perceptions of university students of the basic communication skills module that is offered to first-year students. While the majority of students pointed out that the module was important for their communication skills, some students felt that what they were taught they already knew and thus attending the lectures was a waste of time (Mhindu and Chindedza, 2018).

Conceptual framework

The desire for a theoretically informed understanding of the identity and agency of Zimbabwean EAP practitioners has resulted in this study being grounded within the Specialization dimension of Legitimation Code Theory (LCT). The understanding is that LCT will assist in uncovering the legitimate identity and agency of the Zimbabwean EAP practitioner. LCT is a sociological theory of knowledge credited to Maton and has its roots in Bernstein and Bourdieu's theories (Maton, 2014).

Legitimation Code Theory (LCT)

LCT is a toolkit to analyse knowledge practices with the aim of developing social justice and knowledge building which 'enables knowledge practices to be seen, their organizing principles to be conceptualized, and their effects to be explored' (Maton, 2014: 4). 'LCT sees social practices as enacting competing claims to legitimacy via more or less explicit or tacit languages of legitimation deployed within a wide area of social fields' (Jackson, 2017: 5). Maton (2014) explained that actors within social fields cooperate and struggle over resources and status.

LCT has five dimensions: Specialization, Autonomy, Semantics, Temporality and Density. LCT's Specialization assists in the analysis of practices in terms of knowledge–knower structures. This study uses the Specialization dimension of LCT. The Specialization dimension is chosen as it is the best dimension for the analysis of the trials and tribulations of Zimbabwean EAP practitioners given its emphasis on knowledge–knower structures.

Specialization dimension

The Specialization dimension distinguishes between two relations, that is, epistemic relations (ER) and social relations (SR). According to Maton (2014: 29), epistemic relations are those that are between knowledge claims and the object of focus, that which can be legitimately claimed as knowledge, while social relations consist of those relations between knowledge claims and 'who' is making them, who can claim to be a legitimate knower. Specialization therefore considers 'what' or 'who' is viewed as 'legitimate' in various disciplines. There are four possible Specialization codes that can be envisaged. These four are SR and ER which can be strengthening or weakening (+/−) and can be represented on a Cartesian plane as shown in Figure 5.1. The top left corner on the Cartesian plane houses the **knowledge codes** (ER+, SR−), where value is placed on the possession of specialized knowledge with the attributes of the author being downplayed (Maton, 2014). In this knowledge code, an EAP practitioner will have the required qualifications to teach EAP but does not possess the personal traits valued in the field such as having English as a first language. The bottom right corner houses the **knower codes** (ER−, SR+), where specialized knowledge is less valued, and value is rather placed on actor attributes (Maton, 2000: 86). These knower codes pertain to valued EAP practices that are focussed on being a first-language speaker of English. The top right corner on the plane houses the **elite codes** (ER+, SR+).

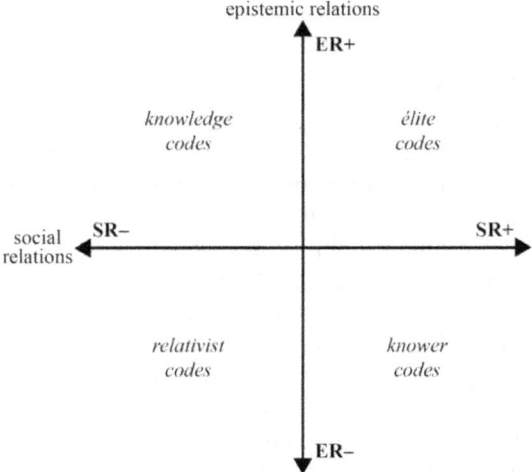

Figure 5.1 The Specialization Plane (Maton, 2014: 30) (permission obtained).

This is where legitimation is drawn from both knowledge and knower attributes. An EAP practitioner will claim legitimacy by having specialized field knowledge, that is, an English language-related qualification and social/innate English skills like being a first-language speaker of the language. The bottom left houses the **relativist codes** (ER–, SR–) whose legitimation is drawn from neither knower nor knowledge. These are EAP practitioners who possess neither the specific qualifications nor what is perceived in the field as 'natural' skills or attributes like being an L1 speaker of English.

Methodology

Given that the study examines the lived experiences of EAP practitioners in Zimbabwe, the ideal methodology would be a combination of ethnography and autoethnography as the researcher has been teaching EAP for some years. While the researcher observes other EAP practitioners (ethnography), with autoethnography, the researcher 'describe[s] and systematically analyse[s] personal experience in order to understand cultural experience' (Ellis, Adams and Bochner, 2011: 1). The journey that I walked, from teaching EAP (referred to as communication skills in Zimbabwe) at a polytechnic college to teaching it at university level, has been an incentive for me to tell a reflexive story of my journey. However, for objective purposes and to avoid researcher bias, this chapter, through triangulation, also uses questionnaires to collect additional data and reduce subjectivity in the study and also does content analysis of communication skills department websites across Zimbabwean universities. As put by Denzin (1978), triangulation involves a combination of methodologies in studying a single phenomenon with the intention of eradicating personal bias. Triangulation provides 'a confluence of evidence that breeds credibility' (Eisner, 1991: 110).

Ethnography and autoethnography

Ethnography and autoethnography are a research approach that is viewed as a bridge between the observer and the observed. An ethnographic approach has to do with the study of relationships between people and other aspects of their life (Harwati, 2019), while autoethnography is a form of knowledge acquisition that acknowledges the feelings of the researcher about their own experiences (auto) within a larger culture (ethno) through data analysis (Ellis, Adams and Bochner, 2011; Rambo and Ellis, 2020). While the researcher is an observer within ethnography, the researcher also becomes the subject or participant in autoethnography (Ellis and Bochner, 2000). Within autoethnography, the researcher is not only the observer but also the subject or the participant (Ellis, Adams and Bochner, 2011). As a self-reflexive practice, autoethnography has two major styles, that is, evocative and analytical styles. The evocative style is confessional and creative (Ellis and Bochner, 2000), while analytical autoethnography is more objective and seen as more academic than evocative

(Anderson, 2006). In this chapter, I use both evocative and analytical, I am creatively confessional and objective. Just like Kumar (2021), besides being objective, there is a trace of confessional elements together with academic creativity.

While both ethnography and autoethnography have been criticized for being subjective, Ellis and Bochner (2000) assert that the quality of an autoethnographic study can be judged by the researcher availing of concrete detail that may include past and present feelings and profound personal engagements, highlighting any changes that have taken place in the course of the journey.

Questionnaires

Questionnaires, as posited by Young (2016), are frequently used in determining a number of things that include reporting behaviour, expressing attitudes and reporting opinions. Participants for this study were communication skills lecturers from one state university in Zimbabwe. The questionnaires were emailed to twenty-one members from the state university and thirteen responded, giving a 61.9 per cent response rate. The questionnaire specified that members could respond to it out of their own volition and they had the choice to respond or not to. Given that the researcher was dealing with human participants, all efforts were made to ensure the safety and confidentiality of participants. The researcher also had to abide by his employer's ethical code of conduct when dealing with human participants.

Content analysis

Content analysis, as proposed by Krippendorff (2013: 24), is 'a research technique for making replicable and valid inferences from text (or other meaningful matter) to the context of their use'. It is this methodology that suits in complementing questionnaires, ethnography and autoethnography. Content analysis was done in the analysis of documents relating to the tenure and promotion of state university teaching staff and departmental communication skills websites. The triangulation assisted in reducing if not eradicating researcher bias. All data was analysed through LCT's specialization dimension. The texts that were analysed using this methodology are documents and communication skills departmental websites that are already within the public domain.

Translation device

Researchers, especially those whose research falls within the qualitative approach, usually face a problem in failing to explain their data through their chosen theory. In most cases, researchers 'sense a gap between their theory and data but lack the means of translating between them' (Maton and Chen, 2016: 27). When faced with such a problem, researchers are encouraged to develop a translation device. Table 5.1 shows the translation device developed for this study.

Table 5.1 Translation device

Relation	Indicator
ER+	The claim to legitimacy of an EAP practitioner comes from having a qualification that is related to EAP.
ER−	The claim to legitimacy by the EAP practitioner does not come from his/her qualifications.
SR+	The claim to legitimacy comes from the practitioner's social background like being a first-language speaker of English or coming from areas where the language is spoken as L1. Legitimacy also comes from approval from higher education authorities and fellow academics from other departments.
SR−	The claim to legitimacy does not come from social attributes of the knower like speaking English as a first language or coming from areas where the language is spoken as L1. Lack of approval from higher education authorities and other departments also shows weaker social relations.
ER+, SR+	These are EAP practitioners whose legitimacy comes from both their qualifications and a strong social background, being an L1 speaker of English or coming from areas where English is spoken as a first language and approval from higher education authorities and other departments.
ER−, SR+	These are practitioners with qualifications not directly related to EAP but who compensate with a strong social background in being L1 speakers of English or coming from areas where English is spoken as a first language or approval from higher education authorities and other departments.
ER+, SR−	These are EAP practitioners whose qualifications are related to EAP but who lack a good command of English from their social and linguistic background. They are neither first-language speakers of English nor is their repertoire closer to those who speak English as a first language.
ER−, SR−	These are EAP practitioners whose qualifications are not related to EAP and whose social life/innate capabilities do not position them as EAP practitioners. They are neither first-language speakers of English nor is their repertoire closer to those who speak English as a first language.

Results and discussion

Qualifications of EAP practitioners in Zimbabwe

From my academic experience, teaching EAP at a non-degree-awarding polytechnic college, to teaching it at university level within Zimbabwe, I have noticed that there are traits of an EAP practitioner that are regarded as the ideal and those that are deemed peripheral by both the higher education administrators and fellow academic colleagues within sister departments. Any degree that is English related is viewed as the ideal qualification for EAP teaching. Being an English L1 speaker is also seen as an ideal trait of an EAP practitioner in Zimbabwe. While the possession of English as L1 is highly valued in Zimbabwe, a country where English is the home language of less than 1 per cent of the population (Peresu and Masuku, 2002) and is spoken by the majority as a second or even third language (Kadenge and Nkomo, 2011), practitioners with English as L1 are a rare breed in the country. Given that English is a second language to most of the population of Zimbabwe, an English qualification accompanied by an English L1 background is ideally seen as the real capital that legitimizes them as EAP practitioners. The qualifications of Zimbabwean communication skills practitioners are rather diverse. Sixty-one per cent of the practitioners that responded to the questionnaire held qualifications in literature and education. Fifteen per cent even proceeded to a doctorate in literature. Some others have done a literature undergraduate degree and a master's and doctorate in either linguistics or applied linguistics. Participant 6 said:

> My background is not from Communication Skills, I was actually in the Indigenous Languages Department that folded due to poor enrolment and instead of losing my job, the administration moved me to the Communication Skills Department.

Participant 6 is an example of a Zimbabwean EAP practitioner who does not have the valued qualifications in an English-related subject. In this case, practitioners like Participant 6 may emphasize their language background as English L1 speakers to assert their legitimacy (SR+). However, given that Participant 6 pointed out that she was not an L1 speaker of English, she occupies the **relativist codes** (ER–, SR–) rather than the **knower codes** (ER–, SR+) because it is rare in Zimbabwe to find an EAP practitioner who is an L1 speaker of English. An ideal practitioner who would occupy the **knower codes** (ER–, SR+), possessing non-language-related qualifications or non-English-related qualifications but with their strength in the field based on them being L1 English speaker as shown above, is a rare breed in Zimbabwe.

Those practitioners whose qualifications are related to English for academic purposes have strong epistemic relations (ER+) and this constitutes 85 per cent of the respondents. Given that all of the respondents pointed out that English was their second language, no EAP practitioner occupies the **elite codes** (ER+, SR+). Practitioners who occupy the **elite codes** should possess an English-related qualification coupled with being L1 speakers of the English language, a rare breed as shown above.

Participants 1, 2, 3, 5, 7, 8, 9, 11, 12 and 13 (in Table 5.2), like Participant 4 below, have strong epistemic relations (ER+) coupled with a weak social relation (SR–) = (ER+, SR–) and resultantly occupy the **knowledge codes** on the Cartesian plane. These participants have the much-valued English-related qualifications but they are not L1 speakers of English. Considering my own qualifications, I am not an L1 speaker of English and I hold an honours degree in linguistics and a master's in applied English linguistics, qualifications that are viewed as falling within the **knowledge codes**.

However some practitioners, as noted from the data, have the tendency to move from the **relativist codes** to **knowledge codes** if they align their qualifications with those valued. For example, Participant 4 explains:

> I had a Bachelor's degree in Education majoring in African languages and a Master of Education majoring in Educational Administration and got the

Communication Skills post. Soon after I had joined the University, the higher education regulatory authority then came to the University checking on lecturers' qualifications and that is when my qualifications were noted as not aligning. I was forced to enroll for a Bachelors in English.

Table 5.2 Summary of qualifications of participants

Participant	Undergraduate	Postgraduate
1	BA Hons English	MA African and Diasporan Literature
2	BA Hons English	MA English, Dhil (Literature)
3	BeD English	MeD English, MA Applied English Linguistics
4	BeD English	MeD Educational Administration, MA English (Literature)
5	BeD English	MeD English, MA Applied English Linguistics
6	BeD African Language	MA (African Literature)
7	BA Hons English	MA (Literature), Dhil (Linguistics)
8	BA Hons Linguistics	MA Applied English Linguistics
9	BA Hons English	MA English (Literature)
10	BA Hons African Languages	MA African Languages, Dhil African Languages
11	BA Hons English	MA English (Literature)
12	BeD African Languages, BA Hons English	Med African Languages
13	BA Hons English	MA (Applied English Linguistics)

We also find practitioners that are in the **relativist code** (ER–, SR–). These are practitioners who neither have the related qualifications nor speak English as a first language as exemplified by Participant 10 below:

> I teach Communication Skills but my qualifications are in African languages. If I get an African language post elsewhere, I will go as I am not as comfortable in teaching Communication Skills as I do with African languages.

Thus we end up having Zimbabwean EAP practitioners occupying the **knowledge codes** and the **relativist codes**. Thus the **knower codes** and the **elite codes** remain unoccupied. This is because the Zimbabwean higher education system values qualifications over knowledge of the English language. It is however important to point out that while a first degree in an English-related area is valued and constitutes a strong epistemic capital, those who proceeded to do non-English-related postgraduate degrees are of lesser value if compared to those with English-related qualifications. An example is Participant 4 who had to do another master's degree in English as his first master's was in educational administration and was found not to align with the first degree.

Contracts of EAP (communication skills) practitioners

The contracts for communication skills practitioners in Zimbabwe have no disciplinary segregation. The practitioners are treated just like any other lecturers from other departments. The appointment and requirements for tenure and promotion are similar. On appointment, communication skills lecturers need to have either a master's or doctorate degree and for them to be tenured they should have at least five publications, satisfactory teaching, university service and progress in innovations and industrializations of some sort. What this means is that EAP practitioners have strong epistemic relations as legitimacy is achieved through qualifications and scholarship (ER+). For members to then be considered for tenure and any other promotions, they need to have satisfied university-wide requirements. They must have the requisite level of scholarship, must have successfully taught and must have proof of university service through being a member of one of the university's committees, a philosophy referred to as Education 3.0 because of the three pillars. Of late the ministry that oversees higher education added two more pillars, innovation and industrialization, thus shifting from Education 3.0 to Education 5.0. The argument from the government was that Zimbabwean universities were producing graduates who were not innovative and their destiny was to be employees rather than employers. The traditional curriculum has been accused of producing graduates who could not fit into the Zimbabwean economy (Kurasha, 2015; Dzvimbo, 2015), which is more informal than formal. The backdrop was that the comatose Zimbabwean economy was in intensive care resulting in a high unemployment rate; thus universities, as citadels of knowledge, are now expected to not only be innovative themselves but also produce innovative graduates. Thus for one to apply for tenure, a minimum of five publications is needed. The applicant should have successfully taught, verified through peer and student evaluations. Furthermore, the applicant must also satisfy university service conditions by being a member of one of the university's committees. For appointment to the senior lecturer grade, EAP practitioners, just like any other academics within the university, must satisfy the teaching and university service pillars plus six post-tenure publications. An applicant for the associate professorial grade should have fourteen to sixteen publications in refereed journals. The same process takes place for those applying for full professorship but the applicants should have at least twenty-one publications as well as satisfying the teaching and university service pillars.

It is however, the new additions, innovations and industrialization, that have been marred by controversy. The argument especially from EAP practitioners is that, unlike in the sciences, goods and services production and industrialization are always difficult to attain. The communication skills practitioners are not alone in this predicament; even other disciplines especially from the arts are struggling to justify how the two can be assessed. For EAP practitioners in Zimbabwe, innovation and industrialization demands are difficult to achieve; what actually constitutes innovation and industrialization in EAP remains vague.

Identity of EAP practitioners

The identity of communication skills practitioners in Zimbabwe is very elusive. The failure to establish a unitary identity stems from the qualifications and research background of people who find themselves teaching communication skills in the country. While many are teaching communication skills, their research focus is not on what they teach.

I have often witnessed many communication skills practitioners applying for vacancies within languages departments in the same university or at sister universities. The urge is always to move away or move back to literature or language areas that they were already publishing in. The desire to move away from the communication skills departments stems from the way academics from the departments are viewed not only by fellow academics but by administrators within the higher and education institutions. The general belief is that the communication skills departments or centres teach soft skills which can be taught by anyone who has tertiary education, sentiments that were also echoed by Participant 3:

> When we complain about the times of slots we are usually given on the timetables, the faculties always claim that they always teach their students Communication skills during their lectures and there may not be need for our lectures.

The other thought is that, because communication skills practitioners do not have students of their own and do not deliver qualifications, they are a service department that imparts academic literacy to all university departments, so they don't have as much power as other academics have. Unlike Fulcher's (2009) findings that some EAP departments in the UK offered master's programmes in TESL and applied linguistics, the Zimbabwean communication skills units do not have any degree programme of their own. Some students even look down upon the modules that are taught by the department to the extent that some students reach their fourth year of studies still carrying and neglecting their first-year communication skills modules. When semester timetabling takes place, in most cases communication skills are scheduled during odd hours. Either they are slotted in very early in the morning or very late in the afternoon or, in serious cases, during weekends. The argument of the academic departments is always that communication skills modules/courses should not disturb the flow of teaching in their departments. The communication skills modules/course are seen by content departments as peripheral to them and as a result students also take the same negative approach to the extent that some students fail the module/course in the first semester of studies and 'carry' this course until they are about to graduate. The response from participants was rather ambivalent; Participant 4 retorted: 'Some departments actually see us as a private organization, they don't see us as part of the University'. The sentiments of Participant 4 gives credence to the long-echoed observation that 'Communication Skills lectures are slotted late in the afternoon when students are tired', especially on a Friday afternoon (Kahari and Takavarasha 2013: 40), Similar observations were noted by Kahari and Takavarasha (2013) when they found out that medical students usually either nap or study for other medical courses during the communication skills lectures. This points to an EAP profession that is underrated.

Conclusion

The above discussion, which exposes the trials and tribulations that EAP/communication skills practitioners face in Zimbabwe, has shown that their professional experiences can be challenging. Attributes that are valued include having English language-related qualifications, and the failure to have such results in weaker epistemic capital. Those practitioners that speak English as a first language are deemed to have a strong social capital compared with those who speak English as a second language and are a rare breed in Zimbabwe. What is however highly valued is a practitioner who has strong epistemic relations in the form of English-related qualifications and stronger social relations in the form of being L1 speakers of English (ER+, SR+), again a rare breed in Zimbabwe. The majority of EAP practitioners occupy the **knowledge codes**; they have strong epistemic capital in the form of an English-related qualification but have weaker social relations as English is a second language to them. The other class of EAP practitioners found in Zimbabwe are those that neither have the English-related qualifications nor are they L1 speakers of the language. These practitioners occupy the **relativist codes**. These tend to struggle to claim their legitimacy with some acquiring further English-related qualifications in an endeavour to legitimize their EAP identity. When they acquire the much-valued English-related qualifications, they then move from the **relativist codes** to the **knowledge codes**. It should also be pointed out that, while many EAP practitioners have English-related qualifications, specializations do differ especially in postgraduate studies; some focus on literature while other focus on language. This then points to the fact that the journey towards a unitary identity among Zimbabwean EAP practitioners is still challenging. Given that the study envisaged that the qualifications of Zimbabwean EAP practitioners and their linguistic backgrounds are diverse, it is suggested that, if given time, space and funding, EAP practitioners in Zimbabwe can actually be involved in research that directly feeds into their teaching, and the founding of a well-coordinated association of EAP practitioners might motivate and bring more confidence to the practitioners in the country. Such an association may provide support in reducing the gap among the practitioners, and any funding will incentivize collaborative scholarship and, in the process, help in the development of an academic identity.

References

Anderson, L. (2006), 'Analytic Autoethnography', *Journal of Contemporary Ethnography*, 35 (4): 373–95. https://doi.org/10.1177/0891241605280449

Basturkmen, H. (2014), 'LSP Teacher Education: Review of Literature and Suggestions for the Research Agenda', *Iberica*, 28: 17–34.
Basturkmen, H. (2019), 'ESP Teacher Education Needs', *Language Teaching*, 52 (3): 318–30. https://doi.org/10.1017/S0261444817000398
Bruce, I. (2021), 'Towards an EAP without Borders: Developing Knowledge, Practitioners, and Communities', *International Journal of English for Academic Purposes: Research and Practice*, 23–36. https://doi.org/10.3828/ijeap.2021.3
Beijaard, D., P. C. Meijer and N. Verloop (2004), 'Reconsidering Research on Teachers' Professional Identity', *Teaching and Teacher Education*, 20 (2): 107–28. https://doi.org/10.1016/j.tate.2003.07.001
Campion, G. C. (2016), 'The Learning Never Ends': Exploring Teachers' Views on the Transition from General English to EAP', *Journal of English for Academic Purposes*, 23: 59–70.
Clarke, M., A. Hyde and J. Drennan (2013), 'Professional Identity in Higher Education', in B. Kehm and U. Teichler (eds), *The Academic Profession in Europe: New Tasks and New Challenges*, 7–22, Dordrecht, Heidelberg, London and New York: Springer.
Denzin, N. K. (1978), *The Research Act: A Theoretical Introduction to Sociological Methods*, 2nd edn, New York: McGraw-Hill.
Ding, A. (2019), 'EAP Practitioner Identity', in K. Hyland and L. L. C. Wong (eds.), *Specialized English: New Directions in ESP and EAP Research and Practice*, 63–75, London: Routledge.
Ding, A., B. Bond and I. Bruce (2022), '"Clearly You Have Nothing Better to do with Your Time than this": A Critical Historical Exploration of Contributions to the BALEAP Discussion List', *Journal of English for Academic Purposes*, 58: 101109. https://doi.org/10.1016/j.jeap.2022.101109
Ding, A. and I. Bruce (2017), *The English for Academic Purposes Practitioners: Operating on the Age of Academia*, Switzerland: Palgrave Macmillan.
Dobrow, S. and M. Higgins (2005), 'Developmental Networks and Professional Identity: A Longitudinal Study', *Career Development International*, 10 (6/7): 567–83.
Dzvimbo, K. P. (2015), 'The African University in the 21st Century: The Quest for Self-financing in the Zimbabwe Open University', *Zimbabwe Journal of Educational Research*, 27 (2): 187–203.
Eisner, E. W. (1991), *The Enlightened Eye: Qualitative Inquiry and the Enhancement of Educational Practice*, Toronto: Collier Macmillan Canada.
Ellis, C., T. Adams and E. Bochner (2011), 'Autoethnography: An Overview. Forum', *Qualitative Social Research*, 12, Article 10.
Ellis, C. and E. Bochner (2000), 'Autoethnography, Personal Narrative, Reflexivity: Researcher as Subject', in N. K. Denzin and Y. S. Lincoln (eds), *Handbook of Qualitative Research*, 2nd edn, 733–76, Thousand Oaks: Sage Publications.
Fulcher, G. (2009), 'The Commercialisation of Language Provision at University', in J. C. Alderson (ed.), *The Politics of Language Education: Individuals and Institutions*, 125–46, Bristol: Multilingual Matters.
Gonye, J., R. Mareva, W. T. Dudu and J. Sibanda (2012), 'Academic Writing Challenges at Universities in Zimbabwe: A Case Study of Great Zimbabwe University', *International Journal of English and Literature*, 3: 71–83.
Harwati, L. N. (2019), 'Ethnographic and Case Study Approaches: Philosophical and Methodological Analysis', *International Journal of Education & Literacy Studies*, 150–5. Australian International Academic Centre PTY.LTD.

Jackson, F. (2017), 'Plotting Pedagogy in a Rural South African English Classroom: A Legitimation Code Theory Analysis', *Per Linguam*, 33 (2): 1–21. http://dx.doi.org/10.5785/33-2-682

Kadenge, M. and D. Nkomo (2011), 'The Politics of the English Language in Zimbabwe', *Language Matters*, 42 (2): 248–63. https://doi.org/10.1080/10228195.2011.581679

Kahari, L. and P. Takavarasha (2013), 'A Study of University of Zimbabwe Medical Students' Attitudes towards the Teaching and Learning of Communication Skills', *International Journal of Advance Research*, 1: 35–42.

Kaivanpanah, S., S. M. Alavi, I. Bruce and S. Y. Hejazi (2021), 'EAP in the Expanding Circle: Exploring the Knowledge Base, Practices and Challenges of Iranian EAP Practitioners', *Journal of English for Academic purposes*, 50: 1–13.

Kohnke, L. and D. Zou (2021), 'Reflecting on Existing English for Academic Purposes Practices: Lessons for the Post-COVID Classroom', *Sustainability*, 13: 11520. https://doi.org/10.3390/su132011520

Krippendorff, K. (2013), *Content Analysis: An Introduction to Its Methodology*, 3rd edn, Thousand Oaks: Sage Publications.

Kumar, K. L. (2021), 'Understanding and Expressing Academic Identity through Systematic Autoethnography', *Higher Education Research & Development*, 40 (5): 1011–25. https://doi.org/10.1080/07294360.2020.1799950

Kurasha, P. (2015), 'The Future of Higher Education in Zimbabwe: A Constantly Moving Target', *Zimbabwe Journal of Educational Research*, 27 (2): 204–21.

Lund, B. and A. Shamsi (2021), 'Richly Resourced Researchers: Work with Developing-World Scientists', *Nature*, 596 (7872): 343. https://doi.org/10.1038/d41586-021-02235-w

Maton, K. (2000), 'Recovering Pedagogic Discourse: A Bernsteinian Approach to the Sociology of Educational Knowledge', *Linguistics and Education*, 11 (1): 79–98.

Maton, K. (2014), 'A TALL Order? Legitimation Code Theory for Academic Language and Learning', *Journal of Academic Language & Learning*, 8 (3): 34–48.

Maton, K. and R. T.-H. Chen (2016), 'LCT in Qualitative Research: Creating a Translation Device for Studying Constructivist Pedagogy', in K. Maton, S. Hood and S. Shay (eds), *Knowledge-Building: Educational Studies in Legitimation Code Theory*, 27–48, London: Routledge.

Mhindu, A. and W. Chindedza (2018), 'Students' Perceptions of Basic Communication Skills Training at a Selected State University in Zimbabwe', *International Journal of Linguistics, Literature and Translation*, 1 (1): 66–73.

Peresu, M. and J. Masuku (2002), 'The Role of Primary Language in Bilingual-Bicultural Education in Zimbabwe', *Zambezia*, xxix (1): 27–39.

Rambo, C. and C. Ellis (2020), 'Autoethnography', 1–3. https://doi.org/10.1002/9781405165518.wbeosa082.pub2.

Young, T. J. (2016), 'Questionnaires and Surveys', in Z. Hua (ed.), *Research Methods in Intercultural Communication: A Practical Guide*, 165–80, Oxford: Wiley.

Chapter 6

'BE MORE PIRATE'

HARNESSING THE POWER OF LIMINAL SPACES IN CREATING ACADEMIC LITERACY PRACTITIONER IDENTITY AND AGENCY

Michelle Joubert and Sherran Clarence

Introduction

Ultimately, I think we're just trying to be pirates . . . within the structure, but not the structure . . . trying to push back against the structure and create different ways of thinking and different ways of doing things. I mean, a lot of what pirates did in the 16th and 17th centuries was also expose . . . the hypocrisy in the ruling classes, and they were very much not trying to be lawless, but they were trying to actually say, 'there's no space for us here. This is unfair, we have to create a new space' . . . if the system is broken, I have to figure out how to not be part of this broken system. I don't want to be complicit in this. Yeah, I just love that metaphor.

– Sherran

This is not a chapter about pirates. But this extract, taken from a conversation between the authors about their work, encapsulates how working in the field of English for academic purposes (EAP), or academic development more broadly, can involve simultaneously working within *and* against systems that act to constrain who we are as practitioners and teachers. These systems can also enable or constrain how we work, what spaces we (are allowed to) occupy and what we are and are not allowed to do. Indeed, building a career in EAP or academic development means that we unconsciously sign up to 'fight the good fight'; part of the EAP or academic development practitioner's mission is to help their institution understand that the kind of work we do is central to student success. This is especially true in the South African context where students need academic language and literacy support due to constraints within the schooling system (Spaull, 2015, 2023; du Plessis and Mestry, 2019). Despite this centrality to access and success, however, EAP is still a marginalized field in higher education, typically positioned within the periphery due to a misrecognition of its value to student learning. Functioning from the periphery impacts upon practitioner agency in both constraining and enabling what kinds of support they can provide; it also has a constraining effect on the ways in which EAP practitioners are able to construct a firm professional identity. The focus of this chapter is thus on the ways in which practitioners work out how to, in effect, be (or not be) pirates – working out their role and identity in conversation with their environment and with themselves, their goals and ambitions.

The name, 'English for academic purposes' or 'EAP' is infrequently used in the South African higher education landscape. Rather, reference is made to academic literacy/ies development (ALD), which encompasses a wide range of practices, including formalized writing development modules, ad-hoc generic and discipline-specific writing workshops, faculty-based extended studies programmes focussed on disciplinary literacy development, formal academic literacy programmes (taking a modular format) and writing centres (see A. Archer, 2010; Boughey, 2013). For the purposes of this chapter, we will use the term 'EAP' with the attached caveat that the shape and format of EAP practices in South African higher education vary considerably from institution to institution, and even intra-institutionally. EAP (or academic literacy/ies development) may be positioned as an integral part of students' curricula (i.e., within the academic space) or as external support to the 'mainstream' academic project (i.e., within the support space). Further, theorized understandings of literacy, language, writing and learning do not consistently inform EAP praxis across South African universities. This results in a range of approaches to academic literacy development work, from embedded and disciplinary to 'bolt-on' or generic provision (Wingate, 2018; Macnaught et al., 2022). Ultimately, the uneven valuing of research-led, theorized EAP curriculum and pedagogy, combined with inconsistent positioning in the university space and a skewed institutional understanding of what EAP is and aims to do, means that many EAP practitioners still operate on the 'edge of academia' (Ding and Bruce, 2017: 107).

The positioning of EAP practitioners within different kinds of support and/ or academic spaces is not necessarily in itself an issue. At some institutions, the support space is a well-funded and highly legitimate space. At others, it is less so. Ultimately, whichever space provides an EAP practitioner with legitimacy and influence is a generative space within which to work. However, positioning and space become problematic when they work to constrain practitioner agency, their sense of professional identity and their value to the institution. For example, when an institution's understanding of EAP is that it is remedial, meant to 'fix' students' 'language problems' (Boughey, 2013), it may result in EAP being positioned as an undervalued and underfunded support service. This ultimately impacts on the work practitioners can do to enable greater student success, which is a significant concern in South Africa as elsewhere (Ellery, 2017; Clarence, 2021). This positioning can be frustrating when practitioners have a different sense of themselves as *academic* literacy specialists. This tension may lead to a fractured sense of identity and cast agency as fighting the system for recognition and space to work, rather than working with the university system as it has been created.

EAP in South Africa, as in many other parts of the world, is marked by an underlying tension between an 'academic' view of EAP and a 'support service' view (Ding and Bruce, 2017). This tension is further entrenched by the traditional structuring of higher education institutions into two spaces which may stand in binary opposition. The first is the academic space which is occupied by the academic staff of the institution. The second is the 'non-academic' space which is generally occupied by student and academic support service staff, administrative or professional staff and management (Whitchurch, 2008; Clarke, Hyde and Drennan, 2013). This binary positioning is evident in both the South African and UK contexts where EAP practitioners are either structurally positioned in the academic space as academics themselves or as support professionals in the non-academic/support space. However, we argue that EAP practitioners do not structurally or operationally occupy one space *or* the other. Rather, they inhabit both and, in so doing, inhabit what we are calling liminal space – that space betwixt and between the support and academic spaces. They use this space as a web or bridge to move between the support and academic spaces enacting both academic *and* support roles and functions (Joubert, 2023).

Constructing a professional identity within the liminal space is influenced by structures and cultures from both the support and academic spaces; it can thus be a complex task. Reflexivity is thus a useful tool for practitioners to bring to light aspects of who they are (how they see themselves and their roles), how they work, what resources they draw on that help or hinder them, and how external perceptions might impact upon their own identity construction and reconstruction. We argue in this chapter that this is important because it brings to consciousness the resources needed to do our work effectively, to create the conditions necessary for ongoing learning and professional development, and to construct a meaningful professional identity within our roles.

In this chapter, then, we will reflect on our own professional journeys within the framework of borderlands, heartlands and liminality. We have constructed this framework with the help of Margaret Archer's notions of reflexivity and the 'internal conversation' to externalize our own processes, over many years, of conceptualizing and (re)constructing our own identities and roles. We offer these insights to argue that seeing and understanding how we do the work we do, what enables and constrains us, and who supports us is vital to creating more supportive and enabling environments for all EAP and other academic development practitioners in higher education, especially those who are joining these environments as early career professionals.

Heartlands, borderlands and 'webs' of liminality

Important for the research that informs this chapter is the fact that practitioners' professional identities are most often shaped by understandings of EAP (and wider academic development) in binary terms as predominantly support *or* as predominantly academic. This is partly because of the ways in which universities manage academic and professional service/support roles, including how staff are contracted, supported and remunerated in these spaces. This binary view is further influenced by institutional views of EAP work – is it predominantly understood and positioned as academic development central to student success or more likely to be understood and positioned as support outside of or parallel to students' main curriculum and learning? (See, for example, Ding and Bruce, 2017; Macnaught et al., 2022). The answer to that question has significant implications for how EAP and other academic development practitioners are positioned, supported and developed further as professionals. Their development and the sustenance of a professional identity and the forms this takes have implications for the work these practitioners do with, and for, students and staff within the university.

The aim of this chapter is to better understand the connections between identity, agency and the more and less visible ways in which practitioners are positioned and supported. As we have argued thus far, even though academic development work, encompassing EAP and academic literacy/ies, has become less peripheral in many university contexts (see, for example, Quinn and Vorster, 2014; Vorster and Quinn, 2015), there is a lingering legacy of its 'remedial' and 'bolt-on' positioning that still creates an 'either/or' binary between 'academic' and 'support' in terms of institutional positioning, staffing, funding and recognition (Whitchurch, 2008; Clarke, Hyde and Drennan, 2013; Leibowitz et al., 2015). Yet EAP and academic development practitioners tend to straddle these positions, moving between these spaces and engaging with work that is *both* academic *and* support. In essence, when it comes to creating and holding a sense of professional identity and clarity of role and purpose, we conjecture here that practitioners move between 'heartlands' and 'borderlands' through a liminal space that is neither wholly one nor the other.

Continuing from the previous section, we use liminality to mean a space of 'betwixtness' or 'betweenness'. This in-between space does not precede a threshold to be crossed (see Cousin, 2006); rather it can be visualized as a web that connects different spaces together, that is created, undone and recreated over the course of a practitioner's career as the environments in which they carry out their roles change or shift (Joubert, 2023). Liminality here, then, captures the understanding that what feels like a borderland to some may be a heartland to others, and different kinds of identity and agency attach to these experiences and positionings.

In this study, we conceive of borderlands and heartlands in terms of their relation, proximity and meaning to the practitioner. This means that borderlands are further away from the practitioner, either practically or metaphorically, and heartlands are closer, specifically in terms of their pertinence to the practitioner's sense of agency and own identity: who they are, what they do and what their work means to the university and students. To illustrate, a borderland could be a professional space such as a committee or working group that defines an EAP practitioner's work as additional to or outside of the 'mainstream' academic curriculum. For example, could they run a short workshop on writing skills, please? Could they give up some of their tutorials or time to 'core' learning students need time for? A heartland, in this conceptualization, may then be a space the practitioner retreats to or calls upon to bolster their sense of agency and identity in relation to this borderland positioning. They could, for example, respond by drawing on the scholarship of teaching and learning or examples from their and colleagues' experience to explain why a 'quick skills workshop' will not have the desired outcome or resist being further marginalized within the timetable.

We suggest that all practitioners move within this liminal space, whether they realize it or not. Thus, a greater awareness of the liminal space and of their own borderlands and heartlands can offer new ways for academic development practitioners to consider, define and nurture agency and professional identity. This awareness may also offer tools with which to 'be more pirate' (Coniff Allende, 2018) and push back against limiting and self-interested university systems that undermine wider student success. We offer, in what remains of this chapter, an account of how we have captured and reflected on our own career journeys, specifically how we have both experienced the liminal space and the borderlands and heartlands that have had meaning and power in our own attempts to carve out agency, a meaningful professional identity and a sense of purpose – sometimes in spite, rather than because of – the environments in which we have worked. Considering the answers to these questions is important not only for continuing to critique narrower approaches to EAP and academic literacy/ies that cast our work as 'skills development' and therefore limit agency, creativity and constructive change, but for enabling greater student access, success and belonging as well.

To capture our stories and reflect on them with rigour and credibility, we have constructed a theoretical framework using Margaret Archer's notion of the 'internal conversation' (2007, 2010). This will be explained in the following section, including our enactment of reflexivity in relation to the generation and analysis of our data. The design we chose for this study will then be explained before we delve into the data.

Reflexivity and the 'internal conversation'

We have worked as academic development and EAP practitioners in multiple university contexts in the UK, Sweden and South Africa. Yet despite the contextual differences, our experiences of the liminality and marginalization discussed earlier has been a constant feature of our careers thus far. This has necessitated regular and intentional reflection on our roles, positioning and positionality – the aspects of our selves that we bring into our roles, such as gender, race, social class and so on – and on how we have shaped our professional identities and professional ambitions in response to our roles, how we are positioned and who we are in our respective contexts. To enact this reflection in an intentional way for the purposes of this chapter, we turned to Margaret Archer (2010) and her insights into the 'internal conversation' with which, we argue, practitioners engage as they move through their careers, whether consciously or not. Even though these internal conversations may not always be completely intentional, Archer argues that our internal conversations allow us to access our own reflexivity (Archer, 2010: 2).

Archer (2010: 2) explains that the internal conversation is about referential reflexivity or the 'bending-back' upon one's thoughts. It is essentially a person's ability to think about reality, the world and our position within it; it allows us to understand the interplay between ourselves (the conditioned) and those structures and cultures that do the conditioning. For example, the university lecturer (conditioned) and the curriculum and departmental ethos that informs what goes into the curriculum and how it may or should be taught and assessed (conditioning). To examine this interplay more closely, we must first specify *how* structural and cultural powers either enable or constrain our actions as agents. Secondly, we must examine *how* we use our personal powers to act in ways that are 'so rather than otherwise' (Archer, 2007: 10). Ultimately, we use our internal processes of conversation to mediate the impact of structural and cultural powers upon us, making choices and enacting agency as we do.

In reality, these processes are not neat and linear, largely because the conditions we are positioned within and within which we position ourselves change over time. For example, the university appointing a new line manager who makes changes to established ways of working or changes we make to a curriculum in line with new research and scholarship. Thus, we do not just talk to ourselves about ourselves in a vacuum. Our roles implicate society and social interaction, as well as pre-existing and new structural and cultural arrangements within the university. In other words, 'we talk to ourselves *about* society in relation to ourselves and about ourselves in relation to society, under our own descriptions' (Archer, 2007: 88).

Going into the process of generating data for this chapter, we thought that we would be speaking mostly about cultures and structures and their determining effects on our career paths. But what we experienced instead was conversations about ourselves and how we have made sense of and manoeuvred within our different professional environments, rather than the structures and cultures as entities in themselves. Our original aim, using Archer's framework, was to map out structures and cultures and analyse the extent to which they impacted on our professional agency (and identity development). But in the end, we found that what came through were our stories about the aspects of our careers thus far – people, places, perceptions – that have shaped who we think we are, what we think we do and how we have moved along our own career paths. In other words, we focussed more on what personal powers we have and how we have used those personal powers to either play or disrupt the game – be more pirate, so to speak – in the institutions, departments and centres in which we have thus far worked. The aim in the analysis that follows is to draw out how we have named and used these personal powers and what our reflections may illuminate for the support and development of other EAP and academic development practitioners.

Generating the data through purposeful conversation and reflection

The method of generating data for this chapter was a modified form of narrative research, in essence, storytelling. We chose this method because narrative retelling allows us to reconstruct our *lived* experiences into meaningful *learning* experiences. The narrative method also provides a doorway into how we construct our identities through unravelling our experiences – the researcher can recount and reform their past and present selves and who they hope to become (Clandinin, 2016; McAlpine, 2016). We constructed our process in three steps.

The first step was to co-create six questions we both answered in writing to begin to externalize our internal 'conversations'. We posted our responses in a shared Google Drive folder.

1. What are the three dominant feelings that come to mind when you think about your AL/EAP role (don't think too hard)?
2. Elaborate on why these feelings came to mind first.
3. If you knew about yourself and role then what you know now, thinking back to the foundations of your career, what would you change, if anything, and why?
4. Sitting on a bus, you have one minute to explain to a stranger what you do. What do you say?
5. How did you get into AL? How did you learn to 'do' AL/EAP? How did you become 'an expert' in this field?
6. In a typical work week, in what 'space' do you feel you mostly operate? Why?

The aim of these questions (and responses) was to begin to get at underlying issues of agency and choice, of knowledge and ways of working, and of spaces or structures within the university. We read one another's responses and co-created a second, smaller set of prompts which were then used to guide two conversations focussed on telling ourselves and one another the stories of how we have evolved our careers: what did we want, how did we try to get what we wanted, what stood in our way and what helped us? In other words, we were deliberating and discerning, moving between our own heartlands and borderlands, before dedicating ourselves to courses of action that were meaningful and, in some cases, pragmatic given where and how we were working at the time (see Archer, 2007, 2010).

These conversations formed steps two and three. Rather than posing set questions, we used the prompts that emerged from the first step as a guide. The first conversation was audio-recorded and transcribed. We then divided up the transcript into two halves and read half of the transcript each, looking for heartlands, borderlands and evidence of thinking and acting within the liminal webs we were part of. We then shared our findings with one another, read the other half of the transcript we had not initially read and refined and negotiated the emerging threads. In the final step, we had a further, focussed conversation where we dug a bit deeper together into some of the issues especially related to identity struggles and to tensions and upheavals as well as successes and the processes of deliberation and reflection that have been part of our career journeys thus far. This too was recorded, transcribed and carefully read so as to add to and further refine the threads we discuss in the following section.

Throughout this process we were guided by our theoretical lens, primarily drawing on Archer's work and adding concepts of liminality, borderlands and heartlands as they relate to the making, sustaining and evolution of practitioner identities and values.

Traversing our liminal 'lands': Reflecting on career trajectories thus far

Before delving into the findings, we note a key limitation of our analysis: our experiences are shaped by who we are and the options that have been available to us. This is, however, true of anyone engaging in reflective work, as Archer (2007, 2010) points out. To mitigate this limitation and enable our findings to make a useful contribution to understanding how EAP practitioners construct their professional identities and enact their agency, we have leaned on our conceptual framework to focus less on what we have experienced as individuals and more on what our experiences highlight in more widely applicable ways.

In the first conversation we talked about our roles in relation to the titles we have been given and the kind of contracts we have been on (i.e. academic or service/administrative) and what those have implied for the work expected from us. At the time of writing, both of us had titles such as 'training manager' (Sherran) and 'assistant director' (Michelle), both of which imply positions typically aligned with professional services/support within the university. This positioning was experienced as a borderland because this was not how we saw the work we were doing and how that work was related to our professional identities.

> Sherran: I teach people how to write, I teach people how to make knowledge. I teach people how to navigate academia, especially at doctoral level, I teach people how to write for publication, I teach people how to make . . . their knowledge accessible to people outside of themselves . . . I don't go in with my title [of manager] because that's not that's not what I do.
> Michelle: Same, because my title is assistant director of the academic language . . . [but] I tell people that I'm a lecturer. I teach . . . That's just closer to who I feel I am . . . I do accept that I am within those structures . . . but how I see my role, I'm kind of using that as a chance to shape it as something that I know would be pushing the students and the agenda of the field forward.

The word 'teach' is mentioned by both of us as a core part of not just what we do, but who we feel we are in our professional roles. There is a clear sense of resistance to being called a 'manager' or 'assistant director' because neither title (and perhaps associated contract type) highlights teaching and student-focussed work. This is reflected in research in the field, especially in EAP and academic literacies development work, where the types of contracts practitioners are on do not necessarily include academic terms of service (teaching and research-focussed). This tends to be especially the case where EAP and academic development are in service/support structures rather than in academic structures, which are more likely to recognize this work as focussed on teaching and development, both informed by research (Graham, 2012; Joubert, 2023). For those EAP practitioners on academic contracts which do include academic terms of service, there is still a marginalization of the work they do through institutional perceptions of what EAP is, what EAP practitioners do and what role it *should* play in a students' development (Ding and Bruce, 2017; Joubert, 2023). Our assertion that we are teachers and not administrators is echoed in the experiences of other practitioners in similar roles. We argue that this is because, like us, many practitioners in EAP and academic development cultivate identities that are 'academic', or scholarly to be more accurate. They read research, they incorporate it in their teaching, they draw on theorized understandings of knowledge, writing, reading and so on; they are teachers (Harland and Staniforth, 2008; Joubert, 2023).

However, identifying yourself as such when your 'official' role demands other, less scholarly, forms of labour or when the institution's perception of you contradicts how you see yourself can lead to tension – a push and pull between a borderland you are pushed into and heartlands that nurture and support your own sense of purpose and professional self. Finding a space – literal or metaphorical – that makes sense to you can feel like a fight, an act of piracy, because you must subvert or disrupt the existing structure (or culture) to create and hold it.

> Sherran: But what's also interesting is . . . how we try to position ourselves . . . we've both experienced a fair bit of being positioned by others and then trying to position ourselves . . . And that's part, I think, probably issues of power and structure. If you're not on an academic contract, like you aren't, like I wasn't until I fought [for it]. I'm expected to do research, I'm expected to, you know . . . do all of that. But on a service contract, admin contract . . . I think that's something that's common to a lot of contexts, not just ours.

As Michelle noted in the second conversation:

> just because you have structures doesn't mean that the institutional recognition is there . . . things are changing a bit, like academics are more open to realizing that they have to help their students with writing now than maybe they were twenty years ago, even ten years. But that doesn't mean that they're all on board with letting EAP practitioners think of themselves and call themselves academics and climb the academic ladder in the same kind of way.

The longer exchange, of which we have shared just a small part here, highlighted what may be a rather common tension for EAP practitioners: identifying as a certain kind of academic practitioner with grounding in research and theory, and being identified as a *provider* of support, skills training and service to other 'real' academics (see also Ding and Bruce, 2017). In essence, we are suggesting that all EAP and academic development practitioners experience this tension at some point or another, whether they are alive to it or not. Liminality – moving between different spaces in the university, literal and metaphorical, and managing demands that may align and clash with who we are and what we do – is a feature of this work and has been for several decades now (Boughey, 2013). Thus, we all have borderlands and heartlands we move between, at times quite consciously and at others less so, as we enact our agency in doing the work we do, both against the system and 'with the tide'.

A significant heartland for both of us was the use of theory and research in our practice and connections to our formative disciplinary training.

> Sherran: I think of myself as a teacher and an . . . academic developer, actually . . . I see my job as decoding the university for people who don't otherwise have access to the means to decode it . . . And then also more and more in the last few years . . . part of a broader push for social justice . . . encountering the social theory during my PhD and after has given me the tools to be able to say, I can figure out how to help you do this better.
>
> Michelle: I think my academic identity comes from having been in the literature department, having been somebody in an academic space and all of that. And I guess I've wanted to hold on to that.

More than a frame for the formation and evolution of our own scholarly identities, though, theory/scholarship has been a tool we have been able to harness to resist or reframe narrower notions of academic writing and academic development work within the universities we have worked in.

> Michelle: I just noticed that students . . . were struggling with expressing their ideas on paper and their arguments, and I started reading about discipline-specific writing, and some empirical research done on, you know, how do business students write, or how do science students write or that kind of thing. And then I slowly became aware, as you say, the scales start to fall off and you're like, oh, wait, hang on, there's something going on here . . . Because it starts to give you a language to talk about what you, as you say, what you kind of instinctively know . . . I didn't really know EAP was a field or academic literacies. I think at the time, what I wish I'd known was, you're entering into an actual field of study. And that would have, I think, given me some sense of validation.
>
> Sherran: . . . I didn't know that people had theory about this . . . So that was also like a big kind of thing of going, 'Oh, actually, this totally validates everything that I've been thinking around like: This isn't quite working. What's going on here?' I didn't have any kind of connections with lecturers in the disciplines at all for the longest time, even when I ran the writing centre . . . people were like, oh, no, but you do the skills – and the problem is for me, before I really found academic literacies and that language and that theory, it was so hard to fight them. You couldn't actually say, 'well, this is not a skill . . . actually how we write is in no way, shape or form generic or homogenous'. So, yeah, theory's been immensely empowering, in terms of my role.

In our work, we have certainly experienced tensions around who we see ourselves as and how we enact our roles and work, and how the university community sees us and how they wish we would enact our roles and work (viz. 'academic' versus 'service'). Theorized practice has helped us find our feet, stand firmly on them and engage differently with academics and students across the disciplines, building our own practitioner identities in the process.

> Sherran: So we're trying very hard to position ourselves in this like, 'let's collaborate', right? 'If what we're offering is not quite the right thing for your students, rather than just going, well we'll throw that away, do the generalized thing, which may well not serve them, because it'll be too hard for them to move towards the specific, then let's collaborate and maybe tweak the specific to have a bit more of the things in the generalized stuff that you think are useful and also some of the more specific things right, like, let's do that. Let's talk'.
>
> Michelle: And I actually had another lecturer, we were speaking about the [discipline-specific literacy] course and they wanted [their students to take a general humanities writing course rather than [the discipline-specific] writing course we were offering]. And I explained that [their] course out of all of them is the one that's the closest to 'disciplinary'. And she was saying, 'no . . . we don't want you to do anything that is [disciplinary] writing or whatever'. She would much prefer the students to do the humanities course. So, I said, 'I'm happy to talk to you about the module and listen to you, because that's the thing about collaboration. And if you think that we're not hitting the nail on the head, then you need to let us know and we'll relook into things'.

In cases like this, practitioners can draw on theorized understandings of what being academically literate means in and across the curriculum and therefore how to collaborate and talk with lecturers in more productive ways (Jacobs, 2013; Rai and Lillis, 2011). Using scholarship and research to underpin our work has helped us, in a sense, to find our inner 'pirate' when we have needed to advocate for students against generic understandings of writing, for example, that would undermine learning and success, or have conversations with tutors or lecturers about the ways in which their students need to read and write in more specialized ways and communicate that effectively. But what these excerpts also highlight is a further heartland we have consistently found important for developing a professional identity: community.

Communities of practice is a widely used concept in teaching and learning scholarship, which includes EAP and academic development scholarship. Locally and internationally, networks and communities of like-minded practitioners and researchers provide spaces that nurture us and challenge and extend us through encountering the work others are doing in contexts similar to and different from our own (Bathmaker and Avis, 2005; Jawitz, 2009). This has been especially important at points in both of our careers where we have worked within universities that have been unable or unwilling to support our work in ways that align with who we believe we are as academic developer or EAP practitioner, and what we think needs to be done to better enable students to access the recognized ways of knowing, reading and writing and so on that are necessary for their success. Rather than happening upon these communities by chance, we have been cultivating them carefully – something practitioners new to a field can find daunting. Both of us spoke about the value of finding 'our people', usually through conferences, meetings and symposia both locally and abroad. Our contention in sharing our reflections on our experiences of this is that being aware of the borderlands and heartlands and the nature of the liminal space can be empowering and can enable more conscious cultivation of the nurturing elements of your space. This is important for the retention and support of teachers and researchers working in EAP and academic development.

Conclusions, or a way forward?

Undertaking this reflexive process and externalizing our inner conversations was a valuable activity in unearthing the ways in which we have interacted with the structures and cultures in environments and why we have acted in ways that are 'so rather than otherwise' (Archer, 2007: 10). Essentially, our reflexivity has enabled us to more clearly articulate where our heartlands and borderlands lie. We acknowledge that, in general, the process of reflection and even the stories we tell each other are subjective and shaped by who we are. Having said this, however, we still see value in this approach to research since we have focussed on what our experiences highlight about the field of EAP in general, all the while relating our experiences to those recounted in previous research. The value of narrative research in delving deeper into issues of positioning, liminality, agency and identity lies in its ability to challenge the dominant 'common-sense' notions about the remedial and marginal nature of EAP in South Africa and abroad. Instead, we would like the broader university and EAP practitioners themselves to alter their discourse in ways which more accurately reflect the academic and research-informed nature of the field. By not engaging with issues such as this, we risk pushing the field and its practitioners further away from academe, making it more susceptible to sub-degree work status as well as to outsourcing and thus the denigration of expertise, which may have a significant impact on student access and success.

EAP as a field in higher education is filled with contradictions which are largely driven by the contradictory spaces we inhabit. We play an integral role in both the support and academic worlds, yet we do not fully inhabit either. Rather, we inhabit the liminal space and oscillate between our borderlands – those spaces which seem removed from who we are as practitioners and the ways in which we construct our professional identity – and our heartlands, those spaces which feel more like home. Our research and scholarly EAP work as well as our collaborations with academics and within EAP communities have been primary heartlands throughout our careers thus far. These heartlands have provided us with a sense of direction and are ways in which we gain a greater sense of legitimacy in the higher education space, which values certain forms of knowledge production. These heartlands are the ways in which we enact our inner pirate – we use the tools of the institutional structures (e.g. the importance of research outputs) to talk back to the structure itself, which may not have an accurate perception of the work EAP practitioners do and the role/s we play in student learning. A clear borderland for us has been the administrative or managerial space, which has most often been attached to our titles and contract-types and which seems far removed from the professional identity we have constructed over time – that of academic, researcher and teacher.

The externalization and identification of these heartlands and borderlands have essentially allowed us to better understand how and why we have constructed the professional identities we have and the ways in which we have, at times, chosen to be 'pirates' in our roles and at other times have chosen to sail with the tide. It has also allowed us to become cognizant of the ways in which we have held on to our heartlands to mitigate the distancing nature of our borderlands, empowering us in our roles and enabling us to extend this to mentoring and supporting our peers, too. We hope these insights will be useful to, and empowering of, other practitioners and those who mentor and support them.

Ethical permissions granted by the University of the Free State: UFS-HSD2021/2002 (29-11-2021).

References

Archer, A. (2010), 'Challenges and Potentials for Writing Centres in South African Tertiary Institutions', *South African Journal of Higher Education*, 24 (4): 495–510.

Archer, M. S. (2007), *Making Our Way through the World: Human Reflexivity and Social Mobility*, Cambridge: Cambridge University Press.

Archer, M. S., ed. (2010), *Conversations about Reflexivity*, London: Routledge.

Bathmaker, A.-M. and J. Avi (2005), 'Becoming a Lecturer in Further Education in England: The Construction of Professional Identity and the Role of Communities of Practice', *Journal of Education for Teaching*, 31 (1): 47–62.

Boughey, C. (2013), 'What Are We Thinking Of? A Critical Overview of Approaches to Developing Academic Literacy in South African Higher Education', *Journal for Language Teaching= Ijenali Yekufundzisa Lulwimi= Tydskrif vir Taalonderrig*, 47 (2): 25–41.

Clandinin, D. J. (2016), *Engaging in Narrative Inquiry*, London: Routledge.

Clarence, S. (2021), 'Context Is Key', in *Turning Access into Success: Improving University Education with Legitimation Code Theory*, 1–20, London: Routledge.

Clarke, M., A. Hyde and J. Drennan (2013), 'Professional Identity in Higher Education', in *The Academic Profession in Europe: New tasks and New Challenges*, 7–21, Dordrecht: Springer.

Coniff Allende, S. (2018), *Be More Pirate. Or How to Take on the World and Win*, London: Penguin Books.

Cousin, G. (2006), 'An Introduction to Threshold Concepts', *Planet*, 17 (1): 4–5.

Ding, A. and I. Bruce (2017), *The English for Academic Purposes Practitioner. Operating on the Edge of Academia*, London: Palgrave Macmillan.

Du Plessis, P. and R. Mestry (2019), 'Teachers for Rural Schools–a Challenge for South Africa', *South African Journal of Education*, 39 (Supplement 1): S1–S9.

Ellery, K. (2017), 'Framing of Transitional Pedagogic Practices in the Sciences: Enabling Access', *Teaching in Higher Education*, 22 (8): 908–24.

Graham, C. (2012), 'Transforming Spaces and Identities: The Contributions of Professional Staff to Learning Spaces in Higher Education', *Journal of Higher Education Policy and Management*, 34 (4): 437–52.

Harland, T. and D. Staniforth (2008), 'A Family of Strangers: The Fragmented Nature of Academic Development', *Teaching in Higher Education*, 13 (6): 669–78.

Jacobs, C. (2013), 'Academic Literacies and the Question of Knowledge', *Journal for Language Teaching= Ijenali Yekufundzisa Lulwimi= Tydskrif vir Taalonderrig*, 47 (2): 127–39.

Jawitz, J. (2009), 'Academic Identities and Communities of Practice in a Professional Discipline', *Teaching in Higher Education*, 14 (3): 241–51.

Joubert, M. (2023), 'Liminal Spaces, Liminal Identities: Re-evaluating the Role of Academic Literacy Practitioners in the South African University', Unpublished PhD thesis, University of the Free State.

Leibowitz, B., V. Bozalek, S. Van Schalkwyk and C. Winberg (2015), 'Institutional Context Matters: The Professional Development of Academics as Teachers in South African Higher Education', *Higher Education*, 69 (2): 315–30.

Macnaught, L., M. Bassett, V. van der Ham, J. Milne and C. Jenkin (2022), 'Sustainable Embedded Academic Literacy Development: The Gradual Handover of Literacy Teaching', *Teaching in Higher Education*, 1–19. https://doi.org/10.1080/13562517.2022.2048369

McAlpine, L. (2016), 'Why Might You Use Narrative Methodology? A Story about Narrative', *Eesti Haridusteaduste Ajakiri. Estonian Journal of Education*, 4 (1): 32–57.

Quinn, L. and J.-A. Vorster (2014), 'Isn't it Time to Start Thinking about "Developing" Academic Developers in a More Systematic Way?', *International Journal for Academic Development*, 19 (3): 255–8.

Rai, L. and T. Lillis (2011), 'A Case Study of a Research-Based Collaboration around Writing in Social Work', *Across the Disciplines*, 8 (3): 9.

Spaull, N. (2015), 'Schooling in South Africa: How Low-Quality Education becomes a Poverty Trap', *South African Child Gauge*, 12 (1): 34–41.

Spaull, N. (2023), *Background Report, 2030 Reading Panel*. Cape Town.

Vorster, J.-A. and L. Quinn (2015), 'Towards Shaping the Field: Theorising the Knowledge in a Formal Course for Academic Developers', *Higher Education Research & Development*, 34 (5): 1031–44.

Whitchurch, C. (2008), 'Shifting Identities and Blurring Boundaries: The Emergence of Third Space Professionals in UK Higher Education', *Higher Education Quarterly*, 62 (4): 377–96.

Wingate, U. (2018), 'Academic Literacy across the Curriculum: Towards a Collaborative Instructional Approach', *Language Teaching*, 51 (3): 349–64.

Chapter 7

FINDING SPACE AND VOICE

DUOETHNOGRAPHIC EXPLORATION OF TEACHER AGENCY IN EAP

Iwona Winiarska-Pringle and Ania Rolińska

Introduction

Research into English for academic purposes (EAP) practitioners' journey into the profession highlights the lack of prior socialization into the field and consequently the in-situ nature of professional development (Ding and Bruce, 2017; Bruce, 2021). While some accounts of entry experiences exist (Alexander, 2007; Campion, 2016), in-service training and development have not been explored much (Fitzpatrick, Costley and Tavakoli, 2022; Webster, 2022). Responding to this blind spot in the EAP knowledge base, this chapter investigates two EAP practitioners' lived experience of transitioning to EAP scholarship and English for specific academic purposes (ESAP) teaching through the lens of agency. To capture the nuances of how agency is enabled or hindered, we have adopted the ecological model proposed by Priestley, Biesta and Robinson (2015), which positions the concept as an emergent and context-specific phenomenon. Aware of the risk of becoming uncritically entangled in our own life stories, we chose duoethnography (Sawyer and Norris, 2013) as a method to 'make [our] current position problematic' (Norris, Sawyer and Lund, 2012: 18) and to embed reflexivity into the inquiry.

Focussing on time, space and caring collaborations as potentially determining factors, this chapter discusses agentic successes and failures in the context of becoming an EAP scholar and an ESAP teacher. Firstly, it briefly overviews the ecological model of agency, benefits and challenges related to developing expertise in EAP and the key tenets of duoethnography. It then presents and discusses the findings, concluding with what we have learnt about agency and the method, limitations we have identified and our suggestions for future developments.

Conceptual background

Ecological model of teacher agency

The ecological model of agency developed by Priestley, Biesta and Robinson (2015) is both multidimensional and complex. It positions the concept of agency at the crossroads between the individual capacity for questioning the present and imagining a different future, and a range of external factors influencing day-to-day decisions in teachers' professional practice. Agency is shaped by three interplaying dimensions: iterational, projective and practical-evaluative.

The iterational dimension consists of the teacher's past experiences, both in terms of personal life experiences, including their own learning experiences, as well as formal and informal professional development and day-to-day socialization into the profession. Interestingly, the significance of personal experiences, sometimes over professional ones, and the experience of working in other non-educational professions have been noted by Priestley and colleagues as important variables affecting teacher agency.

The projective dimension refers to the teacher's future aspirations or their capability to re-imagine their practice. These aspirations can be short-, medium- or long-term and have an inspirational or instrumental character. This ability to imagine a different professional future is largely rooted in teachers' past experiences (iterational dimension), which highlights the importance of teacher education, both pre-service qualifications and in-service development, in shaping (and widening) the repertoire of teachers' responses to policies and practices.

Finally, the practical-evaluative dimension, or the day-to-day environment teachers operate in, is mediated by three factors: material (e.g. physical environment or resources available), cultural (e.g. institutional/team values and beliefs) and structural (e.g. orientation, symmetry, strength of professional relationships, power and trust). In other words, teachers' decisions in the present are affected by wider beliefs and values about the role and purpose of their work, practical considerations of the resources available and evaluations of risks involved in a course of action or inaction. For example, insufficient time for professional dialogue and reflection with peers, identified by Priestley and colleagues as a strong mediating factor inhibiting teachers' agency, can be structural and/or cultural, depending on the quality and strength of relationships in their immediate context and/or values promoted in the teacher's wider environment.

While the above-mentioned dimensions contribute to the achievement of agency simultaneously, they do so to varying degrees. In certain circumstances, one dimension may have more or less impact on one's agentic orientation, subject to constant temporal and/or relational changes. To be agentic in a challenging situation is to be able to make an informed decision how to engage with it and choose the most desirable response even if this means no action at all. Having limited or no options results in decreased or absent agentic engagement, often taking the form of 'routinized patterns of habitual behaviour with no consideration of alternatives' (Priestley, Biesta and Robinson, 2015: 141). So, agency is about the quality of the teacher engagement with contexts-for-action.

Before exploring the quality of our engagement along our respective developmental paths to becoming an EAP scholar and an ESAP teacher, it is important to briefly overview the existing literature on those areas of developing EAP expertise.

Developing expertise in EAP

Research into EAP practitioners' conditions and positionality, although still an under-developed area of EAP knowledge, has been gaining traction recently. In their seminal monograph, Ding and Bruce (2017) call for more inquiries into those who practise EAP as their expertise, development and status in academia are intertwined with the contested position of the field itself. Several reasons contribute to the general marginalization of the EAP field and its professionals. First, entering the discipline is possible with qualifications in cognate disciplines, not an EAP-specific degree, and socialization into the profession is predominantly in-situ, often limited and fragmented (Campion, 2016; Ding, 2019). This is further complicated by the field's diverse and constantly growing knowledge base (Bruce, 2011, 2021) as well as the plurality of spaces EAP practitioners find themselves in (Ding and Campion, 2016), requiring the ongoing need for development throughout their career. Finally, the status of EAP, and by extension the position of practitioners, tends to be viewed in support or service terms (Bell, 2021), as a low-skill activity of commercial, rather than academic, value (Ding and Bruce, 2017). Since EAP is seen by its higher education (HE) institutions as an 'economic and intellectual short-cut' (Turner, 2004: 96), unsurprisingly, little recognition is given to the developmental needs of its teachers.

One area of professional development viewed as crucial in challenging such a view is engagement in scholarship of teaching and learning (SoTL) and research (Ding and Bruce, 2017; Davis, 2019; Bell, 2021). In their SoTL Manifesto, Ding et al. (2018: np) call for scholarship to be underpinned by ethics, shared publicly and concerned with impact, not unlike research; however, they encourage practitioners to experiment with genres, modalities and styles, promoting an inclusive understanding of scholarship outputs beyond what would be conventionally expected from researchers. Scholarship, they believe, can help practitioners 'actively shape their educational contexts rather than be shaped by circumstance, others and powerful ideologies and structures'.

Undertaking and disseminating scholarship can bring numerous benefits to EAP practitioners, for instance increased empathy for students and their challenges, improved writing skills, renewed interest in teaching or stronger connections to other disciplines (Davis, 2019). It can also lead to higher esteem among peers (Webster, 2022) as well as boosting promotion and pay rise opportunities (Bahrami, Hosseini and Atai, 2019; Bell, 2021). However, engaging in scholarship is often not expected of EAP practitioners who are employed on teaching-only contracts. Additionally, as transitioning into the field tends not to require a PhD/

EdD qualification (Ding and Bruce, 2017; Bell, 2021), teachers often lack research training and the associated academic capital, such as experience in the peer-review or publishing process. For all of these reasons, undertaking scholarship in EAP comes at 'a considerable personal investment and time commitment' (Ding and Bruce, 2017: 112).

Indeed, time appears to be one of the main challenges to scholarly work, even for experienced teacher-scholars with a PhD (Bahrami, Hosseini and Atai, 2019; Davis, 2019). Other obstacles include insufficient research and/or writing-for-publication skills, lack of subject knowledge and anxiety about peer review or public scrutiny (Webster, 2022). Ding and Bruce (2017) propose an incremental route to scholarship, building skills and academic capital over time, adding qualifications and seeking collaborative opportunities. A recent account of scholarship of writing in EAP demonstrates that a dedicated time allocation for scholarship promotes a stronger research culture when accompanied by peer mentoring and promoting inclusive dissemination outputs (Webster, 2022). This suggests that supporting 'accidental scholars' (Bond, 2020: 11) is a complex task which requires careful consideration of the challenging contextual barriers and individual needs.

Similarly, becoming an ESAP teacher comes with many challenges. ESAP explicitly concerns itself with teaching the student to 'deploy a repertoire of literacy practices appropriate to different settings, and handle the social meanings and identities that each evokes' (Hyland, 2016: 21), so there is a question of how one engages with the content knowledge and the pedagogy within the specific context in ways that are productive for all of the parties involved (Basturkmen, 2019, 2021). While some content knowledge is required, too much of it may actually disadvantage the ESAP teacher as they may start focussing on teaching the content rather than literacies (Basturkmen, 2019). ESAP is often praised for being motivating and engaging for the students (Woodrow, 2013), but in practical terms its teachers have often been expected to 'deliver maximum assistance in minimum time' (Swales, 1994), foregrounding pragmatic and outcome-driven approaches to designing and delivering curricula, dictated by needs and text analyses, and tasks within parameters prescribed by the discipline (Dudley-Evans and St John, 1998). This focus on the student and their needs often marginalizes the teachers' 'experiences, processes and outcomes of professional learning' (Borg, 2015: 552). How the ESAP teacher positions themselves and/or is positioned towards the new academic community of practice is crucial in the developmental process as is the response from the host academic tribe. There is an increasingly stronger case for embedding academic literacies into the disciplinary curriculum (White and Lay, 2019), best achieved through 'collaboration between writing and subject experts' (Wingate, 2015: 128). It is through such collaborations that the EAP field and its practitioners can win more recognition and status in academia (Bell, 2021). As there are few published examples of such partnerships (e.g. Jacobs, 2010; Northcott, 2019), there is an urgent need to chart out possible ways in which they can be established and sustained.

Methodology

Duoethnography

In duoethnography two (or more) researchers juxtapose their life stories to explore a cultural or social phenomenon which is the object of their study. The presence of the other researcher in this relational and dialogic inquiry aims to emphasize the difference and so helps to disrupt cultural metanarratives and a single-author interpretation of the explored phenomenon. This means that the accounts starting with the investigation of the specific and local context (the ontic) have the potential to move beyond and 'resonate with and be relevant for others' in the wider community, avoiding hermeneutic narcissism (Ding and Bruce, 2017: 154). This process of deconstructing and reconstructing understandings of one's lived experience often becomes 'regenerative and liberating' (Norris, Sayer and Lund, 2012: 18), potentially leading to the transformation of the researcher.

Placing difference as a heuristic requires honesty and vulnerability, which is why mutual trust and ethics of care are needed for the duoethnographic research to reach its transformative potential (Sawyer and Norris, 2013). Although duoethnographers typically do not require institutional ethical approvals, as they explore their own lives and are in control of the data collection, analysis and writing, this does not render ethical considerations superfluous. On the contrary, setting clear expectations, rules and boundaries for the participating researchers to adhere to when critiquing each other's stories is essential (Breault, 2016) to balance the rigour of the academic inquiry with care for the 'other' (Sawyer and Norris, 2013).[1] In the case of this project, sharing physical, intellectual and emotional spaces was not just the method fit for the subject of the research but also a response to our human need for togetherness at the time of COVID-19 pandemic.

Research setting and participants

Since the authors of this chapter are the sites of research, it is important to provide an overview of their relevant characteristics. They are experienced EAP practitioners (Iwona ten years and Ania fifteen years in EAP at the time of writing), and both are, to varying extents, active within the wider EAP community (e.g. committee work for BALEAP and BALEAP[2] Special Interest Groups). Both authors hold master's degrees and have studied at a tertiary level in their home country, Poland, other European countries and the UK. Although both are currently on permanent contracts at UK HE institutions, each experienced extended precarity in ELT and EAP, and part-time employment to balance work with parenting responsibilities or to allow space for other professional commitments. Another shared commonality is that they immigrated from Poland and have been settled in the UK for over fifteen years.

The authors significantly differ in the areas of scholarship experience, professional qualifications and caring responsibilities. Additionally, while Iwona has 10 per cent of her annual workload allocation dedicated to scholarship, Ania's present role has no such explicit arrangement at the moment. The profiles of their institutions and immediate contexts differ, too. Iwona is part of a team of twenty-two teachers in a Russell Group, research-intensive university. Ania, on the other hand, is a sole EAP practitioner working with overseas students in an art school of international repute with a rising research profile.

Data collection and analysis

The data collection process began with individually written responses to a simple prompt: 'How do I understand agency?'. These highlighted some differences in our understandings and opened space for discussion during the subsequent nine reflective meetings held online or in person between October 2021 and February 2022. The meetings were loosely structured around the three dimensions of the ecological theory of agency (Priestley, Biesta and Robinson, 2015). They generated fourteen hours of audio/video-recorded material which was then transcribed and re-read for accuracy.

The transcripts underwent a multi-step data analysis. First, each author applied InVivo coding (Saldaña, 2021), noting high-frequency words which were then refined collaboratively into more conceptual code sets such as 'transitions', 'belonging', 'othering', 'development'. The secondary coding cycle entailed code mapping (Saldaña, 2021), visually supported by the Miro application, which categorized the sets into five higher-level themes: 'time', 'liminality and border work', 'space and materiality', 'care and people' and 'transformation'.

The resulting vastness of agentic experiences across the dataset felt overwhelming, clearly exceeding the scope of this chapter if explored in depth. Rather than insisting on investigating how all five themes reflect the dimensions from the ecological model, we stepped away from the themes and, through a duoethnographic dialogue, we asked each other which of these agentic experiences mattered to us most at the time. It was then that we realized that the most poignant successes and failures were related to developing expertise in scholarship (Iwona) and ESAP (Ania), and we decided to focus on these trajectories in the final written reflections on agency to capture further details, emotions and any new insights. In retrospect, this turned out to be a reconfiguring or cathartic moment, embodying the transformative potential of the method (Sawyer and Norris, 2013).

Coding these final reflections revealed differences in strength and distribution between the five themes. As a result, certain 'liminality' codes now matched 'time' more closely while many 'transformation' codes became aligned with 'care and people', which we extended in meaning to 'caring collaborations'. Additionally, some codes from the 'border work' category were moved to the 'time' and 'space' themes; however, we excluded the codes related to our multilingual and bicultural identities because, while important, they determined our development as an EAP scholar or ESAP teacher to a lesser degree than the three selected themes: 'time', 'space' and 'caring collaborations'.

Finally, we needed to consider how to present our data. Typically, duoethnographic publications allow the reader to 'hear' each author's individual voice in the form of reconstructed dialogues between the researchers (e.g. Lowe and Kiczkowiak, 2016) or narrative vignettes illustrating the main themes (e.g. Rose and Montakantiwong, 2018). We chose the latter approach, using extracts reconstructed with relevant material from the final written reflections as well as earlier reflective meetings and presented in the authors' individual styles.[3]

Findings and discussion

Time

Time-related codes appeared consistently in our dataset and across all three dimensions of the ecological framework, reflecting the importance and multifaceted nature of temporality in the context of professional development. For example, although time appears to be essential in and for the process of developing scholarship and ESAP expertise, our data also suggests that the rhythm and length of that process can be deeply affected by significant events or encounters, marking moments of profound impact on our agency. To illustrate some of these temporal aspects of our agentic orientations, the extracts below focus on the first turning moments in our respective developmental paths and their rippled effects over time.

> Iwona's extract
>
> Teaching EAP without [engaging with] scholarship is like teaching a language you yourself don't use, so I read papers and, attended reading groups and local events. But when I got a permanent post, I discovered that for promotion purposes, evidence in SoTL criterion means outputs such as monographs, external policy and professional reports, book chapters or peer-reviewed publications of international standing to name a few.
>
> Monographs on part-time contract with year-round teaching and no PhD knowledge and experience???? The gap between my abilities, contractual conditions and institutional expectations was colossal. I realised that I was to stay put; forever churn out courses and make money for others.
>
> Shocked and angry I first looked for courses/modules on how to research and disseminate, but CPDs[4] offer only generic guidance with no feedback or collaboration opportunities. EdD/PhD? Costly and/or with rigid timetables: I had two small kids, precarity debts and wanted practical research skills, not a title. 10% allocation for SoTL only added pressure to perform and produce. But how? For a long time, I was stuck and wanted to quit. One day, I stopped looking for short cuts and decided to use all the time I had, paid and unpaid, for scholarship. It was slow but kind of worked, except after years of scholarship, events and volunteering outside my contracted hours, I'm tired and want my private time back.

Ania's extract

When I got the students from the Art School I jumped with joy; I had taught on subject-specific courses and I am interested in art; so, I've got experience, it should be fun! Yet I struggled for a long time; so many disciplinary practices were unfamiliar. Say, writing; as expected, dense with theories and concepts, but the style is more personal at times – in a way easier, but how do you balance the abstract and the affective? Many genres are fluid and multimodal – sketches and drawings on par with writing, far different from a bar chart analysis!

I love teaching writing so I thought I'd figure out those visual essays, but then the studio seemed more about speaking, and not so much the familiar presentations or seminars; I needed to prepare students for unscripted conversations about their work during critiques. Every time I went to observe one, I could see how demanding it was, conceptually, linguistically, emotionally. So complex!

The needs analysis was useful but how do you teach those genres that seem to escape any rules? No wonder I felt unprepared and failed by the 'conventional' EAP methods. As I was a part-timer, I was unable to focus solely on teaching in art and design. The briefs changed ever so slightly every year so any materials I created had to be changed significantly again and again. Whenever I felt I'd made a step forward, it seemed it was three steps backwards during the next class. I felt demotivated, stuck and alienated. And I felt my students saw language learning as a burden, taking their precious studio time away. I felt like an intruder trying to mould them in all that regimented academic protocol. It was a torture. There were moments I wanted to quit.

As can be seen in both extracts, the iterational dimension of the ecological model, encapsulated in our previous academic and professional knowledge and experience, can hinder teachers' agentic orientations. Iwona's academic abilities and scholarly engagement cannot match the institutional expectations of scholarship outputs while Ania's prior expertise in EAP proves an insufficient preparation for teaching in art and design. An unexpected change in circumstances forces both authors to re-orient themselves towards new areas of expertise, illustrating the in-situ (Ding and Campion, 2016; Ding and Bruce, 2017) and ad-hoc (Alexander, 2007; Ding, 2019) nature of becoming an EAP professional. Our findings also offer further insights into the possible consequences of disproportionately prioritizing the needs of students and institutions over those of teachers (Basturkmen, 2019). Specifically, for both authors, developing in a new area of required expertise is not only reactive but to a large degree disruptive, marked by extended periods of stalled growth, demotivation and a corroded sense of purpose. This is despite the authors' strong projective orientations towards their professional future: Iwona's belief in the value of scholarship in EAP and Ania's enthusiasm and interest in creative disciplines, which confirms, in line with the ecological model, that agency requires favourable contextual circumstances to sustain it.

The extracts suggest several barriers within the practical-evaluative dimension, stemming from how time is perceived and valued at the institutional level (cultural factor) and what consequences it has for EAP teachers (material factor). For instance, as the neoliberal universities require EAP units to deliver education as a commodity with maximum teaching hours (profit) at a minimum cost (e.g. time for training and development), EAP teaching responsibilities tend to be undertaken 'year-round' and given priority over professional development (Hadley, 2015). In Iwona's case, a 10 per cent-time allocation for scholarship, a rare acknowledgement of its value and place in the field of EAP (Webster, 2022), is perceived as 'added pressure to perform and produce', highlighting a further clash between managerial efforts to raise the profile of the EAP unit through scholarship and the institutionally recognized outputs not fit for 'the abilities and contractual conditions' of its EAP practitioners. In Ania's case, no contracted time for learning means it becomes an add-on luxury rather than a timetabled essential while 'briefs chang[ing] ever so slightly' require regular updates to the in-house produced materials, reducing time for other development needs.

Although opportunities for professional development in EAP do exist, not least via institutional or BALEAP events and networks, Iwona's extract provides some insights into the possible reasons for their limited impact, such as financial cost, a 'rigid timetable' or insufficient responsiveness to personal circumstances and individual developmental needs. Consequently, and as highlighted before (e.g. Ding, 2019), the burden of professional development is placed upon individual EAP teachers who undertake it largely in their private time and in addition to their regular teaching commitments, which, as our extracts reveal, causes stress and fatigue, especially when stretched over time.

Overall, our findings echo the argument that EAP practitioners' socialization into the profession is, indeed, a slow, often ad-hoc process (Ding and Bruce, 2017), mostly invisible to and unacknowledged by their institutions which, nevertheless, hugely benefit from it. This process lengthens even further in the case of those working part-time even if, as in our extracts, non-contracted time is used to counteract it. Achieving agency in such circumstances can be a bittersweet experience as agentic successes often come at a significant cost. The authors' inability to meet the institutional, students' and their own expectations regarding their role resulted in frustration, alienation and, at times, resentment. The intensity of these emotions indicates the issue of not only teachers' lack of preparedness for the realities of EAP practice but, more importantly, insufficient institutional understanding of the real needs and value of their work. As seen in our extracts, the consequences of limited opportunities for development and marginalization, also in the eyes of students, can seriously impact the retention of practitioners in the field.

Space

Our discussions of the ecological framework's practical-evaluative dimension recurrently touched on space in its different manifestations. At a very situated level, space is the immediate physical or 'practical' environment where the professional practices and processes, including development, are done. These arrangements of and within the material space are often decided, implicitly or explicitly, by the institution or department, demonstrating how individual experiences of space are affected by structures and cultures. The notion of space, therefore, is not transparent, it is political. Also crucial is our changing relationship with physical spaces, that is, positionality. This is shaped by the factors listed above but, more importantly, by how we 'evaluate' the given circumstances, how we react or respond to the physical space and work with, or against, its material, structural and cultural aspects. It is at the crossroads of the practical and the evaluative, where agentic work may happen, as the following extracts illustrate.

Iwona's extract

Even without the extremes of a global pandemic, working and caring for a family is tough. I share my office with up to six teachers so it's usually busy and noisy while at home, familial sounds and needs demand my undivided attention. Becoming a scholar in those spaces has been extremely convoluted.

I started by reading extensively about EAP and research in general. Reading and reflection are essential for SoTL, but they require a space away from external interruptions, so for me, this means a campus bench on a warm day, public transport of all sorts, home when kids are asleep or at school, or a dog walk. Frankly, this is tiring, and the results are often invisible to others. Writing in such stolen spaces is even more challenging, especially for a novice.

What helped? Funding and volunteering. An annually allocated budget [for professional development] allowed me to attend more events: ResTes, PIMs, BALEAP conferences, where I could listen and speak to the practitioners whose work I admire, while joining a SIG offered peer reviews, write-ups and collaborative projects. However, very little of all this learning for scholarship has actually happened in my office or on campus...

Ania's extract

In my second year of teaching art and design students, even though I was still employed by the University, I decided to cross over to the Art School campus hoping this would help my students enjoy English classes more. However, that meant teaching in a space that was completely unfamiliar to me. Now it was me who was an outsider! What is more, the teaching space at the Art School was significantly different from the EAP classrooms I was used to.

Their space is always in flux: fascinating and very frustrating. In the studio, there is no place for my handouts on tables sprayed with paint; maintenance people, studio colleagues, external visitors frequently walk through it. There is a lot of milling and mingling. The tutors and students often work side by side, their conversations shifting from formal to informal within one sentence.

On a typical EAP course, the object of the student's study is often somewhere else, in a different classroom, and so a bit abstract and not necessarily relatable. In the studio, that something the student is passionate or angry about is right there in front of you, the fabric they're draping on a mannequin or the game they're designing . . . it's sitting there, requiring your attention. That object cannot be ignored, it wants to participate in the conversation! How can I talk to it?

The studio with all its messiness and flux was an overwhelming space for me to teach in those first years. I tried other rooms like the cinema or lecture theatres in the hope of restoring some order in my teaching practice. But it was a lost cause really, and I soon realized that resisting the studio space and clinging onto my old ways that were no longer fit for purpose did not make sense. I needed to embrace that space rather than fight it. But how?

Both extracts engage with the complex nature of the materiality of scholarship and pedagogical practice. Working in a busy environment, Iwona does most of her scholarship beyond the physical area of the university, in less official or completely private spaces not intended for this purpose, where support is absent and other commitments such as childcare and private life may compete for her attention. Office availability and allocation may reflect how the value and purpose of EAP is perceived at the institutional level. EAP teachers are often pushed into 'the third space' due to the location of their unit within institutional structures as their role is neither solely academic nor administrative (MacDonald, 2016). For Iwona, this arrangement results in the blurring of identities and roles and requires the constant negotiation of priorities, which echoes similar discussions in publications on gender and academic writing (e.g. Appelby, 2009; McMullan, 2018; Tuck, 2018). However, fragmented, marginal and transient spaces such as public transport, nature and conference halls where Iwona does her scholarship are not discussed in much detail in the EAP literature. Yet, they undoubtedly shaped her agentic orientations, seemingly boosting them but simultaneously occluding much of the work being done, taking the significance and recognition away, leaving Iwona tired and disillusioned. Interestingly, absent from Iwona's extract is the university library which would seem a natural alternative to her busy office, suggesting that creating optimal spatial conditions for scholarly work is possibly more complex than assumed or acknowledged by the institution or teacher-scholars.

Ania, on the other hand, quickly and painfully discovers that space conducive to language teaching is virtually absent from the art school campus as content teaching is mostly conducted in studios or lecture theatres. This may be a manifestation of the language/content dichotomy that often determines the position and value of language and its educators as subservient (Turner, 2004; Bond, 2020). Apart from her 'third space' provenance, Ania is also an outsider to the new academic tribe with its own distinct values and practices shaping their territory and boundaries (Becher and Trowler, 2001). The unfamiliarity with the new institutional and disciplinary context can make it seem overwhelming and insurmountable (Trowler, 2014). The studio space, an illustrative example of Massey's conceptualization of space as 'a rich and fluid constellation of interactions, a simultaneity of many stories, a multiplicity of experiences' (2005: 2), both excites and discourages Ania. Her extract illuminates how educational spaces and objects can blur the concrete and material with the intellectual and cognitive, shaping interactions between teachers, students and content knowledge. Taking the posthumanist lens to look at these situated and embodied knowledges and practices allows us to see the human and non-human participants as 'experiencing an ongoing and nomadic process of becoming' (Braidotti, 2019: 48). For Ania, who has migrated from EAP contexts where content- and language-teaching spaces are separated, it requires a shift in thinking to reconceptualize the teaching space as a non-human agent in the educational process.

Both extracts show how Iwona and Ania position themselves towards the challenging physical spaces available to them, or not, for their scholarly and pedagogical practice. Although it is not a straightforward or risk-free process, they both manage to re-imagine the available spaces in phenomenological terms and even expand them. Iwona, for example, volunteers to join a BALEAP SIG committee, and, with institutional funding, she starts attending conferences. These spaces provide her with meaningful learning resources and social networks that support Iwona's transition to scholarship, pointing to a strong link between learning spaces and social capital in professional development. Ania, by observing, reflecting and having an inner dialogue with herself about the new space, finally acknowledges the sociomaterial aspects of her ESAP practice, which makes 'new connections and unexpected openings' possible (Gravett and Ajjawi, 2022).

McMullan (2018: 24), in her study of the academic writing practices of female graduates, links being able to 're-claim and re-use more conventionalized places in different ways' with agency. Following this thinking, it could be said that Iwona re-creates her space, that being a garden bench or a train seat, as 'space for academic thinking and writing' (McMullan, 2018: 24). A similar conclusion can be drawn for Ania, who at some point re-invents the studio as a space in which she can teach in new ways. The way both authors reposition themselves in relation to the place/location in which they started their journey, from 'nostalgic, regressive and reactionary' to 'progressive and radical' (Agnew, 2011 in McMullan, 2018: 24), provides a powerful illustration of the achievement of agency. When it comes to agentic work within the practical-evaluative dimension of the framework, space cannot be reduced to a physical location, but its phenomenological qualities need to be foregrounded (McMullan, 2018). In other words, the practical and the evaluative go hand in hand.

Caring collaborations

The theme of collaborations with others, colleagues and students, but also with disciplinary knowledge, interwoven into our data, bears strong witness to the relational domain, also referred to as social structures (Priestley, Biesta and Robinson, 2015). The notion of care kept recurring in relation to collaborative experiences, and to account for the relationship between the two, we opted for 'caring collaborations'. Another strong code was that of 'belonging'. The following extracts and analysis provide insight into how these played out in relation to our agency.

Iwona's extract

Convening an in-sessional, credit-bearing course made me see EAP differently, steering my interests to needs analysis, assessment and syllabus design. My students were undergraduate, mostly Europeans, with advanced English and from various disciplines. As there is little research on such context in EAP literature, I read a lot on study abroad and eventually, with a mentor's support, did my first scholarship project. As a result of my findings, I amended the course assessment and shifted course content to problematize study abroad experience so that students would think more critically about it. It was a small project but made me feel I belonged especially when I shared it with the wider university and then EAP community.

Joining a [BALEAP] SIG committee had a similar effect. Being with like-minded colleagues is empowering. Regardless of interests or positions, disagreements or looming deadlines, we share knowledge generously, listen carefully, support each other. Collectively we achieve more. With the SIG, I can be bold, experiment, and make mistakes.

Ania's extract

Last spring, I went into the studio to work alongside the design tutor. During tutorials, the student's art or design was brought to the fore and the language could be used authentically. This experiment felt so exciting. Suddenly I saw many possibilities opening up for my ESAP practice, but also of value to the students and the studio tutors.

I'd like to do more co-teaching with the studio tutors in the future. All those years ago, I felt I was on the periphery of that community of practice, which just felt so unfamiliar. But now I feel more comfortable and I want to be in it. I've had conversations with my studio colleagues about embedding the language even more into the studio. And they are up for it because like me they are interested in building holistic experiences for the students.

For me successful collaborations work when we share some beliefs and values, have complementary strengths and expertise, there is mutual trust and respect and so together we are able to produce a kind of synergy. There is a lot of vulnerability in such partnerships. What if I make a fool of myself? What if I ask wrong questions or don't know the answer? But that's ok, I feel I can take that risk. And that feels good, at last!

Both extracts evidence commitment to investigating the professional context and its actors' needs through inquiry and collaborations with a view to creating meaningful educational experiences. Iwona, having taken up convening responsibilities, conducts a scholarship project to gain insights into the relevant institutional practices and extend her knowledge about a niche EAP space she had come to occupy. In Ania's case, due to her repositioning herself within the studio context alongside her studio tutor colleagues, she is able to reignite her excitement about the pedagogical practice and start innovating.

What these experiences have in common is, first, the evolving sense of belonging and, second, the notion of care. The former is commonly understood as an emotional attachment, an act of identification or feeling safe, accepted and connected. While these infuse the extracts above, it is also palpable that this coming home is 'a situated, processual and evolving practice' and 'experienced relationally' (Gravett and Ajjawi, 2022: 2). In both cases there is a sense of realizing one's own value, feeling seen and validated due to the change in the relational positioning within the collaborations. For both authors, the sense of belonging, becoming part of their respective groups, offers a safe space to open up to vulnerability, experiment, make mistakes and take risks, contributing to their growth as a scholar and an ESAP practitioner. Priestley and colleagues (2015) argue that notions of power and trust that emerge within social structures as relational resources can shape the actors' agency. For Iwona it was the flat power structure and shared mindset within the SIG Committee while for Ania it was the value and belief systems that she realized she shared with her studio colleagues that seem to have afforded the authors with an expanded sense of empowerment resulting in a qualitative change to their agentic orientation. Priestley, Biesta and Robinson (2015: 86) suggest that more horizontal relationships and/or strong dialogical structures tend to encourage sense making and innovation in the event of change or challenge while 'coercive power structures [. . .] or relationships which are predominantly vertical, hierarchical and not reciprocal may prevent the spread of new thinking'. Both authors' experiences support that claim, adding belonging as another determining characteristic of those social structures.

As for care, we extend its understanding beyond instrumental caregiving in response to immediate needs; rather it is about 'a life-sustaining web of relations' (Mariskind, 2014: 318) that includes 'caring about' and 'taking care of', 'care-giving' and 'care-receiving' (Mariskind, 2014: 308). As illustrated in the extracts, collaborations where we cared about and took care of the student, courses, subject knowledge or EAP community, AND (our emphasis) where the caring was reciprocated seemed to have the most transformative impact on our sense of agency. While we do not insist that all professional collaborations must be caring to be constructive, based on our experience we believe the relational dimension of teacher agency may be a strong contributing factor in the ecological system. In relation to higher education, care is often positioned in dichotomy to academic practice, as belonging to compulsory education, eroding intellectual rigour (Mariskind, 2014) and infusing therapeutic culture (Walker and Gleaves, 2016).

Yet, with a broader understanding of care as 'a core academic value' (Tuck, 2018: 32) encompassing 'a deep commitment and engagement' (Tuck, 2018: 33), the university can provide a much-needed holistic experience to the student. We argue that, by fostering caring and reciprocal collaborations, a similar experience could, and even should, be offered to EAP practitioners so that, in the process of their agentic orientations being actively shaped, they respond to professional challenges more constructively and creatively (Biesta and Tedder, 2007: 147).

Conclusion

The main learning takeaways from the research project relate to our expanded understanding of agency not as action or individual capacity but as a complex, constantly evolving phenomenon, enhanced by the relational factors whereby time and space are not 'neutral, binary, concepts, but . . . a dynamic and sociomaterial assemblage' (Gravett and Ajjiawi, 2022). The lived experiences analysed in the chapter stress the importance of relationships and cultures in the workplace. To advance the EAP profession and develop much-needed expertise, for example in scholarship and ESAP, in-situ socialization needs flexible, carefully considered and built-in opportunities for development, preferably negotiated with the teacher to complement generic and fit-for-all approaches. This would help to re-assert care as the core academic value emphasizing 'receptivity, relatedness and responsiveness' (Sailsbury, 2013: 53 in Tuck, 2018). As to the method used for the research, duoethnography turned out to be time- and emotion-heavy, but it offered invaluable moments of revelation, transformation and togetherness, resonating with the value of care.

This research is not without its limitations. Firstly, although we collected vast amounts of valuable and insightful data, in the end, much of it did not feed explicitly into the write-up. For example, despite frequent and emotional discussions regarding our agentic orientations in the context of being a Polish native speaker and a long-term migrant teacher of EAP in the UK, not foregrounding these identities in our respective developmental journeys was a difficult agentic choice we matured into over this two-year project. We admit that, at least implicitly, they may have coloured our beliefs and understandings, but this, we believe, deserves a separate investigation.

Secondly, although the chapter discusses three themes separately, in day-to-day EAP practice, they overlap and interplay with each other, boosting or hindering the achievement of agency. Socialization into EAP happens in material spaces and involves interactions with others enacted in and through time. Separating these themes for analysis and writing-up imposed selectivity and linearity on the findings section, which risks overshadowing the true nature of developing EAP expertise which, for us, had a slow, meandering and individual rhythm with hidden detours eluding quantification. Having said this, our data suggest that certain contextual factors, such as collaborations infused with trust and care, are conducive to agentic orientations while others, for instance insufficient time for development, diminish our responsiveness. Interestingly, in Priestley, Biesta and Robinson's (2015) investigations of agentic experience in compulsory education contexts, material aspects did not seem to play a defining role. In contrast, in an HE setting, material spaces and our positionality seemed of importance and so this may be something worth further investigation, especially in the light of general EAP marginalization within academia.

Ultimately, the reconceptualizations of agency offered in this chapter are by no means declarative or universal but rather they constitute 'placeholders, stepping-stones, milestones, or temporal epiphanies, since changes can and will take place with each new experience' (Sawyer and Norris, 2013: 94). We believe our contribution adds some granularity to existing accounts by illustrating some consequences of in-situ development for two experienced EAP practitioners who navigated time, spaces and relationships to become the experts they aspired to be. We hope that some of our agentic failures and successes will resonate with the reader and encourage further investigations of in-service development in other EAP contexts, particularly beyond the UK, which currently dominates the discourse about the EAP profession (Ding and Campion, 2016). While our dialogues with each other, our contexts and colleagues continue, we hope the reader will join the conversation by drawing and sharing their own 'insights' about agency in their practice to contribute to the growing body of research on the developing needs and experiences of EAP teachers.

Notes

1 For more on ethics of care in ethnographic research see, for example, Ellis (2007), Stahlke (2016), Edwards (2021).
2 The global forum for EAP professionals https://www.baleap.org/
3 For more examples of other formats, please see *Duoethnography in English Language Teaching* edited by Lowe and Lawrence (2020).
4 CPD stands for Continuous Professional Development.

References

Alexander, O. (2007), 'Groping in the Dark or Turning on the Light: Routes into Teaching English for Academic Purposes', in T. Lynch and J. Northcott (eds), *Educating Legal English Specialists and Teacher Education in Teaching EAP. Proceedings of IALS Teacher Education Symposia, 2004 and 2006*, Institute for Applied Language Studies, University of Edinburgh.

Appleby, R. (2009), 'The Spatial Politics of Gender in EAP Classroom Practice', *Journal of English for Academic Purposes*, 8 (2): 100–10.

Bahrami, V., M. Hosseini and M. R. Atai (2019), 'Exploring Research-Informed Practice in English for Academic Purposes: A Narrative Study', *English for Specific Purposes*, 54: 152–65.

Basturkmen, H. (2019), 'ESP Teacher Education Needs', *Language Teaching*, 52 (3): 318–30.

Basturkmen, H. (2021), 'Is ESP a Materials and Teaching-Led Movement?' *Language Teaching*, 54 (4): 491–501.

Becher, T. and P. R. Trowler (2001), *Academic Tribes and Territories*, 2nd edn, Buckingham: Open University Press.

Bell, D. E. (2021), 'Accounting for the Troubled Status of English Language Teachers in Higher Education', *Teaching in Higher Education*, 1–16.

Biesta, G. and M. Tedder (2007), 'Agency and Learning in the Lifecourse: Towards an Ecological Perspective', *Studies in the Education of Adults*, 39 (2): 132–49.

Bond, B. (2020), *Making Language Visible in the University: English for Academic Purposes and Internationalisation*, Bristol: Multilingual Matters.

Borg, S. (2015), 'Researching Language Teacher Education', in B. Paltridge and A. Phakiti (eds), *Research Methods in Applied Linguistics*, 541–60, London: Bloomsbury.

Braidotti, R. (2019), 'A Theoretical Framework for the Critical Posthumanities', *Theory, Culture & Society*, 36 (6): 31–61.

Breault, R. A. (2016), 'Emerging Issues in Duoethnography', *International Journal of Qualitative Studies in Education*, 29 (6): 777–94.

Bruce, I. (2011), *Theory and Concepts of English for Academic Purposes*, Basingstoke: Palgrave Macmillan.

Bruce, I. (2021), 'Towards an EAP without Borders: Developing Knowledge, Practitioners, and Communities', *International Journal of English for Academic Purposes: Research and Practice*, 2021 (Spring): 23–37.

Campion, G. C. (2016), '"The Learning Never Ends": Exploring Teachers' Views on the Transition from General English to EAP', *Journal of English for Academic Purposes*, 23: 59–70.

Davis, M. (2019), 'Publishing Research as an EAP Practitioner: Opportunities and Threats', *Journal of English for Academic Purposes*, 39: 72–86.

Ding, A. (2019), 'EAP Practitioner Identity', in K. Hyland and L. L. C. Wong (eds), *Specialised English: New Directions in ESP and EAP Research and Practice*, 63–76, Oxon: Routledge.

Ding, A., J. Bodin-Galvez, B. Bond, K. Morimoto, V. Ragni, N. Rust and R. Soliman (2018), 'Manifesto for the Scholarship of Language Teaching and Learning', *The Language Scholar* [blog], 6 December. https://languagescholar.leeds.ac.uk/manifesto-for-the-scholarship-of-language-teaching-and-learning/ (accessed 10 January 2023).

Ding, A. and I. Bruce (2017), *The English for Academic Purposes Practitioner: Operating on the Edge of Academia*, Cham, Switzerland: Palgrave Macmillan.

Ding, A. and G. Campion (2016), 'EAP Teacher Development', in K. Hyland and P. Shaw (eds), *The Routledge Handbook of English for Academic Purposes*, 547–59, Oxon: Routledge.

Dudley-Evans, T. and M. J. St John (1998), *Developments in English for Specific Purposes*, Cambridge: Cambridge University Press.

Edwards, J. (2021), 'Ethical Autoethnography: Is it Possible?', *International Journal of Qualitative Methods*, 20: 160940692199530.

Ellis, C. (2007), 'Telling Secrets, Revealing Lives: Relational Ethics in Research with Intimate Others', *Qualitative Inquiry*, 13 (1): 3–29.

Fitzpatrick, D., T. Costley and P. Tavakoli (2022), 'Exploring EAP Teachers' Expertise: Reflections on Practice, Pedagogy and Professional Development', *Journal of English for Academic Purposes*, 59: 101140.

Gravett, K. and R. Ajjawi (2022), 'Belonging as Situated Practice', *Studies in Higher Education*, 47 (7): 1386–96.

Hadley, G. (2015), *English for Academic Purposes in Neoliberal Universities: A Critical Grounded Theory*, Educational Linguistics Series, 22, Cham, Switzerland: Springer.

Hyland, K. (2016), *General and Specific EAP. The Routledge Handbook of English for Academic Purposes*, London: Routledge.

Jacobs, C. (2010), 'Collaboration as Pedagogy: Consequences and Implications for Partnerships between Communication and Disciplinary Specialists', *Southern African Linguistics and Applied Language Studies*, 28 (3): 227–37.

Lowe, R. J. and M. Kiczkowiak (2016), 'Native-speakerism and the Complexity of Personal Experience: A Duoethnographic Study', *Cogent Education*, 3 (1): 1264171.

Lowe, R. J. and L. Lawrence (2020), *Duoethnography in English Language Teaching: Research, Reflection and Classroom Application*, Bristol: Multilingual Matters.

MacDonald, J. (2016), 'The Margins as Third Space: EAP Teacher Professionalism in Canadian Universities', *TESL Canada Journal*, 34 (1): 106–16.

Mariskind, C. (2014), 'Teachers' Care in Higher Education: Contesting Gendered Constructions', *Gender and Education*, 26 (3): 306–20.

Massey, D. (2005), *For Space*, London: Sage.

McMullan, J. (2018), 'Becoming a Researcher: Re-inventing Writing Spaces', *Journal of English for Academic Purposes*, 32: 21–31.

Norris, J., R. Sawyer and D. E. Lund (2012), *Duoethnography: Dialogic Methods for Social, Health, and Educational Research*, Walnut Creek: Left Coast Press.

Northcott, J. (2019), 'Academic Writing Feedback: Collaboration between Subject and EAP Specialists', in K. Hyland and L. L. C. Wong (eds), *Specialised English: New Directions in ESP and EAP Research and Practice*, 214–27, Oxon: Routledge.

Priestley, M., G. Biesta and S. Robinson (2015), *Teacher Agency: An Ecological Approach*, London: Bloomsbury.

Rose, H. and A. Montakantiwong (2018), 'A Tale of Two Teachers: A Duoethnography of the Realistic and Idealistic Successes and Failures of Teaching English as an International Language', *RELC Journal*, 49 (1): 88–101.

Saldaña, J. (2021), *The Coding Manual for Qualitative Researchers*, 4th edn, London: Sage Publications.

Sawyer, R. D. and J. Norris (2013), *Duoethnography*, Oxford: Oxford University Press.

Stahlke Wall, S. (2016), 'Toward a Moderate Autoethnography', *International Journal of Qualitative Methods*, 15 (1): 160940691667496.

Swales, J. (1994), 'From the Editors', *English for Specific Purposes*, 25: 131–2.

Trowler, P. (2014), 'Academic Tribes and Territories: The Theoretical Trajectory', *Österreichische Zeitschrift für Geschichtswissenschaften*, 25 (3): 17–26.

Tuck, J. (2018), '"I'm Nobody's Mum in this University": The Gendering of Work around Student Writing in UK Higher Education', *Journal of English for Academic Purposes*, 32: 32–41.

Turner, J. (2004), 'Language as Academic Purpose', *Journal of English for Academic Purposes*, 3 (2): 95–109.

Walker, C. and A. Gleaves (2016), 'Constructing the Caring Higher Education Teacher: A Theoretical Framework', *Teaching and Teacher Education*, 54: 65–76.

Webster, S. (2022). 'The Transition of EAP Practitioners into Scholarship Writing', *Journal of English for Academic Purposes*, 57: 101091.

White, S. and E. Lay (2019), 'Built-in not Bolted-on: Embedding Academic Literacy Skills in Subject Disciplines', *Creative Pedagogies Imprint*, 1 (2): 33–8.

Wingate, U. (2015), 'Towards an Inclusive Model of Academic Literacy Instruction', in U. Wingate (ed.), *Academic Literacy and Student Diversity: The Case for Inclusive Practice*, 126–49, Bristol: Blue Ridge Summit: Multilingual Matters.

Woodrow, L. (2013), 'Motivation and the Transition to University', in E. Ushioda (ed.), *International Perspectives on Motivation: Language Learning and Professional Challenges*, 117–32, Basingstoke: Palgrave Macmillan.

Chapter 8

RESPECTED TEACHERS OR A MARGINALIZED, STIGMATIZED PROFESSION? AN EXPLORATION OF UK EAP PRACTITIONER IDENTITY

Sarah Taylor

Introduction

EAP is not widely recognized as an academic discipline, and, as there are few high-level EAP academics in universities, EAP practitioners lack cultural capital in comparison to other academics (Ding, 2019). This lack of cultural capital reduces the agency of practitioners and excludes them from certain theoretical debates in higher education (Burke and Hermerschmidt, 2005), thereby limiting their involvement in decision-making processes and their ability to implement change within the field (Ding and Bruce, 2017). The lack of recognition or understanding of EAP has been articulated by Ding and Bruce (2017) as a corollary of a tension between two views of the field: as a profit-making support activity that focusses on outcomes, and as a complex, research-informed academic field. In light of this lack of recognition, and the relatively small body of literature around the professional identity of EAP practitioners (Ding and Bruce, 2017), for my EdD thesis, I conducted a study into the ways in which EAP practitioners in the UK construct their professional identities (Taylor, 2020), which revealed fragmented identities that either aligned with one of the conflicting views of EAP articulated by Ding and Bruce (2017) – academic or support service activity – or occupied a more liminal space. This chapter examines one theme that emerged from this larger study: how practitioners may perceive their identities as stigmatized.

Certain labels or terms used by EAP practitioners and others in higher education to describe EAP are problematized in the literature. These terms include the word 'support', often used to distinguish EAP from 'content' and to distinguish EAP practitioners from 'content lecturers' (Gavriel, 1999) or 'subject specialists' (Flowerdew and Peacock, 2001), and the word 'service' – often a synonym for support – which may be used to exclude EAP from traditional academic activities (Turner, 2012) and position 'EAP teachers as lower-status members of the academic hierarchy' (Benesch, 2001: 53). A further aspect of this labelling is the job titles used for EAP practitioners – usually 'tutor' or 'teacher' – which contrast with the traditional academic title 'lecturer', and which may be a means of allocating different, less favourable, working contracts to EAP practitioners (Ding and Bruce, 2017). Although these labels tend to be problematized in the literature, a recent study of contributions to the BALEAP discussion list (Ding, Bond and Bruce, 2022) suggests that there is disagreement among practitioners as to the acceptability of these labels. This chapter examines data from interviews with EAP practitioners in the UK in an attempt to understand how EAP practitioners may construct their identities in response to these labels, using the symbolic interactionist theories: the *looking-glass self* (Cooley, 1998), Goffman's notion of stigmatized identity (1968) and Becker's (1963) labelling theory. It also examines how they 'manage impressions' (Goffman, 1959) when discussing their identities as a means of effecting agency.

Theoretical framework: Symbolic interactionism

Symbolic interactionism (SI) is an approach to the study of social life and behaviour (Blumer, 1969) that developed from the ideas of the American pragmatists, who argued that there is no objective, true reality, but that knowledge is acquired actively and dynamically (Pascale, 2011). The premise of SI was that individuals and society are inseparable and are developed through shared meanings (Pascale, 2011). Although SI is a broad and heterogeneous approach, there are similarities in the ways its scholars view human group life (Blumer, 1969), the key tenets being that meanings are collective and created through interaction (Pascale, 2011).

Interaction and interpretation are key aspects of SI (Blumer, 1969). Individuals construct meaning from their own actions and from those of others – meaning is not inherent in actions but must be interpreted (Blumer, 1969). Individuals take different positions and act accordingly, but they also note and interpret the positions of others in working out their own line of action (Azarian, 2017). Thereby, a 'larger collective form of action' known as 'joint action' (Blumer, 1969: 70) is created through the construction of a shared interpretation of one another's actions. This chapter uses the following four symbolic interactionist theories to elucidate the responses of the interviewees.

The looking-glass self

One useful theory for understanding identity construction is Cooley's (1998) *looking-glass self*, the social self that develops through individuals' perception of how others view that self, and which develops from social interactions (Scott and Marshall, 2009). This idea of self has three main components: individuals imagine how others view them; then they imagine how others judge that view; and finally, their feelings are affected by that imagined judgement (Cooley, 1998). The imagined judgement is essential in creating the self-feeling, and, importantly, 'the character and weight of the other [. . .] makes all the difference with our feeling' (Cooley, 1998: 164). Thus, identity is a social construction which is constantly being adjusted according to people's perceptions of how others judge them. The remaining three theories below relate to how individuals construct their own identities in response to this *looking-glass self*, and how they may behave in relation to that construction.

Impression management

In response to this *looking-glass self* view that has been constructed, individuals attempt to manage the impressions of others in order to influence this view (Goffman, 1959). In other words, they perform for others, verbally and through other means of communication, and move towards forming a working consensus; they may not necessarily have the same views but maintain a harmonious relationship by acting as if they do (Goffman, 1959). Thus, identity is a result of collaborative interactions, which the actor uses to manage the impressions of others, and, in order to manage impressions, the actor presents an idealized version of the self which generally conforms to the norms of the group (Goffman, 1959; Hyland, 2012).

As implied above, the purpose of impression management may be to establish a 'collective identity', which Johnston, Laraña and Gusfield (1994) describe as 'the (often implicitly) agreed upon definition of membership, boundaries, and activities for the group' (1994: 15). Creating this collective identity involves negotiation and conflict, through which members 'construct the collective "we"' (1994: 15). In order to construct this collective identity, groups often engage in 'boundary maintenance', which involves setting boundaries around the social group, and 'the sharper the boundaries [...] the stronger the collective identity' (Johnston, Laraña and Gusfield, 1994: 20).

Labelling theory

Becker's (1963) labelling theory explores how labels applied to individuals may impact on their identities. Individuals may construct their identities in response to *looking-glass self* perceptions of the meanings they believe others attach to those labels. Becker (1963) used the concept of deviance to discuss how labelling is used in identity negotiation and formation. He argued that the concept of deviance is created by society in the sense that society establishes the rules whose infraction is labelled deviance. Deviance is thus not a feature of the person or act, but a consequence of the rules applied to the outsider; society has a shared meaning of deviance, and that meaning is then attached to the perceived deviant. Deviant behaviour is thus behaviour that is so labelled.

Being caught engaging in deviant behaviour has consequences for the identity of an individual, as it often results in the person being labelled a deviant. Related to this is the difference between one's 'master'– or main – status and one's auxiliary status traits (Becker, 1963). For instance, a doctor's master status might be her occupation as a doctor, but as a doctor, she might, for example, be expected to have certain auxiliary traits, such as being middle-class. If one is labelled a deviant, this becomes the master status assigned to (and possibly accepted by) the 'deviant', and various auxiliary traits are expected. For example, if a man is labelled a criminal, he might be expected to exhibit auxiliary traits such as dishonesty or further criminal activity.

Being labelled a deviant can often be a self-fulfilling prophecy (Becker, 1963). First, the branded deviant is cut off from certain social groups, which may then lead to the person being forced into activities which are deviant. For example, someone labelled a criminal might have difficulty finding legitimate work and may, therefore, be forced to resort to crime to survive. This labelling becomes complete when the deviant joins an organized deviant group and develops a feeling of commonality or belonging, which solidifies the identity as a deviant (Becker, 1963).

Becker's (1963) theory specifically explores the labelling of deviants, but it is not difficult to see how it may shed light on certain labels that are applied to EAP practitioners. For example, the labels of 'service' and 'support', which are frequently applied to EAP, may be accepted as a master status (with auxiliary traits such as being positioned within a support service department rather than an academic one, or being employed on a 'teaching-only' contract) by some EAP practitioners, thus solidifying their identity as a support service, while others may reject this label and construct an academic master status instead.

Stigmatized identities

Goffman's (1968) concept of stigmatized identities has some parallels with Becker's (1963) theories on deviance and labelling. Goffman (1968) distinguishes between the 'virtual social identity' – an identity created through the 'joint action' by which societies categorize people and associate certain traits with each category – we may attach to new acquaintances based on the first impression they make on us and the characteristics we attach to them because of this first impression and the 'actual social identity' which that person possesses. If characteristics emerge that conflict with the virtual social identity that has been constructed, and if these characteristics are viewed as less desirable than those we anticipated, the new acquaintance then becomes tainted. This is what Goffman refers to as stigma. The stigmatizing attribute is not undesirable in itself – it is undesirable in relation to the virtual social self that has been constructed. For example, if the 'virtual social identity' of a university teacher is seen to possess characteristics such as research activity or the job title of 'lecturer', EAP practitioners may perceive themselves – through a *looking-glass self* construction of their identities – to be stigmatized by having an 'actual social identity' that is characterized by a teaching-only role and the job title of 'teacher'.

Goffman refers to 'those who do not depart negatively from the expectations at issue' (1968: 15) as 'normals'. The stigmatized person may feel 'normal' but may perceive that others 'do not really "accept" him [or her] and are not ready to make contact with him [or her] on "equal grounds"' (1968: 18). Stigmatized individuals may form in-group alignments with fellow stigmatized individuals and this group may claim to be the 'real group [. . .] to which [the stigmatized individual] *naturally* belongs' (Goffman, 1968: 137 original emphasis). They are considered loyal if they align themselves with their 'real' group and foolish if they align themselves with others. Those who align themselves with the in-group may exaggerate their stigmatized identities, resulting in further alienation from 'normals' and reinforcing the in-group as a 'real' group. Stigmatized individuals might also join out-groups by aligning themselves with 'normals'. Furthermore, stigmatized individuals construct their own identities in relation to 'the degree to which their stigma is apparent or obtrusive' (Goffman, 1968: 130) and may then distance themselves from those who are more stigmatized. The more stigmatized individuals align themselves with 'normals', the less stigmatized they feel (Goffman, 1968).

These ideas around stigma may help to elucidate how labels applied to EAP practitioners may be perceived to be stigmatizing and how this may affect practitioners' construction of their own professional identities. The idea of in-group or out-group alignments might also shed light on the ways in which practitioners position themselves as either academics or support service workers.

Criticism of symbolic interactionism

Some scholars have suggested symbolic interactionism is overly focussed on the social nature of identity and neglects the individual (e.g. Hyland, 2012). Conversely, Archer (2000) argues that Goffman's self 'operates in a social arena by merely donning and doffing masks [. . .] without becoming anything through the social relations it sustains (too much self; too little of the social)' (p. 78). In response to Archer, I would argue that Goffman's (1959) impression management is by nature social, as one needs to interpret the actions of others before one can attempt to manage their impressions. There may be some merit to Hyland's argument, but it seems to me that the individual is clearly apparent in theories within the approach, as evidenced by notions such as impression management – a manifestation of agency, as Archer suggests – and the choice of stigmatized individuals to align themselves with either in-groups (choosing to internalize labels) or out-groups (choosing to reject them). As Archer (2002) also points out, the difficulty in theorizing agency is understanding how an individual can both be shaped by society and also influence it, but that individuals are active and reflexive and that they are continuously reflecting and reacting to life. SI may have limitations, but it is a very useful lens through which researchers can attempt to interpret that reflection and reaction.

Methodology

In-depth interviews

This study employed qualitative in-depth interviews in line with the symbolic interactionist research principle that 'human interactions form the central source of data' (Berg and Lune, 2012: 12). As my aim was to understand how practitioners construct their own professional identities, it was important to examine their views and feelings in depth and to allow the voices of the practitioners themselves to be heard (Esterberg, 2002).

Recruiting participants

Participants were recruited through the BALEAP email discussion list because this was the most efficient way to contact a large number of EAP practitioners, and I wanted participants with a broad range of experience, qualifications and working conditions. One limitation of this method is that it meant restricting participants to BALEAP members, whose engagement with BALEAP might suggest that they are likely to be more experienced. Those enrolled on the email list are also likely to be those practitioners with a certain level of engagement in the profession. A further disadvantage was that practitioners on temporary contracts are less likely to have access to institutional membership of the organization and might not be able to afford the fee for individual membership. I recruited seventeen volunteers (eleven women, six men) with a reasonable range of experience, qualifications and contract types (see Table 8.1), who were, or had been, employed at universities in England, Scotland and Wales.

Designing the interview schedule

The interview schedule comprised several questions to guide proceedings but also with the freedom to evolve according to what was said (Newby, 2014) in order to gain a rich understanding of participants' beliefs about their own identities. I was interested in a number of issues that are frequently discussed in various EAP forums and how these may be tied up with practitioner identity, including how job titles and roles are related to EAP professional identity, whether practitioners identify themselves as academics or support service workers and how practitioners feel about the language we use to talk about ourselves. These issues are fairly frequently discussed in the literature (e.g. Bell, 2016; Ding and Bruce, 2017; Turner, 2004) or in less formal settings, including conferences (e.g. Bruce, 2017) and the BALEAP discussion list, but they are also issues that resonate with my professional experience and identity. The interview questions related to the findings presented in this chapter were:

1. In job descriptions, EAP practitioners are more often referred to as 'tutors' or 'teachers' than as lecturers. Does this matter to you?
2. We are often referred to as 'support', which has been critiqued in the literature. What do you think about this terminology?
3. How would you describe the status of EAP practitioners in higher education?
4. Are there any aspects of your professional status/identity that you would like to improve?
5. How do you think others in the academy view you?
6. What do you consider your professional identity to be?

8. A Marginalized, Stigmatized Profession?

Table 8.1 Overview of participants

Pseudonym	Job title	Contract type	Experience	Teaching qualification + highest qualification
Jane	Senior Lecturer	Permanent	25 years in ELT; 12 of those in EAP	CELTA, PhD in EAP
Ingrid	EAP Teacher	Permanent	1 year in EAP	CELTA, MA Applied Linguistics
Paul	Pathways Manager	Permanent	Over 20 years in ELT, over 7 years EAP	MA + MPhil Anglophone Studies, CELTA
Maria	Teaching Associate	Fixed term	14 years in ELT/ESP; 2 pre-sessionals in EAP	MEd
Pete	EAP Tutor	Fixed term (soon to be permanent)	25 years in ELT, about 5 years in EAP	CELTA, Delta, undergraduate degree
Dave	-	Freelance	Over 40 years in ELT, ESP and EAP	MA Applied Linguistics
Kim	EAP Tutor (soon to be Lecturer)	Permanent	13 years in ELT; several years in EAP	MA Ancient Greek, Delta
Emily	EAP Tutor (soon to be Lecturer)	Permanent	About 20 years in ELT; 5 of those in EAP	CELTA, Delta, doing MA TEAP
Mike	EAP Tutor	Permanent	About 14 years in ELT; about 5 of those in EAP	MA Applied Linguistics and TESOL
Sue	EFL Tutor	Fixed term	14 years in ELT; about 5 of those in EAP	CELTA, PGCE ESOL, MA Applied Linguistics
Ildiko	EAP Subject Leader	Permanent	32 years in ELT	PhD US Literature, PhD Applied Linguistics
Tina	EAP Lecturer	P/T (0.5) permanent	30 years in ELT, 6 of those in EAP	PhD
Rebecca	EAP Tutor	Permanent	11 years in EFL/ESOL, 6 of those in EAP	CELTA, Delta, MA Media and Culture
Steve	Senior Language Tutor	Permanent	36 years in ELT, more than 20 years in EAP	Cert Ed, DELTA, PhD
Maureen	Course Director	Permanent	5 years in ELT, then 18 in EAP	TEFL course, Delta, MA TESOL
Beth	Lecturer	Permanent	At least 7 years in ELT, writing and EAP	MA ESP, CELTA
Graham	Not employed	Fixed term (previously)	Two EAP pre-sessionals; about 11 years in EFL	CELTA, BA English Language and Linguistics

Data coding and analysis

I used thematic coding to analyse the data. The coding was iterative, involving many attempts at coding and recoding in three different stages, in line with King and Horrocks' (2010) advice. The first stage, descriptive coding, involved labelling pieces of data that might be helpful in answering the research questions. Stage 2, interpretive coding, involved grouping descriptive codes that might have a common meaning and then attempting to capture this meaning in the form of an interpretive code. The final stage was to identify the main themes that emerged from the interpretive coding, being mindful of what my SI theories might be able to offer in terms of interpreting what the interviewees were saying.

Ethical considerations

Ethical approval was obtained for the study and ethical guidelines carefully followed. Participants were fully informed of their rights and what the study involved, and every effort was made to preserve their anonymity.

Findings and discussion

A major theme that emerged from the data analysis was that of stigmatized identities, which is explored in the following three sections. Firstly, interviewees sometimes saw the labels associated with EAP – including the term 'support' to refer to what we do and the job titles 'tutor' or 'teacher'– as stigmatizing or marginalizing. Secondly, there was also a considerable amount of derogatory language used by the interviewees to refer to EAP, which suggests a view of the field as stigmatized. However, there was also quite strong resistance to the notion of EAP as marginalized or stigmatized, as discussed in the third section. The way interviewees articulated these views suggests that they tended to position themselves within either the support service or the academic field view of EAP.

Stigmatizing labels: Support, tutors and teachers

Labels such 'support', 'service', 'tutor' or 'teacher' do not hold inherent meaning; EAP practitioners construct meaning through their interaction with others and their interpretation of how others use these labels (Blumer, 1969). Therefore, it is useful to attempt to understand their interpretations in order to gain an understanding of the identity they have constructed for themselves. Interviewees appeared to attach different meanings to these labels, resulting in different identity constructions. There was a sense from a number of responses that the labels attached to EAP, either by ourselves or by others, have a stigmatizing function. The word 'support' connotes positively with notions of facilitating student learning, but it may also be used to 'other' EAP and to create a false dichotomy between so-called content knowledge and language knowledge (Scott and Turner, 2008).

This tension between the two interpretations of the word 'support' was reflected in the participants' responses to questions about the use of the term. Almost all of the interviewees used the word at least once when describing their roles, and responses varied when they were asked their views about the way the word 'support' is often problematized in the literature. Some participants appeared to agree with those in the literature (e.g. Turner, 2012) who argue that the term 'support' subordinates EAP to content knowledge. In the following example, the interviewee appears to suggest that positioning EAP as a 'service' or 'support' makes it 'subservient' and less than a 'full member' of the academy:

> You do feel that you're providing a service rather than a full member of an academic university, which is ironic because we've got three people with PhDs in our department [...] and it's a bit of a kick in the teeth, I think, when you've got your PhD, or you are research active [...] but you're not recognized outside of that within the university. I don't think they have a clue sometimes what we do. I think they see us as subservient. We are a support role for their *real* stuff. (Kim)

Some participants connected the use of the word 'support' with administrative positioning in departments such as Corporate Services or Professional Services rather than in academic departments. For some practitioners, the terms 'service' and 'support' seem to have a marginalizing or stigmatizing function, particularly in terms of indicating that EAP is not an academic activity, as suggested by Kim's reference to not being a 'full member of an academic university' and to being support for 'their *real* stuff'. This also appears to be reflected in the following comment:

> Initially it was the Language Centre – academic English for international students – then we merged with the Modern Languages department, which they didn't like at all because they thought they were proper academics, and we are just supporting people. (Tina)

Here the word 'supporting' seems to have been constructed as a 'deviant' label in the sense that 'supporting people' are perceived as inferior to the 'proper academics'. Both Becker's (1963) notion of deviance and Goffman's (1968) stigma are socially constructed in the sense that stigma or deviance are not undesirable in themselves – they are undesirable in relation to a socially constructed view of how individuals should be. In other words, both Kim and Tina seem to view this label as stigmatizing or othering in relation to the 'normal' (Goffman, 1968) identity of an academic, and this seems to reveal feelings of vulnerability in their position. Kim, in particular, seems to align herself with the academic 'out-group' (Goffman, 1968) when she refers to EAP practitioners not being recognized despite having PhDs and being research active.

However, the tension between the positive and negative connotations of support meant that interviewees might have a more nuanced view on the extent to which the term is stigmatizing:

> A word I don't like used with regard to EAP is 'support' because . . . Joan Turner wrote about metaphors used, and she imagined support with walking sticks and Zimmer frames and things like that, and I agree with that. A couple of years ago, I saw an advert for a prestigious university wanting a senior lecturer in law, *so it's a serious job*. It said: 'in this job, you will support undergraduate and postgraduate students', and I thought, 'that's alright if a senior lecturer at a prestigious university can use the word "support" about their teaching at master's and PhD level, then we shouldn't worry about it'. (Dave)

Although Dave seems to be suggesting that perhaps the term 'support' should not be stigmatized, I detected a note of sarcasm in his words 'if a senior lecturer [. . .] can use the word "support" [. . .] then we shouldn't worry about that' and his reference to 'a serious job' in juxtaposition to EAP, which suggests that he does not necessarily subscribe to that view. This is borne out by his agreement with Turner's metaphorical conceptualization of Zimmer frames and walking sticks. Therefore, there was a definite sense that he felt the label was stigmatizing when used in conjunction with EAP.

The job titles 'teacher' or 'tutor' also appear to have been perceived by some to have an 'othering' or stigmatizing function. Some appeared to feel that job titles were an important signifier of status and worth within the academy. For example, Jane, a senior lecturer at her institution, explains that this title is very important to her in terms of status:

> I'm very proud to have that job title because I know not all professionals in my field have that [. . .] I care very much what I'm called. I think that's because I'm not new to the profession, and I'm not at a stage when I feel those things don't matter – they *do matter* – and they can be taken away so easily by some private provider coming in and saying 'now you're going to be an instructor' [. . .] It concerns me when I see EAP staff who are called things like Language Fellow, Language Tutor or Instructor. I do feel that unfortunately there are lot of EAP departments where staff don't have the posts, recognition and stability as well – I think stability is a major issue – that they deserve. (Jane, Senior Lecturer)

Goffman (1968) argues that the stigmatized person may feel 'normal' but may perceive that others 'do not really "accept" him [or her] and are not ready to make contact with him [or her] on "equal grounds"' (1968: 18). Jane appears to feel on 'equal grounds' with other academics at her university but that a non-academic job title would render her less acceptable to others. The job title 'senior lecturer' is an insignia of her rank and, therefore, forms part of the personal front (Goffman, 1959) she presents to her audience in order to maintain the identity she has constructed for herself. Her reference to 'some private provider coming in and saying: "now you're going to be an instructor"' suggests that she feels her position within the academy is vulnerable, so she uses impression management techniques – such as engaging in PhD research related to EAP – in order to validate the identity she ascribes to herself. She also makes the point that job titles may also have practical implications in the form of job instability linked to the contracts that often accompany these titles.

The symbolic nature of job titles as insignias of rank, and therefore a means to subordinate EAP practitioners, was also highlighted by the following interviewee:

> Titles often exist for other people, as a sort of symbol, something on the CV, and we are, therefore, disadvantaged by having these different titles and lesser-seeming titles. To most, 'lecturer' or 'professor', or whatever our academic colleagues get, seems far more important than 'tutor' or 'teacher', and that's an issue. So we are disadvantaged by these titles [. . .] These titles *do* make a difference, if we want to be treated as equal in this field, if people don't recognize what we do, etc., and even just for our own sense of what we do – so many of us are getting PhDs and getting so highly specialized – there should be some signifier for that, so the titles are important [. . .] It's not just important for me and my colleagues but for the field and people coming into it, this should be recognized. (Beth, EAP Lecturer)

Despite having the job title 'lecturer', Beth still expresses concerns about the use of other titles for EAP practitioners. It seems her identity is not just constructed around her current status and position in her own work, but also situated within the field of EAP as a whole. She appears, thus, to be engaging in sensemaking, a kind of 'joint action' (Blumer, 1969) in which members of a group develop shared meanings (Patriotta and Spedale, 2009). Identities are constructed through social interaction, during which sensemakers are constantly redefining themselves (Weick, 1995). Our own perceived identity has an effect on how outsiders perceive us and behave towards us, which then 'stabilizes or destabilizes our identity' (Weick, Sutcliffe and Obstfeld, 2005: 22). Thus, the symbolic nature of job titles appears important to Beth because 'who we are lies in the hands of others' (Weick, Sutcliffe and Obstfeld, 2005: 22). In other words, Beth's own identity as a lecturer is reliant on a shared meaning – within the field of EAP as well as the academy as a whole – of EAP practitioners as lecturers (academics) rather than the less prestigious job titles of 'tutor' or 'teacher', which undermine the specialist nature of what we do.

Stigmatizing words we use to describe ourselves

Another suggestion that participants constructed their identities as stigmatized was the derogatory terms they sometimes used to refer to the field or EAP practitioners. These did not appear to be the participants' own representations of the field, but rather a *looking-glass self* identity they had constructed from how they felt they were perceived by others in the academy. The following are examples of this kind of *looking glass self* identity:

> We described ourselves once in semi-jest as being 'pond life'. (Pete)
> Currently [EAP] is in the gutter with all the support providers. (Ildiko)

> We're supposedly in this commercial bubble. (Sue)
> We felt like the Cinderellas of the department. (Sue)
> The poor relation. (Maureen)

What these terms seem to have in common is a sense that EAP practitioners have a stigmatized outsider identity. The interviewees quoted here appear to view EAP practitioners as marginalized because they are perceived to be inferior in some way.

When asked, a number of participants identified themselves as 'teachers', and this core identity was apparent through many of the topics discussed in the interviews. It seemed to represent, to an extent, a collective identity that interviewees were proud of. This identity as teachers, and as effective teachers in particular, seems to be a form of boundary maintenance through which participants appeared to 'construct the collective "we"' (Johnston, Laraña and Gusfield, 1994: 15) of EAP, in that many EAP practitioners may be denied an academic identity through administrative positioning in non-academic departments, or through teaching-only contracts, but their identity as effective teachers was something that could not be challenged. The following example highlights how the teacher identity may be constructed as something valued and of equal status to other academic identities, even though EAP is often positioned in support service departments:

> I see myself as a teacher, and I think there's a reason we all pick the term 'teacher'. I think there's something there where we see our role as giving [. . .] students the understanding and the skills they need to succeed, so that to me is a direct fit with HE because very few students come in with that, even the cleverest in your native language, there are always ways they can do better [. . .] It should be on equal footing with other academics. Here at X University, we're sort of put in this weird student support side of it. (Beth)

This suggests that practitioners may construct their own identities as effective teachers who consider themselves to be professionals in order to assert their own self-worth in the face of perceived stigmatization.

Another word used to describe EAP practitioners that seems to contrast with how practitioners see themselves was 'gatekeepers':

> [The students] see us as gatekeepers. (Pete)
>
> I do feel that some of the departments we certainly deal with have that kind of gatekeeper approach of, you know 'On the IFP[1] you should only be sending us those who're really good. Make sure anyone who's not going to get a first doesn't come across'. (Paul)

These participants appear to attach a stigmatized meaning to the notion of gatekeeping. This role may conflict with their identity as effective teachers engaged in supporting students and might be seen to contradict the 'moral purposefulness'

(Nixon et al., 2001: 234) associated with being a professional. As in earlier examples, the notion of EAP practitioners as gatekeepers seems to be a *looking-glass self* perception of how EAP is viewed by outsiders; however, this sort of stigmatizing language was not always used to indicate a perceived outsider view. In the following examples, the participants appear to accept that EAP should be positioned differently:

> A lot of us are glorified EFL teachers. (Paul)
>
> It's a little bit pretentious to be called a lecturer if you don't do lecturing. I suppose I have a very simplistic view of the hierarchy. The teacher comes right at the bottom of the ladder, the lowest of the low of those who teach at university [. . .] we're still at the bottom of the heap. (Graham)

As will be discussed in the next section, participants sometimes resisted the notion that EAP should have greater status, and the above comments seem to suggest that EAP has the status it deserves. This may be 'face-work' – the adjustments and repairs individuals make to the image they present to others when managing impressions (Goffman, 1967) – in response to the 'face threat' (Goffman, 1967) implicit in my questions about the status of EAP practitioners. For example, Graham's response to any perceived stigmatization appears to be to accept the 'deviant' label – aligning himself with the 'in-group' (Goffman, 1968) – and to construct his identity around that label so as to avoid being seen as status-seeking.

The following comment suggests that these stigmatized identities are self-constructed, and that more successful impression management might mitigate them somehow:

> Is it a self-fulfilling prophecy that because sometimes we *think* we're the poor cousins, we *become* the poor cousins? [. . .] I think it's very easy to feel the poor cousin, and I think to a certain extent that's how we are made to feel by academics. But if we continue to believe that there is a deficit model, and that we are the poor cousins, and if we don't take stock of ourselves and our positions and say: 'Actually, hell no! We are pedagogically really really strong, so, you know what, we're not going to buy into this. We're going to put ourselves forward as being every bit as good as you are, just differently'. (Pete)

Again, the effective teacher identity seems to be used to assert Pete's agency and self-worth in response to a perception that EAP is viewed as the 'poor cousin' and something that should be 'shouted loudly' (as he put it earlier in the interview) in order to counter the perceived stigmatized identity.

Resistance to the notion of a stigmatized identity

Although, as described above, some participants appeared to view their identities as stigmatized, there was also strong resistance to the notion of EAP as stigmatized or marginalized. The following comment is an example of this:

> I've got a colleague who has bought into this notion that I hear a lot of in EAP circles, that we are not respected and the academy looks down on us [. . .] If you go to Physics and say 'what do you think of Law?', they'll say 'Law is a waste of time', and if you go to Law, they'll say that the Marketing people, 'that's not a proper academic subject'. I don't think there's a cohesive core, the academy; I don't believe that exists. I mean it's basically a bunch of individuals and they probably all think their particular subject is very important and not given enough respect. (Mike)

Mike appears to reject any collective identity (Johnston, Laraña and Gusfield, 1994) of EAP as marginalized, but instead seems to position EAP within a disparate academic community composed of fragmented identities, of which EAP is merely one, and not one that is stigmatized in relation to the others. He also distances himself from the idea that the job titles assigned to EAP practitioners have a stigmatizing function:

> I'm not embarrassed to be a tutor, I don't think I'm a lecturer, whatever that means. It's just a name. I'm only impressed with what someone has done or what they're saying than what their title is. (Mike)

The fact that he uses the word 'embarrassed' suggests that he has constructed a *looking-glass self* view that other EAP practitioners may feel embarrassed by the title, and he is managing impressions so as to distance himself from this perception, perhaps to avoid it becoming a self-fulfilling prophecy, as Pete suggests above. In a similar vein, the participant below does not seem to feel that being viewed as support confers any inferior status to EAP:

> I *do* see it as support [. . .] they need help to be able to succeed in their studies and they need different types of help or information or knowledge or skills. And some of that information, knowledge and skills is provided by their content lecturers, and some is provided by us. My view is we are different, but that doesn't make it hierarchical, so it doesn't mean that what they get from their content tutor is better or more important because for some of them, it's not. (Emily)

By setting boundaries between the support offered by EAP practitioners and the knowledge provided by 'content lecturers', and thereby making a 'we–they distinction', Emily may be aiming to create a stronger collective identity for EAP (Johnston, Laraña and Gusfield, 1994: 20) and rejecting the positioning of EAP as stigmatized.

The apparent desire to distance EAP from EFL was a thread that ran through many of the discussions, echoing a persistent theme in the literature of defining EAP in terms of its differences from EFL/general English (Campion, 2016) and frequently presenting EAP as superior (Ding and Bruce, 2017). EAP practitioners seem to distance themselves from EFL in order to maintain boundaries around their EAP identity and perhaps position themselves as less stigmatized than EFL teachers. This boundary maintenance is somewhat complex because, although practitioners sometimes distanced themselves from EFL, there was also a sense that this background was linked to their identity as effective teachers. The following comment suggests that the participant wishes to distance himself from an identity that considers titles to be important, but he also sets a boundary between EFL teachers and EAP practitioners, perhaps indicating that in some ways status is important to him:

> People take their titles or positions a bit too seriously. I'm not saying this is 100% of people, but a lot of us are glorified EFL teachers. Not all of us(!), but a lot of us have come from that background and we're in positions which are much much better than working in a language school, and for me I'm happy about that every day. (Paul)

Although he suggests that titles are unimportant to him, he appears to construct EFL teachers as stigmatized and EAP practitioners as being in a higher status position with better working conditions. Therefore, by maintaining boundaries around his EAP identity, he is able to distance himself from any stigmatized identity. These boundary-maintaining discourses, including the self-identification of EAP practitioners as effective teachers, provide 'security for individuals by making the world meaningful and populated by others who have similar understandings and ways of sharing ideas' (Hyland, 2012: 11).

Conclusion

This chapter has examined how the labels and terms we EAP practitioners use to talk about ourselves may reveal stigmatized identities. Interviewees' perspectives on these labels reveal fragmented identities that appear to mostly align with either the stigmatized in-group – support service teachers who take pride in their teaching ability and view themselves as support – or the out-group – academics who 'are getting PhDs and getting so highly specialized' (Beth). The main implication of these identity constructions is that the lack of shared meanings with regard to EAP identity results in a fragmented profession. This suggests that EAP needs to carve out a unique identity for itself, as expressed by a number of participants. However, attempts to carve out this identity by distancing EAP from EFL may alienate practitioners who construct their identities around their EFL backgrounds. It may also create hierarchies in the field by suggesting that novice EAP practitioners with an EFL background are somehow 'other' within the profession.

Another implication is that practitioners might be alienated by discourses of marginalization and stigmatization if they do not attach the same meanings to these discourses or view them as reflective of their own identities and practice settings. As discussed above, some interviewees resisted these discourses, which they perceived to be prevalent 'in EAP circles' (Mike). This may result in increased fragmentation if they do not align themselves with this 'collective "we"' (Johnston, Laraña and Gusfield, 1994) that is often presented in the literature. Most participants appeared to view themselves as having agency, either in embracing their role as service workers and exhibiting pride in their teaching ability, or obtaining the insignias of rank of academics, such as obtaining PhDs or engaging in research activity in order to align themselves with that identity. The main implication of this is the need to construct a stronger collective EAP identity. We cannot attempt to effect agency unless we confront the fragmented nature of the EAP profession and understand what agency means to those involved.

Note

1 International Foundation Programme.

References

Archer, M. S. (2000), *Being Human: The Problem of Agency*, Cambridge: Cambridge University Press.

Archer, M. S. (2002), 'Realism and the Problem of Agency', *Alethia*, 5 (1): 11–20. https://doi.org/10.1558/aleth.v5i1.11

Azarian, R. (2017), 'Joint Actions, Stories and Symbolic Structures: A Contribution to Herbert Blumer's Conceptual Framework', *Sociology*, 51 (3): 685–700. https://doi.org/10.1177/0038038515609029

Becker, H. S. (1963), *Outsiders: Studies in the Sociology of Deviance*, New York: Free Press.

Bell, D. E. (2016), 'Practitioners, Pedagogies and Professionalism in English for Academic Purposes (EAP): The Development of a Contested Field', PhD thesis, University of Nottingham, UK. http://eprints.nottingham.ac.uk/38570/

Benesch, S. (2001), *Critical English for Academic Purposes: Theory, Politics and Practice*, Abingdon: Routledge.

Berg, B. L. and H. Lune (2012), *Qualitative Research Methods for the Social Sciences*, London: Pearson.

Blumer, H. (1969), *Symbolic Interactionism*, London: University of California.

Bruce, I. (2017), Discussion paper. Presented at *BALEAP ResTes: Knowledge and the EAP Practitioner: A Symposium*, The University of Leeds.

Burke, P. J. and M. Hermerschmidt (2005), 'Deconstructing Academic Practices through Self-reflexive Pedagogies', in B. V. Street (ed.), 346–65, *Literacies across Education Contexts: Mediating Learning and Teaching*, Philadelphia: Caslon Inc.

Campion, G. C. (2016), 'The Learning Never Ends': Exploring Teachers' Views on the Transition from General English to EAP', *Journal of English for Academic Purposes*, 23: 59–70. https://doi.org/10.1016/j.jeap.2016.06.003

Cooley, C. H. (1998), *On Self and Social Organization*, Chicago: University of Chicago Press.

Ding, A. (2019), 'EAP Practitioner Identity', in K. Hyland and L. L. C. Wong (eds), *Specialised English: New Directions in ESP and EAP Research and Practice*, 63–76, London: Routledge.

Ding, A., B. Bond and I. Bruce (2022), '"Clearly You Have Nothing Better to do With Your Time than this": A Critical Historical Exploration of Contributions to the BALEAP Discussion List', *Journal of English for Academic Purposes*, 58. https://doi.org/10.1016/j.jeap.2022.101109

Ding, A. and I. Bruce (2017), *The English for Academic Purposes Practitioner: Operating on the Edge of Academia*, Cham, Switzerland: Palgrave Macmillan.

Esterberg, K. G. (2002), *Qualitative Methods in Social Research*, Boston: McGraw-Hill.

Flowerdew, J. and M. Peacock (2001), 'Issues in EAP: A Preliminary Perspective', in J. Flowerdew and M. Peacock (eds), *Research Perspectives on English for Academic Purposes*, 8–24, Cambridge: Cambridge University Press.

Gavriel, A. (1999), 'English for Very Specific Teaching: Bilateral Gap-Filling in British Higher Education or How can We Internationalise the Staff?', in H. Bool and P. Luford (eds), *Academic Standards and Expectations: The Role of EAP*, 19–27, Nottingham: Nottingham University Press.

Goffman, E. (1959), *The Presentation of Self in Everyday Life*, Harmondsworth: Penguin.

Goffman, E. (1967), *Interaction ritual: Essays on face-to-face behaviour*, New Brunswick: Transaction Publishers.

Goffman, E. (1968), *Stigma: Notes on the Management of Spoiled Identity*, Harmondsworth: Penguin.

Hyland, K. (2012), *Disciplinary Identities: Individuality and Community in Academic Discourse*, Cambridge: Cambridge University Press.

Johnston, H., E. Laraña and J. R. Gusfield (1994), 'Identities, Grievances, and New Social Movements', in E. Laraña, H. Johnston and J. R. Gusfield (eds), *New Social Movements: From Ideology to Identity*, 3–35, Philadelphia: Temple University Press.

King, N. and C. Horrocks (2010), *Interviews in Qualitative Research*, London: Sage Publications.

Newby, P. (2014), *Research Methods for Education*, 2nd edn, Harlow: Pearson Education.

Nixon, J., A. Marks, S. Rowland and M. Walker (2001), 'Towards a New Academic Professionalism: A Manifesto of Hope', *British Journal of Sociology of Education*, 22 (2): 227–44. http://dx.doi.org/10.1080/01425690124202

Pascale, C. (2011), 'Symbolic Interaction', in C. Pascale, *Cartographies of Knowledge: Exploring Qualitative Epistemologies*, 77–104, Thousand Oaks: Sage Publications.

Patriotta, G. and S. Spedale (2009), 'Making Sense through Face: Identity and Social Interaction in a Consultancy Task Force', *Organization Studies*, 30 (11): 1227–48. https://doi.org/10.1177%2F0170840609347036

Scott, J. and G. Marshall (2009), *A Dictionary of Sociology*, 3rd edn, Oxford: Oxford University Press.

Scott, M. and J. Turner (2008), 'Problematising Proofreading', *Zeitschrift Schreiben*. https://zeitschrift-schreiben.eu/globalassets/zeitschrift-schreiben.eu/2008/scott_proofreading.pdf

Taylor, S. (2020), *An Enquiry into How English for Academic Purposes Practitioners Construct their Professional Identities*. EdD Thesis, The University of Roehampton. https://pure.roehampton.ac.uk/portal/en/studentTheses/an-enquiry-into-how-english-for-academic-purposes-practitioners-c

Turner, J. (2004), 'Language as Academic Purpose', *Journal of English for Academic Purposes*, 3 (2): 95–109. https://doi.org/10.1016/S1475-1585(03)00054-7

Turner, J. (2012), 'Academic Literacies: Providing a Space for the Socio-political Dynamics of EAP', *Journal of English for Academic Purposes*, 11 (1): 17–25. https://doi.org/10.1016/j.jeap.2011.11.007

Weick, K. E. (1995), *Sensemaking in Organizations*, Thousand Oaks: Sage Publications.

Weick, K. E., K. M. Sutcliffe and D. Obstfeld (2005), 'Organizing and the Process of Sensemaking', *Organization and Strategy*, 16 (4): 409–21. https://doi.org/10.1287/orsc.1050.0133

Chapter 9

EAP TEACHER AGENCY IN A DIGITAL AGE

Blair Matthews

Introduction

In English for academic purposes (EAP) there has been an increased recognition of the importance of teacher agency, the power that teachers have over the nature and quality of their practices (Bond, 2020; Ding and Bruce, 2017; Larsen-Freeman, 2019; Qi and Wang, 2022; Tao and Gao, 2021). Teachers know their own students and their own contexts and are best-placed to make decisions about their own classrooms (Priestley, Biesta and Robinson, 2015). Teacher agency is a key concept in teacher development, and it is evident in the BALEAP TEAP Fellowship Scheme (2014) and the TEAP Competency Framework (2008) under personal learning, development and autonomy. Meanwhile, discourses of digital technology emphasize choice, often promising to liberate teachers and students from the constraints of the classroom. Approaches such as blended or flipped learning are presented as empowering for teachers and students, and learning analytics offer opportunities for efficient task selection and personalization. Technology would therefore seem like a good fit for teacher agency. However, for all that technology offers, it can impose practices, values and routines that may be incongruous or inconsistent with a teacher's beliefs about teaching and learning (MacGilchrist, 2019; Williamson, 2017; Watters, 2021). Technical constraints may take the form of the prescription of content or methods. Alternatively, software may involve the technicalized evaluation of students, limiting the judgement of the teacher and working against notions of teacher agency (Selwyn et al., 2020; Knox Williamson and Bayne, 2020). In this chapter, I investigate the agency of five EAP teachers relating to technology, observing its emergence from an assemblage of technical objects, practices and discourses.

Biesta (2008: 20) defines teacher agency as 'the situation where individuals are able to exert control over their (practices)'. There is a consensus in social theory that agency is structured; social structures (interpreted broadly as the complex webs of relations that make up society, such as the family, education or work) constrain and enable individuals, granting opportunities and access to resources or limiting choices (Giddens, 1982; Bourdieu, 1978; Sewell, 1992; Archer, 1995, 2003; Emirbayer and Mische, 1998). Miranda Fricker (2007: 12) distinguishes between two types of structural power: active power, or the capacity for an actor to exercise power granted by their position within a structure, such as a teacher marking a student's work, and passive power, the power that operates purely structurally (where no actor exercises their power directly), for example, the attention that university admissions give to student marks. Without the presence of the passive power, the active power of the teacher will have little effect on students. Technology may grant active power to a teacher by offering new affordances (for example allowing a teacher the option to give feedback electronically, or providing online spaces for collaborative learning). Technology also exerts passive power. For instance, if a technical platform tracks student data and makes it visible, then it may make it necessary for the teacher to use this data regardless of whether the teacher values this approach or not. Similarly, if a classroom is installed with an interactive whiteboard, then there is often an expectation that teachers will use it, requiring classroom practices to accommodate the technology. Therefore, inquiry into teacher agency must consider both the capacity for individuals to act and the contexts within which their choices are realized. Teacher agency is situated within complex arrangements of conflict and compromise with other actors, each with their own agency, providing the contexts in which decisions are made about teaching and learning (Priestley, Biesta and Robinson, 2015).

A key mechanism in how teacher agency is realized is through reflexive thought. As humans make their way through the world they reflect on their experiences, engendering 'a feel for the game'. The nature of the arrangements of various structures, therefore, elicits from their participants a particular logic. For example, a relatively stable assemblage of familiar objects and established processes elicits habitual dispositions ('I know what to do'). However, technical change introduces the potential for rupture to established values and routines (what Archer (2003) calls the *reflexive imperative*); habit is no longer a guide and participants are compelled to think about what to do instead, resulting in the negotiation of new habits and practices. The more that circumstances change, the more there is a need to work hard reflexively to figure things out. The thinking around technical practices is realized through choices and practices regarding technology, which become codified into technicalized social structures. The increased technicalization of classrooms provides an example of the reflexive imperative in action. For example, in a study of the sudden shift to digital learning of language teachers during the COVID-19 lockdowns, Ashton (2022) observes how teachers reflexively redirected their practices to fulfil short-term goals in the sudden absence of long-term orientations.

The reflexive process is complicated, however, by the passive power of technology. For example, the platform Microsoft Teams started off life as a chat-based workspace and videoconferencing platform. It subsequently expanded by offering opportunities for collaboration, sharing and discussion. Over time, new features have been added, including the ability to upload documents, provide feedback, grade assignments and assign breakout rooms. Teachers can monitor and interact with students, and it is also possible for an institution to get a holistic view of all the activity being generated through the platform. While the affordances of such software have been very welcome, in this context it is the technology that is often dictating teaching and learning practices. Rather than teachers reflecting on their own practices ('what do I do?'), the introduction of such software invites its users to exercise reflexive deliberation relating to the functioning of the platform (i.e. what does *it* do?). Digital platforms such as Microsoft Teams represent complex socio-technical systems, hybrids of technical and social processes with their own practices and values coded into the functioning of the software. While the teacher has the autonomy to make choices about the technology, they are still confined to the practices granted by the system. Any alternative approach requires alternative technicalized responses.

Therefore, technology has the potential to take power away from teachers. Tsang and Qin (2020), in a study on the emotional labour of teachers, associate digital technology with the potential for *technical disempowerment* – the deprival of teachers' power to control their teaching practices through the passive power of technology (which they equate with deskilling). Tsang (2019) particularly laments what he sees as the tendency for institutions to ideologically value the technical purposes of teachers' work over its pedagogical purposes (the conflation of technical practices with pedagogical practices). Such disempowerment of teachers, he argues, may result in only a narrow conception of learning (for example to pass a test or achieve the learning outcomes), and consequently technology often becomes associated with the instrumentalization of teaching.

One reason for this, Tsang argues, is a tendency for teacher agency to be conflated with autonomy, which is often presented as an ideal type of agency (though it is possible to exercise agency in any number of ways; Archer (2012) outlines a series of *modes* of human agency). Gershon (2011) argues that autonomy as an ideal type of agency is analytically unsound, as it sees structure as a set of choices (rather than constraints) and subsequently provides no way of understanding how such autonomy is achieved. Tsang observes that autonomy has been given a prominent position within discourses of teacher practice. Drawing on the work of Michel Foucault, he observes that notions of teacher freedom or agency have been re-configured into an ideology of an autonomous self, where teachers are presumed to have power over their choices. Through these discourses, the teacher becomes objectified as an active, responsible and reflective practitioner, while their autonomy is governed at a distance through technical and bureaucratic mechanisms of control (Tsang 2019). Autonomy in this sense represents the *under*-socialization of agency in socio-technical structures, where the concept of the autonomous individual is too independent of the socializing forces of their contexts. There is an increasing recognition of the complexity of agency and that it is contingent on social relations and resources that go beyond autonomy.

If power is not located in the individual (as autonomy demands), the question then is how to locate agency in the technicalized classroom. There is a need to avoid thinking about technology in reductionist terms, which do not allow for the unpacking of complex processes (resulting in deterministic and linear explanations of human agency, Rutzou and Elder-Vass, 2019: 402). The sociologist Jane Bennett (2010) draws on the works of Hannah Arendt and Gilles Deleuze to develop an account of social forms that emphasizes *origin* rather than *causation*. Bennett argues that instead of conceiving structure as a unified whole (such as an institution or a classroom), there is a need to see it as a set of complex relations, not only with other people, but with the world around us: physical objects, discourses and technology, all of which shape how humans engage in certain practices. By tracing the objects which make up a system (and their effects on each other), Bennett argues that it is possible to discern or infer social processes that go beyond what we would ordinarily perceive. Understanding these processes trades the individualistic and mechanistic explanations of agency characterized by autonomy with one that is dynamic, relational and reflexive.

Thinking beyond autonomy, therefore, requires a rejection of the primacy of the individual in technical structures. Instead, there is a need to decentre humans and see our natural state as being together, embedded in complex relations, all of which condition how we engage in certain practices. According to Bennett (2010), actors never really act alone; their capacities to act depend on other actors and objects such as technology (or non-human agency, what Bennett refers to as 'the vitality of things', 2010). Fawns (2022: 9) argues that teachers and technology are in a state of *entanglement* of people, discourses and objects, and agency is made possible through these relations, from which dispositions, practices and beliefs about teaching emerge. Once we understand the distribution of agency through relations of humans and non-human structures, such as technology or discourses (and that it is not, like autonomy, inherent to an individual), the concept looks very different and we can begin to explore teacher agency in relation to the contexts from which it emerges (Bennett, 2010). In this way, it is possible to avoid the determinism of both autonomy and technology in the analysis of teacher agency in EAP.

Methods

In this paper, I offer an account of the agency of EAP teachers as it relates to technology in EAP. First, I identified the technical objects available to participants. This involved participants filling out a mapping document where they listed the technical objects available to them. This was then used as a basis for interview questions as we talked through learning and teaching processes using technology. I interviewed five EAP teachers, representing a range of situations (full-time, part-time, pre-sessional teachers, university teachers, teachers in private institutions), recruited from a call for participants on social media (see Table 9.1). Interviews took between thirty minutes and one hour and were recorded on MS Teams. The recorded interviews were transcribed first using transcription software and then edited to ensure accuracy. Transcripts were read and re-read, and themes were identified and coded using NVIVO. The themes that emerged from the interviews were mapped on to the mapping document in order to identify connections between objects and deeper social and technical processes. As Harman (2016, 2018) suggests, since there is no way of knowing what will shape agency in advance

Table 9.1 Participants

Pseudonym	Context	
Marcus	UK	Teaches EAP at a large private, for-profit pathways provider in the UK. Teaches pre-master's and foundation programmes.
Angela	Spain/UK	English teacher based in Spain, but every summer returns to the same university in the UK to teach on a large pre-sessional programme.
Skye	Greece	Teaches EAP at a large public university in Greece.
Tom	Japan	Teaches EAP at a Japanese university, preparing students for study-abroad programmes.
Jane	UK	Teaches EAP at a large UK university.

(many events happen, but only a few will have an effect), first I established the nature of a participant's agency at the point of maturity (that is, how they exercised agency), then from there traced the events that shaped or conditioned their agency. Participants and their identifiers have been pseudonymized. Ethical permission was granted by the University of St Andrews.

Results

In the mapping stage, participants reported a range of technical objects, machines and software that were available to them. However, while participants encountered vastly different teaching contexts, there was much consistency with the technology that was available. Although participants taught in a wide range of contexts, they could typically draw on synchronous and asynchronous learning platforms (such as Moodle, Blackboard, Zoom or Microsoft Teams) as the primary ways of engaging with learners. These platforms were supported by various apps and classroom-based software. By and large, the participants in this study could do fundamentally the same things in each of their different contexts, and the technology available allowed a range of pedagogical approaches to be applied. However, contexts varied more significantly in their institutional arrangements. While the educational technology was objectively very similar, their contexts differed subjectively, particularly in the interpretations of the way technology was thought about and applied.

Marcus worked for a private, for-profit pathway provider at a Russell Group university in the UK. The college owned a building on the university campus, where they ran foundation and pre-master's courses for international students. Classrooms were designed to a high specification, with 'huddle spaces' (a term borrowed from corporate practices related to collaboration) equipped with tables that fit three students around a computer monitor, on which the teacher could project different things for students to look at. For Marcus, much of the way that technology was applied was governed through institutional values, which drew on common discourses in education such as 'active learning' and 'autonomy'. These discourses were embodied in the choice of technology and often determined the selection and design of tasks, demonstrating the passive power of the technology. Teachers were expected to design classroom tasks around these hubs and, as a result, their presence in classrooms had the potential to significantly shape the choices teachers made about teaching. Marcus acknowledged that his and others' practices, while not embracing the technology, certainly had to accommodate it in some way. However, Marcus observed that teachers did not 'really use the affordances of the room and the technology'. The creation of these spaces was underpinned by the pedagogical values of the company, but

> I mean, they I, I guess they've (the institution) found some, erm, there must be some pedagogical basis for that, I think they've probably found some research articles to come to support (it). I think my suspicion is it's more of a branding exercise.

In this context, the implementation of the huddle spaces, while drawing on pedagogical discourses which presented the technology as enabling and empowering, imposed particular practices onto teachers. One mechanism whereby practices were imposed was through bureaucratic and distanced processes of quality assurance. The private college was part of a network of for-profit colleges in partnership with various universities in the UK, which, while all nominally independent, shared a centralized quality assurance department. During the transition to online learning as a result of COVID-19, the institution attempted to recreate the huddle spaces online in breakout rooms. Nevertheless, there was some space for interpretation:

> So they (the quality assurance department) decide something that's standard across all the colleges and then it's up to you how you interpret, how you do it locally or is it done similar in a similar way across different colleges. In theory it should be done in a similar way across colleges, but I think the reality is. Yeah, things can take different directions.

The gap here between institutional structures and classroom structures represented space which allowed some room for agential manoeuvre, where Marcus could reflexively manage the technology in order to 'make things work'. This space was not formally granted by the institution, but emerged from the tension between quality assurance demands, the affordances of the technology itself and the needs of the teachers. Had Marcus not had this room for manoeuvre, he would not have had much influence on the way technology was applied.

Such tensions between teacher and institutional expectations of the use of technology were evident in other contexts. A good example of how teachers negotiated competing demands was the experience of Angela, a pre-sessional teacher at a large university. Angela worked on pre-sessional programmes which lasted between six and twelve weeks, helping students (mostly postgraduate) prepare for university study prior to them taking part in their university degree.

She was employed on a short-term contract for the duration of the course and was expected to follow a fixed set of materials. Teaching on the pre-sessional was itself a considerable undertaking with a lot of bureaucracy (training, teaching, recording tutorials), which was, according to Angela, 'emotionally demanding'. Angela's experiences represented an interesting entanglement of competing agencies: teachers, institutions, EAP departments and the students themselves all with their own desires, practices and demands, which shaped practices related to technology, though ultimately they shared a common goal – for students to pass the course and begin their master's programme. This example represented a relatively low-agency context, in that Angela had little say in determining choices about teaching and learning.

One way in which tensions became evident was the way that teachers communicated with students. Most institutional communication (e.g. assessment information) was done through the department virtual learning environment (VLE) page (Moodle) due to General Data Protection Regulation (GDPR) constraints. The VLE was typically used as a repository of documents but also hosted discussion forums for communication about important dates, readings, assessments and other course-related information. However, students often ignored the VLE and communicated with each other through self-organized communication on their own media (in this case, the Chinese social media app, WeChat), which was set up by students *before* the course had started and was the primary mode of communication for students with each other. While the institution was reluctant to communicate with students through social media, Angela observed needing to communicate with students who were not checking the VLE, and would ask a student to communicate messages on her behalf on the WeChat group, asking all students to check the VLE. GDPR rules complicated the matter, with Angela remarking, 'I don't even know if that's the right thing to do'. The teacher (and the institution) were absent from these discussions suggesting a rupture in the connectivity of actors, brought about by competing agencies concerning technology, which affected the way important course information was communicated. As in Marcus's case, there was no signal cause that could account for this rupture. Instead this gap emerged from the interplay between competing agencies and desires. This required the teacher to reflexively manage her use of technology in order for institutional processes to function efficiently. Had Angela not exercised agency by intervening here, student–institution communication may have broken down.

Both of the above examples involved teachers having little power to influence technical or pedagogical choices other than to fulfil the functioning of the technicalized system, brought about by the contradictions or tensions within technical structures whereby the actors were subordinate to the performance of the technology and other institutional processes. In each case the technology *preceded* thinking about pedagogical or technical practices, providing examples of teachers negotiating the passive power of technology and their institutions. These experiences contrasted with Skye, who worked at a state university in Greece. Skye often had over a hundred students at a time in her EAP classes, though her context was marked by an absence of institutional support (including the provision of technology; Skye used her own laptop for work). Skye described her experiences as demanding. However, the lack of institutional presence, plus the relatively low status of EAP teaching, allowed her quite a lot of freedom in the way she approached her teaching.

> In the administrative part, the language programme, the English language programming languages are not very well reputed at the university. Mostly there is a reputation of language teachers just doing the same stuff as the private language schools the kids go to ... that's the idea they have. So the university does not really get in the way as an institution. The university does not dictate pedagogical (approaches).

In a stressful environment and without support from her institution, a disposition marked by criticism of her situation emerged. Skye's only option regarding methodology was to rely on webinars on technology and language learning (practices she observed 'with stupid theories that address classes of twenty students') that did not relate in any way to her own struggles.

> People (in webinars) have been bragging about using technology. I have attended seminars and observed classrooms ... people who have been really famous for using technology and actually what they do is most of the time they transfer a traditional mode of teaching with a way of doing things like they haven't changed anything. Yeah, it's a different wrapping.

Skye rejected what she perceived to be traditional methods. For her, the dissonance she experienced opened up opportunities to experiment with technologies. Skye played around with various methods and found a way that worked for her. She favoured practices aligned with 'decision making science and economics, behavioural economics, I draw on everything'. This often took the shape of gamification (the application of gaming techniques, such as rewards and competition, to learning). She also talked in detail about using an app she found which helped students annotate texts. However, Skye's experimentation was often unstructured and drew on her own reading, which she acknowledged was somewhat chaotic. The lack of structure was particularly evident in the transition to online learning during COVID-19 lockdown:

> We didn't have any training. We were told that all we had to switch to online teaching overnight, we didn't even know how to use the platform. At first we didn't know the features of the platform.

Skye demonstrated care in the way she engaged with her students and, in the absence of support, it was her own personal concerns that guided her practice. However, this too had its demands '(be)cause this is a very tiresome process I have about 1,000 students every semester'. Her critical disposition and the space to experiment drove her choices, which at times involved genuinely interesting ways of using technology, though it was hard to see how long this could be maintained. It appeared that there was also always the danger that her practices were not quality controlled. In this way, Skye's autonomy was also her isolation. She was compelled into reflexive thought through the imperative to make sense of technology, though the lack of opportunity to confirm her thoughts through discussion with peers or managers intensified discord and potentially hindered the long-term development of effective practices.

The lack of opportunity for discussion was also evident in Tom's experiences with technology. Tom worked at a high-tier university department in Japan for students who were planning to study abroad. It was his first year in this position after a number of years in precarious work. Tom's experience with technology was marked by dissonant and competing agencies between students, institutions and teachers. Like Skye, Tom enjoyed quite a bit of freedom in terms of choices about the modules he was teaching on, though he was constrained by the amount of teaching he had:

> I could do without using textbooks and I could kind of in theory, pick out whatever technology I wanted the students to use, but because my first year in the department I was advised to use books at least this year, because you'll have just too much on with planning everything. I teach ten courses in this quarter and ten next quarter and the first semester. It's like a full semester.

However, the quality of the technology provided by his department was a little dated. The VLE, which '(seemed) like it's been designed by committee', was useful for enrolment and distributing emails, but not much else. As a result of the sudden shift to online learning, Tom was compelled to deliberate on how to utilize technology. One source of support for Tom was through interaction with the teachers' associations in Japan. Although it was not a requirement for his work, there was an expectation that teachers would be members, particularly university teachers. Tom remarked that 'It's like a kind of service, so if that's blank (on a CV), it's sort of like a red flag'. Tom was an active participant in these teachers' associations, though had changed his membership as a result of unpleasant experiences.

> So I've got a bit of a weird relationship with (one of the teaching associations) because there was previously committee sitting on like working conditions and stuff like that. But actually the committee seemed to not be sitting at all and they were challenged on (working conditions) and they basically brushed it off and said, like you know, we're all tenured university professors so you know, I'm alright Jack. So I let my membership run out.

This limited the extent to which he and others could engage with discourse communities related to technological practices and language learning. While he acknowledged the usefulness of teachers' associations in terms of sharing good practices and techniques, these communities acted like gatekeepers of specialist knowledge of learning technology pedagogy, with barriers to entry that had nothing to do with teaching competence. Like Skye, Tom was afforded what might be termed *autonomy* over his practices and, in contrast with the experiences of Marcus and Angela, thinking about pedagogy informed technical practices. However, his autonomy and an absence of a wider network of support meant he had to rely on his own internal engine of action to develop an effective pedagogy.

Of all the participants in this study, Jane exercised the most authority over her practices. Jane worked at a language centre at a large UK university. She had been on short-term contracts for a couple of years, though was recently employed on a permanent contract after completing a postgraduate qualification in EAP. Jane was highly reflexive about her context, acknowledging how practices had changed as a result of adjusting and transitioning to digital spaces during the first and second waves of the COVID-19 pandemic. However, she was also fortunate to work in a department that she perceived to value and encourage thinking about pedagogy. At the beginning of lockdown, Jane expressed difficulty with managing classroom dynamics, in particular observing that things had changed significantly as a result of the transition to online learning. She remarked that 'we're working in a different space, surely partly the space that you're working in informs the pedagogy'. As a result of her supportive department and from her own studies in EAP, Jane had a strong knowledge base and opportunities for thought and discussion, which guided her choices, remarking that 'I know I'm influenced by the structures around me and by obviously the people I work with and that I sort of seek out to work with'.

At first, Jane encountered an overwhelming choice of platforms, though her practices became more focussed as a result of adjusting and transitioning to digital spaces. Jane's context was very methodologically driven, particularly through the twin mechanisms of reflexivity and discussion, where thinking around pedagogy preceded the selection and application of technology.

> We had so many discussions within small staff teams and at the, you know, bigger kind of whole staff meetings about how we manage things like breakout groups, collaborative documents. All the, you know, the myriad of tools that you can possibly put together for students to interact asynchronously and synchronously. So it was a lot of discussion around how can we make (learning) more meaningful between the asynchronous and synchronous in the live Zoom or Teams room or wherever it was.

In particular, Jane was guided by concepts from systemic functional linguistics, particularly genre theory and pedagogy, which resulted in certain pedagogical choices concerning technology, specifically the way that collaborative spaces were used:

> It's very easy just to use a collaborative Word document or a Padlet, and people are adding as they're discussing in the breakout rooms. So in terms of that

process, I suppose, the asynchronous outside of the live sessions did make it more, how do I say it, uhm? I think it helped.

The opportunities afforded to her, particularly time for thought, experimentation and discussion with others, resulted in the negotiation of effective practices, individually and collectively, informed by pedagogical principles within the constraints and enablements of technical infrastructure. Jane's experiences represented a form of communicative action, where decisions were made in consultation with others by way of deliberation.

In conclusion, technology always has some effect on the shaping of educational practices. Each class, module and programme is embedded in ephemeral arrangements of people, objects and discourses, shaped by the culture, values and policies and also what the students bring. These arrangements are highly fluid, though they also have a tendency to endure and reproduce, through the habituation of ways of thinking about practice. COVID-19 has provided an excellent example of the reflexive imperative and technology – a major disruption that has resulted in significant and sometimes permanent changes to educational practices resulting from people figuring things out. The ways people confront their contexts become habitualized, creating new 'rules of the game' over time.

This research reveals two approaches to technology as it relates to EAP teacher agency: first, technology may be imposed onto teachers, where the application of the technology precedes the thinking about how it will be used. In the cases of Marcus and Angela technical processes were not developed with pedagogy in mind and instead were used as generic technicalized educational solutions. In this way, the selection of technology resulted in a form of technological determinism, where teacher agency was reduced to the functioning of the technology or other institutional processes. Second, technology may be applied as a result of a 'pedagogy first' approach, whereby it is pedagogical choices that drive the selection and application of technology (Fawns, 2022). In this case, theories of learning and second language acquisition precede the development and adoption of technology and the technology is applied to align with what is known about how learning happens. In the case of Skye and Tom, an absence of institutional presence and support resulted in relative isolation. However, Jane demonstrated control over the affordances offered by technology in the form of communicative action – where teachers were given time to think and experiment and opportunities to discuss ideas with others. Key to the successful application of learning technology were the mechanisms of 'thought and talk', opportunities for thinking about pedagogical practices and for discussion with others, plus (in the case of Jane) a solid knowledge of pedagogy, which informed choices of technology and practice.

There is a need to involve teachers in pedagogic processes and decision-making as they relate to technology. Although the benefits of EAP teacher agency are well-established, there is often a natural tendency in institutions towards technological determinism, where technology dictates practices. These tendencies come from a number of different pressures, such as a desire for control or circumstances marked by conflict. There is therefore a need to explore what sort of pressures shape pedagogical choices in technicalized classrooms and institutions. Social theory can be helpful for understanding the sorts of pressures that shape teacher practice. In order for teachers to be able to make good decisions about their own contexts, they need a good knowledge base, resources and space and encouragement and opportunities for thinking about and discussing pedagogy.

References

Archer, M. S. (1995), *Realist Social Theory: The Morphogenetic Approach*, Cambridge: Cambridge University Press.
Archer, M. S. (2003), *Structure, Agency and the Internal Conversation*, Cambridge: Cambridge University Press.
Archer, M. S. (2012), *The Reflexive Imperative in Late Modernity*, Cambridge: Cambridge University Press.
Ashton, K. (2022), 'Language Teacher Agency in Emergency Online Teaching', *System*, 105.
BALEAP (2008), 'Competency Framework for Teachers of English for Academic Purposes'. https://www.baleap.org/wp-content/uploads/2016/04/teap-competency-framework.pdf
BALEAP TEAP Fellowship Scheme (2014), 'Accreditation Scheme Handbook'. https://www.baleap.org/wp-content/uploads/2016/04/TEAP-Scheme-Handbook-2014.pdf
Bennett, J. (2010), *Vibrant Matter*, Durham: Duke University Press.
Biesta, G. (2008), *Learning Lives: Learning, Identity and Agency in the Life-course: Full Research Report*, ESRC End of Award Report, RES-139-25-0111, Swindon: ESRC.
Bond, B. (2020), *Making Language Visible in the University: English for Academic Purposes and Internationalisation*, vol. 82, Bristol: Multilingual Matters.
Bourdieu, P. (1978), 'Sport and Social Class', *Social Science Information*, 17 (6): 819–40.
Ding, A. and I. Bruce (2017), *The English for Academic Purposes Practitioner*, Basingstoke: Palgrave Macmillan.
Emirbayer, M. and A. Mische (1998), 'What is Agency?', *American Journal of Sociology*, 103 (4): 962–1023.
Fawns, T. (2022), 'An Entangled Pedagogy: Looking beyond the Pedagogy-Technology Dichotomy', *Postdigital Science and Education*. https://doi.org/10.1007/s42438-022-00302-7
Fricker, M. (2007), *Epistemic Injustice: Power and the Ethics of Knowing*, Oxford: Oxford University Press.
Gershon, I. (2011). 'Neoliberal Agency', *Current Anthropology*, 52 (4): 537–55.
Giddens, A. (1982), 'Power, the Dialectic of Control and Class Structuration', in A. Giddens and F. R. Dallmayr (eds), *Profiles and Critiques in Social Theory*, 197–214, London: Palgrave.
Harman, G. (2016), *Immaterialism*, London: Polity.
Harman, G. (2018), *Object-oriented Ontology: A New Theory of Everything*, London: Penguin UK.
Knox, J., B. Williamson and S. Bayne (2020), 'Machine Behaviourism: Future Visions of "Learnification" and "Datafication" across Humans and Digital Technologies', *Learning, Media and Technology*, 45 (1): 31–45.

Larsen-Freeman, D. (2019), 'On Language Learner Agency: A Complex Dynamic Systems Theory Perspective', *The Modern Language Journal*, 103: 61–79.

Macgilchrist, F. (2019), 'Cruel Optimism in Edtech: When the Digital Data Practices of Educational Technology Providers Inadvertently Hinder Educational Equity', *Learning, Media and Technology*, 44 (1): 77–86.

Priestley, M. R., G. Biesta and S. Robinson (2015), *Teacher Agency: An Ecological Approach*, London: Bloomsbury Publishing.

Qi, G. Y. and Y. Wang (2022), 'Challenges and Responses: A Complex Dynamic Systems Approach to Exploring Language Teacher Agency in a Blended Classroom', *The JALT CALL Journal*, 18 (1): 54–82.

Rutzou, T. and D. Elder-Vass (2019), 'On Assemblages and Things: Fluidity, Stability, Causation Stories, and Formation Stories', *Sociological Theory*, 37 (4): 401–24.

Selwyn, N., L. Pangrazio, S. Nemorin and C. Perrotta (2020), 'What Might the School of 2030 be Like? An Exercise in Social Science Fiction', *Learning, Media and Technology*, 45 (1): 90–106.

Sewell, W. H. (1992), 'A Theory of Structure: Duality, Agency, and Transformation', *American Journal of Sociology*, 98 (1): 1–29.

Tao, J. and X. Gao (2021), *Language Teacher Agency*, Cambridge: Cambridge University Press.

Tsang, K. K. (2019), 'Ideological Disempowerment of Teachers', *On Education. Journal for Research and Debate*, 2 (5). https://doi.org/10.17899/on_ed. 2019.5.5

Tsang, K. K. and Q. Qin (2020), 'Ideological Disempowerment as an Effect of Neoliberalism on Teachers', *Power and Education*, 12 (2): 204–12.

Watters, A. (2021), *Teaching Machines: The History of Personalized Learning*, Cambridge, MA: MIT Press.

Williamson, B. (2017), 'Learning in the "Platform Society": Disassembling an Educational Data Assemblage', *Research in Education*, 98 (1): 59–82.

Chapter 10

'CHANGING LANES'

BALANCING BETWEEN ROLES OF EAP LECTURER AND RESEARCHER IN A TEACHING INSTITUTION TOWARDS A RESEARCH UNIVERSITY

Eric Cheung

This chapter arises from a larger study investigating how teaching- and research-intensive staff perceive the growing demand for scholarly activities and research output following the recent changes in a Hong Kong self-financed higher education institution ('the college' hereafter) transitioning towards a private university. The chapter focusses on the EAP lecturers changing to the 'research lane' branching from the teaching track. Research-lane EAP lecturers ('REAPs' hereafter) are required to increase research activities and scholarly publications, adding to their teaching, administrative and service roles. The study presented in the chapter reports on how the REAPs, including myself with an autoethnographic lens, reflected on their precarious, complex and liminal identities in the college and critiqued the influence of an increasingly 'managerial' institutional culture on teaching and research, in response to the significant changes that they experienced at the personal, collegiate and institutional levels. Such precarity may be considered pertinent to tertiary EAP practitioners, whose institutions leverage the so-called 'accountability' and 'productivity' in scholarship to advance in institutional rankings or transition into research-intensive universities. The chapter concludes by identifying the REAPs' coping strategies including claiming scholar identities, seeking alignment and collaboration with the broader academic community and finding meanings of engaging in research in their EAP teaching careers and personal dispositions such as determination, passion and resilience. These attributes can be helpful for EAP practitioners who aim to have more agentive control over how 'academic research' and 'scholarship' influence their career prospects aside from informing their teaching decisions.

EAP in Hong Kong HEIs

Adopting a trilingual (Cantonese, English and Mandarin) and biliterate (Chinese and English) language policy, English remains the mainstream medium of instruction (MOI) in most programmes in Hong Kong higher education institutions (HEIs). With the increasing number of middle schools using Chinese as the MOI, the massification of tertiary education and the attempt to recruit both local and international students, there is a constant demand for EAP programmes to support students' English proficiency and academic literacy (Evans, 2016; Ortega, 2018). English, while enjoying a privileged status in Hong Kong, is considered a 'foreign language for the majority of the student body' (Choi and Cheung, 2014), in that it is challenging for them to learn through English (Tse et al., 2001). A seminal study by Evans and Green (2007) reinforced the argument for the necessity of EAP in higher education. Hong Kong tertiary students were reportedly struggling with EAP, especially in vocabulary, grammar and discourse. Ortega (2018) discussed issues of fragmented literacies in Hong Kong, in that the English proficiency of many secondary-school graduates might not fulfil the entry requirements of government-funded universities, as reflected in the results of the English subject in the public examination. As Evans and Green (2007: 14) concluded, students' English proficiency issues may be alleviated 'by focusing existing EAP programmes more sharply to accommodate identified student needs' instead of placing them in so-called 'remedial' English courses.

However, EAP in Hong Kong HE potentially faces three main challenges: constant changes in the higher education landscape, a strong emphasis on vocational training and employability and an instrumental view of EAP learning. Owing to the growth of the tertiary student population thanks to the massification of higher education (Sutherland, 2002; Tang, Tsui and Chau, 2018), the growing demand for EAP courses makes it difficult for EAP teaching units to develop teaching and learning materials that can cater to individual needs and to be critical of their pedagogy (Marr, 2021). Students with lower academic language proficiency are still accepted by the HEIs, who adopt a 'business-as-usual' agenda and prioritize administrative efficiency over pedagogy, such as equally allocating English exposure time to all students regardless of their proficiency (Ortega, 2018). Another possible consequence of HE massification is the inclination towards vocationalism. HEIs emphasize training students for employment opportunities rather than acculturating them with 'cultural ideals [and] humanistic values' (Hadley, 2015: 29). Against the neoliberal backdrop, HE emphasizing vocational training may aggravate student alienation in turn, suggesting that students prefer an instrumentalist approach to learning simply to improve their competitiveness in the business world (Wong, 2022).

The brief description of HE in Hong Kong shows that changes in the HE landscape align with Hadley's (2015) discussion of how EAP in HE is influenced from the top down by globalization and vocationalism: English is still privileged as the dominant medium of instruction (MOI), and programmes often emphasize vocational training and employability to meet industry demands. Such an influence is also motivated from the bottom up by massification, resulting from the growing demands from the increasing domestic and international student population, and by McDonaldization, in that 'similar practices and strategic approaches [are adopted] for "processing" large number of students' (Hadley, 2015: 33–4), potentially turning EAP units into 'knowledge factories' (Harding et al., 2007; Ishikawa, 2009). Following this instrumental sense, EAP seems to privilege preparing students with language proficiency and improving their employability, rather than equipping them with the literacy skills essential for knowledge production. The main role of EAP practitioners, consequently, becomes 'technicians whose intellectual and creative skills have been incorporated into learning packages the consumption of which they now only disseminate, manage and assess' (Allman, 2001: 71).

EAP lecturers transitioning towards scholarship

The influence of neoliberalism in HEIs also transforms the staffing of EAP teaching units in the face of a large student population. In Hadley's (2015) terms, the new role that EAP practitioners take to 'process' a large student population for producing 'quick' results is called 'blended' EAP professional (BLEAP). In Hong Kong HEIs, aside from full-time academic staff, EAP courses may be taught by part-time 'visiting lecturers' or teaching staff on short temporary contracts with little or no fringe benefits (e.g. insurance coverage, dental and medical benefits). To ensure job security or seek promotion, EAP teachers may need to teach fifteen hours or more weekly, while engaging in administrative work and other service duties such as student consultation and organizing student activities. This precarious job situation of EAP practitioners in terms of uncertain employment status and their identities 'recast into service personnel' (Hadley, 2018: 184) may be similar in HEIs in other regions such as Canada (Breshears, 2019), Japan, the UK and the US (Hadley, 2015). Such precarity may further lead to the marginalization of EAP at the tertiary level, in that EAP practitioners' ever-increasing workload gains so little in return.

One of the ways to raise the status of EAP is to consider it as an academic field, instead of a peripheral teaching unit marginalized in HEIs, and to promote scholarship. As Ding and Bruce (2017) advocated, EAP is a theoretically robust discipline, since it draws upon a vast range of theoretical concepts and methodological frameworks. EAP practitioners, many of whom have previously taught TESOL, are also required to be equipped with the theoretical and analytical knowledge to recognize the similarities and differences between EAP and TESOL to prepare for the transition (Ding and Bruce, 2017). EAP units adopting such a shift in academic culture towards research may facilitate their practitioners in normalizing scholarly activities (Webster, 2022). Not confined to writing journal articles, research activities such as conducting literature reviews (Bai, 2018) or teaching reflections (Arhar et al., 2013) may also be considered, which potentially help EAP practitioners construct identities as researchers. However, the construction of EAP researcher identities may be impacted by how teachers consider the nature of their job; time issues in relation to workload are often the primary factor in choosing not to engage in research (Banegas, 2018). While the above scholarly works discussed the notion of precarity and EAP teacher-researcher identities primarily in the context of HEIs with autonomous EAP teaching units, this chapter aims to focus on the EAP unit 'embedded' within an academic department of a self-financed HEI, promoting research as it is undergoing transition into a private university.

The context: EAP teaching teams in a Hong Kong self-financed HEI

The present study was situated in a Hong Kong self-financed HEI. The college consists of four academic divisions offering both post-secondary and undergraduate programmes such as business, design, engineering, health studies, humanities and communication, science and technology and applied social sciences. Cross-division EAP subjects are offered by the languages and communication division ('the division' hereafter), the specific research site where the EAP staff members are stationed.

In the college, the EAP teaching teams comprise staff from the language and communication division. This differs from government-funded universities, which have autonomous language centres offering a wide range of EAP and ESP courses for students from all disciplines. The EAP teams provide college-wide English subjects to other college divisions, to ensure that students acquire academic English for their subsequent undergraduate and postgraduate studies. This difference suggests that the EAP teachers in the college may have to teach other languages, translation or communication subjects. For example, an EAP lecturer in the division typically teaches at least fifteen hours weekly, including content subjects. In the EAP subjects, the lecturers use designated resources instead of self-prepared materials and grade assessments with standardized rubrics. This teaching-intensive profile is common among all college EAP practitioners, especially if they teach only discipline-specific EAP courses. The intensive teaching schedule, with little control over choices of teaching materials, may demotivate these EAP teachers from seeking development in their careers. This may further result in 'stagnation', in Zamir's (2018) terms, meaning that one 'does not feel the need to advance and realize [one's] full potential' (Zamir, 2018: 150).

From teaching-intensive EAP practitioners to researchers

Pursuing a successful transition towards a private university, the college landscape has undergone one significant change, that is, the establishment of research centres and new laboratories. For example, the division has three language laboratories, and the recently established pedagogic research centre has a big data lab, a STEM lab and an upcoming multimodal lab. The research centres conduct conferences, seminars and workshops to encourage intellectual exchange and colleagues' participation in research activities. These changes pave the way for nurturing scholarly activities and encouraging research outputs as some of the college's long-term missions to maintain its advantage in Hong Kong.

Initiating changes in staff deployment strategies also serves to address the issue of stagnation, as briefly mentioned in the previous section. As a teaching-intensive institution, the college introduced a scholar scheme to allow lecturers to transition to a new career 'lane' and increase their intellectual contributions.

This scheme differs from a typical research 'track' in universities: all full-time lecturers belong to the teaching track, but are all eligible for the scheme to enter the research 'lane' on a three-year basis. Becoming a research-lane member involves two main changes. First, to be eligible to apply for external research grants, the REAPs have to take up mostly undergraduate teaching, mostly replacing their teaching duties at the associate-degree level (a post-secondary qualification below the bachelor's degree but above the higher diploma). This change in their teaching profile indicates that the REAPs need to adapt to a different teaching and administrative environment, aside from undertaking scholarly activities. Second, 30 per cent of the lecturer's annual performance in the research lane is appraised based on their 'intellectual contributions'. Such contributions include leading research projects, securing major external funding and publishing in top-tier, peer-reviewed journals. The change in assessment criteria shows that the context in which the present study is situated is always a teaching-intensive one. That is to say, the changes that the research-lane lecturers face are multi-faceted and may destabilize their sense of security as experienced EAP lecturers.

Despite a shift in focus on research, research-lane lecturers in the college are different from tenure-track assistant professors in Hong Kong universities in at least four aspects. First, the job title of the staff as 'lecturers' does not reflect their researcher/scholar status, unlike the academic rank structure in Commonwealth universities such as in Australia and New Zealand, in which lecturers can be considered equivalent to the rank of assistant professors. Second, while teaching remission is granted to the research-lane lecturers, the weekly teaching hours are still higher than the professorial-track staff, who are entitled to sabbatical leaves for scholarly activities. Third, research-lane lecturers have no obligations to undertake research supervision duties, for there are no postgraduate students in the college, while it is optional for academic staff to supervise undergraduate capstone projects. Fourth, teaching remains the focus of the assessment, despite the difference in proportions between teaching-intensive (90 per cent) and research-intensive staff (70 per cent). This means that, unlike the 'publish or perish' tradition of tenure-track professorship in universities, research-lane staff have the flexibility to explore their career options without serious consequences. In other words, after the three-year period, they may 'return' to the teaching lane if they are assessed to be less satisfactory regarding their research performance. In other words, apart from research awards granted internally, there are no specific promotion or demotion pathways reflecting the faculty's research performance.

The above differences may not be seen as constraints, especially the fourth aspect, which actually gives the research-lane staff some leeway as to what kind of academic career to develop. However, conversely, what 'outstanding' research achievements (e.g. securing major grants, publishing numerous journal articles annually) entail is not explicitly stated in the scheme's documentation, as the college does not have a research track. Given teaching is the major assessment criterion (70 per cent of the whole appraisal) and the obscure identity of research-lane staff (the 'lecturer' title in the context of Hong Kong), whether research engagement can be seen as career development or even advancement is questionable.

It is also important to note that, as far as the scholar scheme's documentation is concerned, the terms 'scholar' and 'scholarship' are not clearly defined. As the scheme's full title is 'Enhanced Productive Scholar Scheme', the staff members in the research lane are expected to 'produce' research outputs (e.g. journal articles, book chapters, monographs and conference papers). While participation in conferences and other scholarly activities can be included in their performance profile, only research deliverables (e.g. journal articles and research grants) are considered in the staff performance assessment. This view may be different from views on scholarship in (higher) education from scholars such as Fincher et al. (2000) and Schulman (2000), in that teaching and other activities supporting learning can be seen as 'scholarly'; alternatively, scholarly works can also inform teaching, as they are open to the public for evaluation and developed by other scholars (Glassick, 2000). The emphasis on scholarly output may influence how REAPs view their research and teaching, as well as the hardship they face in the college.

In view of the changes and uncertainties implied in the newly introduced research lane in the college, the present study aims to answer the research questions related to (i) what challenges there may be in the research lane; (ii) what motivates the teaching-intensive EAP lecturers to transition into the 'research lane' (i.e. REAPs) despite the perceived precarity and (iii) how they address and resolve these challenges as they develop.

Research design

The present study adopted an interactive qualitative research design (Maxwell, 2012). The study combined approaches including semi-structured interviews with REAPs and reviewing policy documents regarding the scholar scheme, accompanied by the author's self-reflection, which captures the author's lived experience as a member of the scheme.

The study interviewed six research-lane staff in the division, but two were excluded as they did not teach any EAP subjects. The four selected EAP lecturers taught mainly EAP subjects at the associate-degree and undergraduate levels and engaged in various research projects. The projects included EAP studies and those on literary criticism and social media discourse. The individual interviews followed an interview protocol (see Appendix 1), including questions about their reasons for choosing the research lane, research activities and strategies for coping with challenges and increasing research productivity. The interviewees' views on how the changes impact their teaching and research are accompanied by my own reflections as a division member, who also possesses knowledge about changes in the landscape of the college. As reflected in the documentation on issues such as the scholar scheme, research funding and outputs, such changes contextualize the staff members' experience and perceptions as researcher-intensive faculty.

After removing the interviewees' personal information, the collected data underwent qualitative content analysis to identify subthemes (Miles and Huberman, 1994). The open coding generated 216 codes and 4 relevant themes in axial coding, including the interviewees' views on how changing to the research lane impacted their identities in the college, challenges as an REAP, adopting research to inform EAP pedagogies and coping strategies for innovation and collaboration. With these themes, I related my perception and experience as a lecturer actively engaged in teaching and research activities in the college.

Ethical considerations

As a research study involving autoethnographic reflections, there is a potential bias that the author, as a member of the college, will provide the story that he wishes to tell, particularly one with subjective judgement or conclusions about the objects of study, such as the scholar scheme and its influences on the research-lane staff. The author is reflexively aware of his position; therefore, at least three measures have been undertaken to minimize bias and enhance rigour. First, the present study is not commissioned by the college, nor does it receive any financial support therefrom, in order to eliminate the impression of siding with the college's policy. Second, the main findings of the present study were obtained from semi-structured interviews with research-lane peers, who gave comprehensive and balanced views on their changing roles in the college. The interview protocol contained prompts for eliciting the interviewees' positive and negative perceptions regarding their position in the research lane, in that the author was able to engage in authentic dialogues with the interviewees. Third, the present study does not aim to offer a definitive account of the (dis-)advantages of being a research-intensive EAP practitioner in a teaching-intensive HEI. Instead, it seeks to 'evoke conceptual insights and to become a stimulus for further intellectual discussion' (Poerwandari, 2021: 318). Through the author's and the interviewees' authentic reflections (Amin et al., 2020), the present study aims to inform readers of the phenomena under investigation or those whose experience is similar but has not been shared through scholarly writing (Morrow, 2005). In other words, these reflections may provide EAP practitioners with insights into possible strategies to facilitate the gradual 'shift from a predominantly teaching identity towards a more academic one' (Webster, 2022: 10).

Research-lane EAP lecturers' reflections

The themes in the following subsections arise from the interviews with the REAPs. I first identify the challenges that they encountered as research-lane staff members and consider these challenges a specific kind of 'precarity' of an EAP lecturer-turned-researcher. I then describe why they were determined to take up a new role and how they coped with the precarity of being REAPs. Their responses are also juxtaposed with my reflection, from the perspective of an REAP lecturer. They are then discussed in relation to the research literature on EAP practitioners' identity and agency, their engagement in research, their precarity in possessing liminal roles and their coping measures in response to the changes in HEIs against the neoliberal backdrop.

Precarity arising from the complex identities of REAPs

> You have to be a good researcher, a good teacher and a good administrator . . . but you have only twenty-four hours . . . you have family you have to look after. (Lecturer D)

Teaching taking time away from research

The identity as a lecturer newly inducted into the research lane in September 2020 'legitimized' my position to experiment with different pedagogic approaches for both teaching and research purposes. For example, to make my discipline-specific EAP curriculum 'responsive and situated' (Marr, 2021: 138), I adopted linguistically guided approaches, such as corpus-based language pedagogy (e.g. Ma et al., 2022) and genre-based pedagogy informed by systemic functional linguistics (e.g. Dreyfus et al., 2016), to plan my lessons and develop teaching and learning materials. As I mentioned above, becoming an REAP under the college's scholar scheme meant a change in my teaching profile, that is, teaching new undergraduate courses other than EAP subjects. This means that, in the first year in the research lane, it was difficult to meet the college's requirement in terms of generating research output, while I had been aware scholarly activities involve more than just writing grant proposals and journal articles.

Similar sentiments were reflected in the interviews with the REAPs due to their liminal roles at the college, as they transitioned to their new researcher identity. Despite their new identity in the college, the primary evaluation criterion of an REAP is teaching quality. Under the scholar scheme, which emphasized research output, the interviewed REAPs seemed to consider teaching and research as two separate activities, although other findings from the interviews suggested otherwise (see 'Conducting Research for Informing and Improving Teaching'). Lecturer C lamented that teaching new subjects every year had taken away most of his time 'to sit down quietly for research and publication . . . for reading and brainstorming ideas for future research and good new topics for journal papers'. Lecturer D also felt that 'there's a lot of work . . . but research [was] always compromised'. The strong emphasis on quality teaching had therefore put REAPs in a precarious situation, in that focussing on teaching might mean they would have to sacrifice their research.

The REAPs' precarity also resulted from the ad-hoc duties assigned to them and the over-caring approach to students. All academic staff in the college can be asked to take up additional teaching assignments, especially when there is a shortage of part-time lecturers or an unexpected surge in student enrolment. In both cases, EAP lecturers are the first to be invited to teach extra classes. Despite their research-lane staff status, all interviewed lecturers reported that they would still be called to teach extra classes. Lecturer A said she might have to teach for over fifteen hours, including the additional teaching assignment. Regarding additional assignments, Lecturer D commented that the college might not have 'really made up its mind . . . to leave [research staff] alone', adding that 'the boundary that sets the research and teaching staff apart is not that clear'. In addition, the college's quality assurance approach to assessing teaching negatively impacted the REAPs' ability to integrate teaching and research (assuming that they considered scholarly writing as the major research activity). Measurements such as rubrics, student feedback surveys and other metrics did not seem to help the interviewees other than providing 'analytics' for the college to measure performance and generate findings to facilitate governance. The interviewees commented that the college did not treat students like undergraduates and considered themselves 'babysitters' and 'high school teachers'. Lecturer C expressed his frustration: while he was supposed to focus on research activities during the summer break, he was overwhelmed by meetings and new course preparations. Moreover, detailed grading rubrics added to the already heavy teaching load, when one EAP teacher had to teach and assess large classes in a semester, without the help of teaching assistants or tutors. Lecturer D described fine-grained assessment rubrics for ensuring teaching quality that 'really sounded like a factory', which may harm the staff's academic freedom, that is, to 'teach . . . and research with more flexibility'. The above REAPs' statements suggested that, instead of divorcing research from teaching, they actually hoped for a more distinctive role as granted by the college, so that duties that did not contribute to scholarly works could be warded off.

Growing pressure to achieve research 'excellence'

I also experienced the pressure of securing funds and publishing research, the 'key performance indicators' I was required to accomplish. I found myself constantly distracted from my research and teaching, as much of my time was dedicated to writing grant proposals. For example, after obtaining a major grant to finance my research project on corpus-based language pedagogy, I was 'strongly encouraged' to submit a new proposal to 'help' maintain the college's number of grant applications and increase the chances of getting funded. In the meantime, my performance level would be considered as 'exceeding the expected level' if I was able to publish in 'prestige' journals as indicated in SCImago Journal Rankings (SJR). In this sense, scholarly activities as 'intellectual contributions', according to the college's documentation, were confined to those that were publicly recognized outputs 'subject to peer-review processes'. Other scholarly activities such as convening research interest groups, serving as a member of research centres and coordinating research seminars may not count as valuable 'intellectual contributions'.

The interviewees also voiced their concerns about research outputs, including publications in academic journals and securing project funding. Because of this, research-lane faculty put a lot of time and effort into drafting grant proposals. Lecturer B reflected that limited time was a source of pressure, as '[REAPs] were under review from time to time'. Lecturer C expressed his anxiety as he awaited results from academic journals and grant proposals, in that there was pressure because '[the research lane] seemed not so secure . . . the [performance appraisal] would only evaluate your funding results and your journal publications'. Such anxiety was also echoed by Lecturer A, who was advised not to take up research early in her career, as 'it is possible that [one] works very hard and [does not] have any product'.

Becoming an REAP in the college seemed to have put myself in a dilemmic situation. In the college's context, taking the research lane and engaging in scholarly activities were considered 'value-adding activities', but how exactly this would influence my career outlook was yet to be clearly explained. It was uncertain whether failing to fulfil the research requirements would lead to any penalization. In addition, it was also unclear how success in the research lane would help secure or enhance my current position, as the post of senior lecturer in the college, for instance, implied an emphasis on educational and administrative leadership. As the title of one of the internal grants suggested, academic staff in the college had to achieve 'teaching and research excellence' at the same time, in addition to balancing many different roles (e.g. administration, student advising and other services). Consequently, striking a balance between teaching and reaching the 'yardsticks' of research-lane staff became very challenging.

Aside from balancing multiple roles in the college, the interviewees also attributed a less balanced life to time-related issues, in that their work pressure started impacting their family lives. For example, Lecturer A had to sacrifice time with her children, in that her children seldom saw her as she stayed at school to finish writing manuscripts. Similarly, Lecturer C gave up relaxation time with his family outside and 'stayed at home and worked'. Aside from compromising family lives, the interviewees' well-being also took a toll. While they all agreed that they were 'extremely busy' and 'unbalanced', they also described mental and physical exhaustion. They reported leading a 'not very healthy . . . kind of lifestyle', working very long hours, which they found difficult to maintain in the long run. For example, during the transition period of becoming an REAP, Lecturer A had to go after publication deadlines during the semester with long teaching hours:

> I spent over 16 hours per day. I don't think I can survive . . . for a long term. But it's just temporary because I wrote the proposal to the journal, and then they gave me the deadline I must not miss . . . otherwise I don't think I have another chance in the future.

Summarizing the interviewees' reflections above, the perceived precarity of REAPs is different from what previous research has discussed regarding the precarity of EAP instructors in terms of unstable employment (e.g. Ding, 2019; McCartney and Metcalfe, 2018; Vosko, 2006) or marginalization in HEIs as 'a remedial butler service to the academy' (Marr, 2021: 138). Instead, the sense of precarity of the research lane includes teaching new subjects, balancing multiple roles and, perhaps most importantly, facing uncertainties related to research outputs. Since 'there is no guaranteed way to secure a permanent position in EAP' (Walková, 2021: 98), scholarship does not protect EAP lecturers from such precarity, despite its potential to enhance the lecturers' visibility and personal and job satisfaction. Additionally, the college's governance style and quality assurance approaches seemed to 'push' REAPs to juggle multiple roles at the expense of their personal lives and well-being. Therefore, the sense of precarity may also result from a less distinct lecturer/researcher boundary, which might impact their perceptions of their career outlook, time pressure and overall work-life balance. As a result, REAP lecturers often find it challenging to focus on scholarly activities even though they have been granted the identity of research-lane staff.

In light of this, the intriguing question is how the research-intensive EAP staff balance their liminal roles in the division, overcome the fear of being in a more insecure and less certain position than their teaching-intensive peers and cope with the fact that 'impermanence has remained a consistent feature' (Breshears, 2019: 42).

Coping strategies in response to the precarity of REAPs

Well aware of the conundrums being an REAP in the college, I applied for the scholar scheme as a way of recognizing myself as having career goals and a sense of achievement that differed from a teaching-only career. While a teaching-intensive lecturer may seek the career goal of becoming an administrative and/or educational leader, my new research role corroborates my mission to pursue scholarship for both personal and professional development, aside from informing EAP teaching with my observations and findings from research. Entering the college as a recent PhD graduate in 2019, I worked towards extending my doctorate research on stance and voice in postgraduate academic writing to the associate-degree and undergraduate levels. Aware of my identity as teaching staff at the beginning, I conducted unfunded independent research and presented at conferences and symposia to stay connected with the EAP research and text linguistics fields. Granted the research-lane identity in 2020, I regarded this as the college's recognition of my developing track record, as shown in terms of financial and administrative support and teaching remission. Despite facing uncertainties in relation to my position as an REAP, it was reasonable for me to acknowledge such support, which I could leverage to explore new research interests, enhance my research skills and expand collaborative networks.

The interviewed REAPs demonstrated in the interviews that their scholarly identity was inherited from their doctorate research, their mission to leverage research to improve teaching and their proactive and prosocial mindset to find various means to develop their research careers. These helped them overcome the precarity of being an EAP researcher/lecturer in the college and maintain their perseverance to stay committed to scholarly activities, in addition to publishing their research works.

Claiming a researcher or scholar identity

> I see myself as a researcher, researcher–teacher. So basically, I would like to prioritize my teaching research because I just don't want to be a teacher–teacher.

I would use research to inform and improve my teaching, so it's not a sacrifice. (Lecturer B)

The sense of mission as doctorate holders motivated the interviewees to proceed to the research lane. In addition to the resistance to being just 'teacher–teachers', they were also aware of their research identity inherited from their PhD graduate status. Aside from enthusiasm and a lifelong dream to become a scholar (Lecturer A), the interviewees found that 'it is quite normal [to be] interested in research' (Lecturer C) as 'a trained PhD [who] reaches [his] mission' (Lecturer B) and that their PhD training should not be wasted (Lecturer D).

Therefore, their 'core identity' as trained PhDs contributed to their positive views on transitioning into scholars. Lecturer A felt happy about the college's changing attitude towards encouraging research through the scholar scheme, in that she could 'have more time to focus on research and then recycle the data collected before to write research papers and proposals'. Lecturer B benefitted from teaching remission for 'focus[ing] on writing and design projects'. Similarly, Lecturer C found such a change 'a good direction . . . allow[ing] opportunities to pursue research', whereas Lecturer D thought 'there was nothing to lose' as she would use the opportunity to 'test out [her] ability as a researcher'. Meanwhile, the interviewees understood that this new role and the 'lecturer' title could not compare with the assistant professorship at universities, although they recognized certain similarities between the two positions:

> We are in a transition period and that is why the title is still 'lecturer', but I see the requirement for a research-lane staff is actually quite high . . . what [the college has] required us to do is equivalent to assistant professors in [government-] funded universities. (Lecturer A)

> We do need to teach, we do need to publish, we have the same mission or we have the same kind of responsibilities and roles as a university faculty. (Lecturer B)

The interviewees' responses showed a stronger academic identity from scholarship writing and their alignment with the broader academic community (Webster, 2022). The sense of mission as scholars and researchers seemed to take precedence over overcoming the pressure of publication and uncertainties arising from the scholar scheme.

Conducting research to inform and improve teaching

Without the 'publish or perish' dictum or clear promotional prospects, it seemed to the interviewees that pursuing research 'excellence' was not a pragmatic goal. They admitted that repeatedly teaching the same EAP materials for years in the teaching post was a safe choice to 'teach and finish . . . complete the task' (Lecturer A). They considered themselves in a secure job position, since 'when [teaching-lane EAP lecturers] have finished teaching, they don't have any evaluation of their research publication, so it seems quite secure' (Lecturer C). However, the interview data showed that the lecturers' intention to advance to the research lane would be more than just a desire to keep up with the fast-moving academic world, but also to provide quality EAP teaching through their engagement in scholarly activities. Lecturer D expressed her fear of 'go[ing] back to that main ... teaching-only thing', and 'recognize[d] some numbness', so much that she hoped to 'avoid that complacency because the world is changing very fast.' Now focussed more on research, they expressed their aspiration of providing quality EAP teaching based on research, or informing teaching with pedagogical and theoretical knowledge, as they believed that teaching and research feed each other.

They reported that they leverage their expertise in linguistics or other EAP-related knowledge to teach their students or to increase their understanding of their students:

> I think that's very important to know the theoretical background of those pedagogies ... so that I can have a lot of skills to motivate students and pass knowledge to them. (Lecturer A)

> I will always introduce to them some learning strategies, or even I use corpus tools for [showing] examples. (Lecturer C)

The interviewees' reflections suggest that the merging of 'researcher' and 'teacher' identities represents an alignment of their professional identity with credibility arising from scholarly works. Although this view seems to contradict their earlier comments on the teaching-research distinction, their perspective on teaching-scholarship integration may also show the reflexiveness of their conflicted views and awareness of the need for informing teaching with scholarship. In constructing a researcher identity, EAP lecturers should prioritize their scholarly practices that have an impact on their teaching practices as 'meaningful' ones instead of pursuing 'meaningless' activities only for the sake of measurement (Barkhuizen, 2021). While research interests may vary among individuals, REAPs should develop classroom-based research that can encourage reflection and reflexivity, in order to improve practice in turn. Additionally, to promote EAP research, new EAP practitioners need to be better informed about the connection between research and the language-teaching profession (Barkhuizen, 2021) and seek support through induction programmes or mentorship (Billot and King, 2017).

Embracing an 'entrepreneur' mindset

The major intellectual contributions of emerging scholars in the college include submitting grant proposals and writing journal articles. In view of the challenges, they developed strategies across personal and social levels to make their research efforts efficient and meaningful. Three main solutions are identified from the interview data: developing research motivation, expanding collaboration and adjusting research orientation.

With a reduced teaching load, transitioning into becoming a research academic implies that their daily schedule can be more flexible than teaching-intensive staff. Intrinsic motivation for research engagement becomes essential, as reflected in one's self-discipline, passion and time management capability, the personal attributes which the interviewees were continuously developing:

> I need to have a very clear pattern . . . to have a very self-regulated study pattern for myself . . . for my personal development as well. (Lecturer A)

> [One has] to save some time and use it more efficiently; during the semester, I'd spend more time focussing on my teaching . . . but during the semester break I'll change back to . . . focus more on my research. (Lecturer B)

> Time management is an issue . . . and self-discipline as well . . . most of the things that I do . . . are what I choose to do. Even with these grant proposals . . . I still get a lot of pleasure writing them. (Lecturer D)

Personal motivation also originates from the staff's strategic articulation of their research ideas, through proposal writing to gain control of the project 'once you have the idea . . . when your logic is good and coherent', as Lecturer B put it. When I asked him how to get projects involving linguistic analyses funded, he advised that one has to address and solve problems and 'sell [one's] ideas' that are 'ground-breaking'. These reflections may resemble a 'business-like' thinking approach, in that research-lane staff develop themselves as 'personal brands' through 'pitching' research solutions to secure funding. It seems to be at odds with scholarship's higher goals of knowledge advancement and solving real-world problems; however, considering research in business or marketing terms apparently motivates researchers to visualize their achievements as they attempt to overcome hardships in research.

To resolve challenges due to limited time amid a busy teaching schedule, all the interviewed REAPs considered expanding collaborative networks in the college to be crucial, such as cross-disciplinary research within the division; Lecturer C mentioned his collaboration with colleagues from Chinese literature, in order to analyse literary texts through quantitative methods, which was his area of expertise. They were also aware that their expertise might require complementary efforts from their peers. As Lecturer D put it figuratively, REAPs 'try to piece the puzzles together' to 'speed up the outcomes', to 'add something onto our research repertoires' (Lecturer B) and, in general, to be 'more productive' (Lecturer A). In a broader sense, the REAPs might also adjust their research foci from their original expertise or EAP-related studies to the latest research trends in the college. As a linguist whose main focus is EAP written text analysis, I have been exploring new research opportunities in different areas such as data-driven language pedagogy, language assessment and teaching staff's research engagement. These areas are relevant to research related to teaching professional development, one of the main research directions that the college's pedagogic research centre pursues. With regards to the establishment of the college's big data laboratory, Lecturer C regarded this trend as 'a good signal' since it was pertinent to his research area, in that '[he could] use what [he had] learnt before for the future research'.

From the above reflections, the REAPs match the descriptions of 'teacher- and research- entrepreneurs' (Davis, 2006; Kurek, Geurts and Roosendaal, 2007). The notion of 'entrepreneur' in higher education assumes the existence of a 'consumer':

students consuming educational products or the institution capitalizing on research output (Clark and Jackson, 2018). That said, the presumably 'good' qualities of 'entrepreneurship' may actually help REAPs build resilience to face challenges arising from the constant changes in their work context. As Keyhani and Kim's (2021) systematic review pointed out, teacher 'entrepreneurs' possess many proactive and prosocial attributes such as being innovative, opportunity-minded, dedicated, resourceful, risk-tolerant, visionary, self-improvement oriented, collaborative and socially motivated. In terms of collaboration, Kurek, Geurts and Roosendaal's (2007) notion of 'research entrepreneurs' suggested that scholars are able to establish relationships with the surrounding environment to form alliances and joint adventures, while maintaining autonomy to engage in research and develop long-term goals. These attributes can also be applied to describe the interviewees, because the highly competitive and stressful context in which the interviewees were situated suggests the natural and inevitable process of turning REAPs into 'entrepreneurs' as a coping mechanism. Motivation for and engagement in research may require a strong sense of 'business-like' thinking and determination to eliminate the precarious factors in the research lane.

Concluding remarks

This chapter has reported on how REAPs address the tension between teaching and research excellence in a self-financed HEI transitioning into a university. The precarity arising from the insecurity of the position as a research-lane faculty member is, however, different from that described in Ding (2019) regarding employment stability. Instead, the REAPs cope with changes in the teaching profile and the pressure of competing for major external grants and producing research outcomes. Their less demarcated roles as lecturers/researchers do not seem to undermine their scholar identity, as their reflexive response to their status is reflected in their agency in research engagement, despite heavy teaching and administration duties. Their research engagement is not solely for their personal career development, but for informing and improving their teaching in the EAP classroom. It is therefore apparent that the REAPs interviewed in the present study possess the self-determining and agentive mindset, resisting the status-quo, seeking collaborations proactively and being more innovative regarding research activities. While they might not see themselves as effectively balancing their multiple roles, their determination and passion for research overcome the sense of insecurity resulting from the precarity of being an EAP lecturer/researcher. Their reflections suggest that, while 'managerial' measures in HEIs aim to ensure the healthy development of the institution (Lau et al., 2023), a 'professional' logic (e.g. autonomy, collegiality, knowledge creation) seems to be more desirable than a 'corporate' logic that focusses predominantly on metrics and rankings (Vican, Friedman and Andreasen, 2020), as demonstrated by their undertaking scholarly activities to resist result-oriented, monotonous teaching, developing their careers and advancing their fields. This is not to suggest that resistance to the managerial culture in HEIs is necessary; however, institutional administration should look into what elements of the 'corporate' logic result in the faculty's dissatisfaction and ensure that the priorities of the institution are communicated clearly and transparently (Vican, Friedman and Andreasen, 2020).

As this chapter has focussed primarily on the REAPs' perceptions of a myriad of changes amid the college's transition, future research seeks to incorporate voices from teaching-lane EAP lecturers, who may provide insights into why they do not move to the research lane, and the college management, who may offer a bird's-eye view on how staff deployment strategies can better motivate academic staff to engage in research and innovation. Additionally, this chapter has illustrated the interviewees' coping strategies in response to the precarity of being in the research lane. Future studies can also introduce psychological analytical frameworks, such as Herzberg's (1966) two-factor model, to understand how to increase lecturers' motivation for research engagement, aside from maintaining or enhancing job satisfaction as EAP lecturers.

Appendix 1. REAP interview protocol

Background information

1. Qualifications
2. Subjects you're currently teaching
3. Physical (e.g. single/shared office) and administrative position (e.g. programme leadership) in the institution

For REAPs

1. In a very general way, what is/are the major research project(s) you are working on?
2. Why did you choose to engage in the research lane rather than staying in the teaching lane?
3. How would you describe the key changes as you have transitioned from a teaching practitioner to research staff?
    1. How much have recent changes in the institution (i.e. greater emphasis on research and grant applications) influenced the way you work here?
4. How would you describe your current career since you have transitioned to research?
    1. What is your greatest achievement so far?
    2. What are your greatest challenges so far?
    3. How much has your teaching load influenced the way you work?
5. Can you comment on working on solo projects and interdisciplinary research collaborations?
    1. Specifically, how are they similar/different to you?

6. How do you see yourself in comparison with the research-track staff in government-funded universities?

   1. What kind of professional do you consider yourself?
   2. How much do you see your transition as equivalent to taking up an academic position as 'assistant professor'?
   3. To what extent does the job title influence your perception of yourself as research staff?

7. How do you see yourself in comparison with teaching-lane colleagues?
8. How do you balance your career and other parts of your life?

References

Allman, P. (2001), *Revolutionary Social Transformation: Democratic Hopes, Political Possibilities and Critical Education*, Westport: Bergin & Garvey.

Amin, M. E. K., L. S. Nørgaard, A. Cavaco, M. J. Witry, L. Hillman, A. Cernasev and S. Desselle (2020), 'Establishing Trustworthiness and Authenticity in Qualitative Pharmacy Research', *Research in Social and Administrative Pharmacy*, 16 (10): 1472–82.

Arhar, J., T. Niesz, J. Brossman, S. Koebley, K. O'Brien, D. Loe and F. Black(2013), 'Creating a "Third Space" in the Context of a University–School Partnership: Supporting Teacher Action Research and the Research Preparation of Doctoral Students', *Educational Action Research*, 21 (2): 218–36.

Bai, L. (2018), 'Language Teachers' Beliefs about Research: A Comparative Study of English Teachers from Two Tertiary Education Institutions in China', *System*, 72: 114–23.

Banegas, D. L. (2018), 'Towards Understanding EFL Teachers' Conceptions of Research: Findings from Argentina', *Profile: Issues in Teachers Professional Development*, 20 (1): 57–72.

Barkhuizen, G. (2021), 'Identity Dilemmas of a Teacher (educator) Researcher: Teacher Research versus Academic Institutional Research', *Educational Action Research*, 29 (3): 358–77.

Billot, J. and V. King (2017), 'The Missing Measure? Academic Identity and the Induction Process', *Higher Education Research & Development*, 36 (3): 612–24.

Breshears, S. (2019), 'The Precarious Work of English Language Teaching in Canada', *TESL Canada Journal*, 36 (2): 26–47.

Choi, T. H. and K. L. Cheung (2014), 'Enhancement of Student Learning with English as the Medium of Instruction: Introduction', in *Briefing Paper, Enactment of Medium of Instruction Policy: Enhancement of Student Learning in Courses with English as a Medium of Instruction Project*, Hong Kong: Hong Kong Institute of Education.

Clark, J. O. and L. H. Jackson (2018), 'Ideology in Neoliberal Higher Education: The Case of the Entrepreneur', *Journal for Critical Education Policy Studies (JCEPS)*, 16 (1): 313–45.

Davis, V. 'The Classroom is Flat: Teacherpreneurs and the Flat Classroom Project Kickoff', *Cool Cat Teacher Blog*. http://coolcatteacher.blogspot.com/2006/11/classroom-is-flat-teacherpreneurs-and.html

Ding, A. (2019), 'EAP Practitioner Identity', in K. Hyland and L. L. C. Wong (eds), *Specialised English: New Directions in ESP and EAP Research and Practice*, 63–76, New York: Routledge.

Ding, A. and I. Bruce (2017), *The English for Academic Purposes Practitioner: Operating on the Edge of Academia*, Cham: Palgrave Macmillan.

Dreyfus, S., S. Humphrey, A. Mahboob and J. R. Martin (2016), *Genre Pedagogy in Higher Education: The SLATE Project*, Basingstoke: Palgrave Macmillan.

Evans, S. (2016), *The English Language in Hong Kong: Diachronic and Synchronic Perspectives*, London: Springer.

Evans, S. and C. Green (2007), 'Why EAP is Necessary: A Survey of Hong Kong Tertiary Students', *Journal of English for Academic Purposes*, 6 (1): 3–17.

Fincher, R. M. E., D. E. Simpson, S. P. Mennin, G. C. Rosenfeld, A. Rothman, M. C. McGrew, P. A. Hansen, P. E. Mazmanian and J. M. Turnbull (2000), 'Scholarship in Teaching: An Imperative for the 21st Century', *Academic Medicine*, 75 (9): 887–94.

Glassick, C. E. (2000), 'Boyer's Expanded Definitions of Scholarship, the Standards for Assessing Scholarship, and the Elusiveness of the Scholarship of Teaching', *Academic Medicine*, 75 (9): 877–80.

Hadley, G. (2015), *English for Academic Purposes in Neoliberal Universities: A Critical Grounded Theory*, vol. 22, London: Springer.

Hadley, G. (2018), 'The Games People Play: A Critical Study of 'Resource Leeching' Among 'Blended' English for Academic Purpose Professionals in Neoliberal Universities', in R. L. Raby and E. J. Valeau (eds), *Language, Education and Neoliberalism: Critical Studies in Sociolinguistics*, 184–203, Bristol: Multilingual Matters.

Harding, A., A. Scott, S. Laske and C. Burtscher (2007), *Bright Satanic Mills: Universities, Regional Development and the Knowledge Economy*, New York: Routledge.

Herzberg, F. I. (1966), *Work and the Nature of Man*, Cleveland: World Publishing Company.

Ishikawa, M. (2009), 'University Rankings, Global Models, and Emerging Hegemony: Critical Analysis from Japan', *Journal of Studies in International Education*, 13 (2): 159–73.

Keyhani, N. and M. S. Kim (2021), 'A Systematic Literature Review of Teacher Entrepreneurship', *Entrepreneurship Education and Pedagogy*, 4 (3): 376–95.

Kurek, K., P. Geurts and H. E. Roosendaal (2007), 'The Research Entrepreneur-an Analysis of the Research Environment', *Third Organization Studies Summer Workshop: Generation and Use of Academic Knowledge about Organizations*, Crete, Greece, 7–9.

Lau, Y., L. M. E. Cheung, E. M. H. Chan and S. W. Lee (2023), 'The Perspective of New Managerialism on Changes in Hong Kong's Self-financing Post-secondary Education Institutions: Progress, Challenges and Outlook', *International Journal of Educational Management*. https://doi.org/10.1108/ijem-05-2022-0207

Ma, Q., R. Yuan, L. M. E. Cheung and J. Yang (2022), 'Teacher Paths for Developing Corpus-based Language Pedagogy: A Case Study', *Computer Assisted Language Learning*. https://doi.org/10.1080/09588221.2022.2040537

Marr, J. W. (2021), 'The Promise and Precarity of Critical Pedagogy in English for Academic Purposes', *BC TEAL Journal*, 6 (1): 132–41.

Maxwell, J. A (2012), *Qualitative Research Design: An Interactive Approach*, Sage.

McCartney, D. M. and A. S. Metcalfe (2018), 'Corporatization of Higher Education through Internationalization: The Emergence of Pathway Colleges in Canada', *Tertiary Education and Management*, 24 (3): 206–20.

Miles, M. B. and A. M. Huberman (1994), *Qualitative Data Analysis: An Expanded Sourcebook*, Sage.

Morrow, S. L. (2005), 'Quality and Trustworthiness in Qualitative Research in Counseling Psychology', *Journal of Counseling Psychology*, 52 (2): 250.

Ortega, A. G. (2018), 'A Case for Blended EAP in Hong Kong Higher Education', *The Asian EFL Journal*, 20 (9.2): 6–34.

Poerwandari, E. K. (2021), 'Minimizing Bias and Maximizing the Potential Strengths of Autoethnography as a Narrative Research', *Japanese Psychological Research*, 63 (4): 310–23.

Schulman, L. S. (2000), 'Fostering a Scholarship of Teaching and Learning', *Paper Presented at the Annual Louise McBee Lecture*, Institute of Higher Education, The University of Georgia.

Sutherland, S. (2002), *Higher Education in Hong Kong* (Report of the University Grants Committee: Commissioned by the Secretary for Education and Manpower; Hong Kong: University Grants Committee, Hong Kong).

Tang, H. H. H., C. P. G. Tsui and C. F. W. Chau (2018), 'Sustainability of Massification in East Asian Higher Education: Community Colleges in Hong Kong in Retrospect and Prospects', in R. L. Raby and E. J. Valeau (eds), *Handbook of Comparative Studies on Community Colleges and Global Counterparts*, 63–82, Cham: Springer International Publishing.

Tse, S. K., M. S. K. Shum, W. W. Ki and C. P. C. Wong (2001), 'The Transition from English to Mother-Tongue Chinese as Medium of Instruction; Issues and Problems as Seen by Hong Kong Teachers', *L1-Educational Studies in Language and Literature*, 1 (1): 9–36.

Vican, S., A. Friedman and R. Andreasen (2020), 'Metrics, Money, and Managerialism: Faculty Experiences of Competing Logics in Higher Education', *The Journal of Higher Education*, 91 (1): 139–64.

Vosko, L. F. (2006), *Precarious Employment: Understanding Labour Market Insecurity in Canada*, Canada: McGill-Queen's Press.

Walková, M. (2021), 'Scholarship is a Journey', *The Language Scholar*, 9: 97–104.

Webster, S. (2022), 'The Transition of EAP Practitioners into Scholarship Writing', *Journal of English for Academic Purposes*, 57: 1010–91.

Wong, Y.-L. (2022), 'Student Alienation in Higher Education under Neoliberalism and Global Capitalism: A Case of Community College Students' Instrumentalism in Hong Kong', *Community College Review*, 50 (1): 96–116.

Zamir, S. (2018), 'A Teaching Career: Mobility and Stagnation', *Athens Journal of Education*, 5 (2): 145–60.

Chapter 11

RESPONDING TO STUDENTS' DISCIPLINARY WRITING IN A UNIVERSITY-WIDE WRITING REQUIREMENT

NEGOTIATING AGENCY THROUGH POSITIONING

Shari Dureshahwar Lughmani and Svetlana Chigaeva-Heddad

Introduction

English language teaching in English-medium tertiary contexts often places EAP practitioners in cross-disciplinary, collaborative and policy-driven institutional environments. Decisions about language teaching are highly regulated, and faculty are often required to allocate curricular space, time and resources towards language input that is sometimes received with caution or resentment by non-language faculty as such services are provided by language centres (Craig, 2012). At the same time, as English language standards are considered a benchmark of graduates' quality by senior management and employers, language centres respond by formalizing and structuring language education for visibility across the university and accountability to the departments that they service, the funding bodies and the senior management while trying to receive recognition for their work as an academic discipline with its own knowledge structures and practices (Ding and Bruce, 2017). Such positioning often places language teachers in highly restrictive environments in which they provide formalized language education services to stakeholders across the university. The writing programme described in this chapter is an example of this kind of environment.

In 2012, when switching over from a three- to four-year curriculum for undergraduate studies in Hong Kong, one university introduced a highly structured writing-intensive general education (GE) programme that undergraduate students had to complete as part of their graduation requirement. It was decided by the task force that implemented the new expanded curricular structure that all the university faculties would develop and teach GE subjects and that each GE subject would include a written assignment taking up at least 40 per cent of the final grade. English language centre teachers were mandated to offer two rounds of feedback on students' assignment drafts while the final draft would be assessed by GE teachers (Lughmani et al., 2016). This requirement is now known as the English Writing Requirement (EWR). The programme is large in scale as it involves twenty to twenty-five GE teachers from across various faculties, around 2,000 students, most of whom are Cantonese L1 speakers, and around 80 language teachers each semester. Given the scale of the programme, its impact on students' graduation results and the cross-disciplinary collaborative structure, it was important to develop clear communication lines between the various stakeholders and to ensure fairness and parity across various GE subjects as well as to develop strategies for managing language teachers' workload. As a result, a liaison team consisting of five to six language teachers was created.

Liaison team members co-construct assessment guidelines with GE teachers, develop support tools for language teachers and students, communicate with all the stakeholders involved and evaluate the programme on a regular basis. They also support language teachers in providing assignment-specific genre-based feedback on disciplinary assignments (Gardner and Nesi, 2013). When commenting on the first draft, language teachers are asked to focus on assignment task fulfilment and text organization and present feedback as three to five actionable points. They are asked explicitly not to focus on surface-level linguistic features of writing at this stage. Draft 2 feedback is expected to build on the first round of feedback and provide further advice regarding the assessment task and its genre, including its lexico-grammatical realization. All in all, language teachers have a clearly defined duty within the programme with clearly communicated expectations regarding preferred kinds of feedback but, as our studies show, they also exercise the right to develop their own approaches to providing feedback, sometimes ignoring or reinterpreting the liaison team recommendations (Burns, Chigaeva-Heddad and Leung, 2019).

Understanding language teachers' experiences within this highly regulated programme is important so that their expectations become more visible and their preferred feedback practices are recognized in this and similar programmes in the future. This chapter addresses this by reporting findings from positioning analysis of three language teachers' narratives about their feedback and their experiences with the programme. Our goal in conducting this study was to understand whether and how these teachers exercised agency while being positioned to provide very specific types of feedback within this highly structured programme.

Agency and positioning

Positioning refers to the phenomenon of individuals continually adopting different selves and assigning roles (Langenhov and Harre, 1994). Individuals take up positions made available within the discourses (Bomer and Laman, 2004). Such acts of positioning are agentive and occur in conversational contexts called storylines by Harre and Langenhov (1994). *Storylines* and *positions* are part of the larger cultural context, and individuals adopt the positions within the storylines that occur within cultural contexts rather than invent completely new positions or storylines. *Agency* – 'an individual's ability to choose acts of positioning' – does not extend beyond the boundaries of these cultural contexts. Agency is exercised through subject positions that individuals can ascribe themselves in relation to others (Kayi-Aydar, 2019). Studies have also explored language teachers' agency within various given and potentially restrictive contexts, tracing the ways in which language teachers position themselves and others to find agentic ways to exercise their rights and perform given duties. In her 2015 study, Kayi-Aydar reveals how, in one storyline, Janelle positions herself as superior and more agentic after having learnt another language (Spanish) compared with her family members who knew only English (2015). The discursive nature of the link between positioning and agency is further highlighted when Janelle, later, in another storyline, after an unsuccessful attempt to become a teacher of Spanish as a second language, decided to give up on her career as a Spanish teacher as the social context and her lower grades in a teacher exam nudged her towards making that decision (2015: 151).

Positions come with *rights*, *duties* and obligations relevant to the context. Although, within a storyline, positions are usually coherent, these can change in different storylines (Davies and Harré, 1990). Duties and rights are intimately related, reciprocal and can be resisted and ascribed as Harré has elucidated in two steps (Harré, 2009: 7–8).

1. Rights and duties are distributed among people in changing patterns as they engage in performing particular kinds of positioning actions.
2. These patterns are themselves the product of higher-order acts of positioning through which rights and duties to ascribe or resist positioning are distributed. (Harré and Moghaddam, 2012: 7)

Storylines create coherence between the I/you and speech/text triad. Research investigating teacher positioning has identified both broader – taken for granted or institutionalized – storylines as well as more discursive and conversation-based and thus evolving storylines (Kayi-Aydar, 2021). There could be many storylines in which individuals navigate and take up subject positions as was evident in Bomer and Laman's 2004 study observing a children's writing workshop as they developed their texts in groups (2004). Examples of storylines that emerged in our data include broader storylines that consist of typical pedagogical relationships such as student–teacher and less explored subject–language teacher relationships. However, it is the discursive, evolving, conversation-based storylines that are the focus of this chapter as they revealed the dynamic nature of positioning, that is, what positions teachers take, contest and attribute to other characters in the storylines and how this helps them exercise their agency.

Methodology

Social, discursive or 'new paradigm psychology' (Davies and Harré, 1990: 43) with a focus on 'dynamic aspects of encounters' provides the theoretical framework used in this study as it aims to understand why individuals act in certain ways through the narratives they share (Harré, 1979; Harré and Secord, 1972). This framework views agency as constructed through social interactions and suggests that people position themselves and others to achieve their goals.

Participants

The English Language Centre hires language instructors with an MA in linguistics and ELT or TESOL and at least five years of post-secondary teaching experience. Hence, even the new instructors are not really new to university-level teaching, but they may be new to the EWR programme that is the focus of our paper. The instructors' teaching experience has been taken into consideration with regard to the EWR programme as well as overall experience in the field.

Three teachers working on the same GE subject participated in the study. The written assignment in this subject required students to read a book containing ten chapters on topics related to earth conservation and natural disasters, summarize the book and then analyse one of the book themes in more detail.

Mike, the most experienced of the three teachers, has been teaching for thirty-four years and has been with the unit for about twenty years. Originally from the UK, he has made Hong Kong his home for more than two decades. His expertise lies in professional as well as academic communication. He has experience of teaching ESL to secondary-school students and sub-degree students, as well as working adults at the British Council and various corporations. He has been involved in the writing programme since its inception, has worked on a number of different EWR assignments and has marked this assignment numerous times.

Becca has been an ESL teacher for eleven years during which she has taught post-secondary and degree-level students. Prior to teaching, Becca was in the banking field. She joined the university about seven years ago and has been contributing to the programme since then. During this period, she has worked on assignments from three to four different subjects; she has worked on the assignment under study for at least three times.

Jane, the teacher with the least EWR experience compared to the other two, joined the university in the same academic year that the study was conducted. She has four years of teaching experience overall that includes sub-degree and degree-level teaching. This was her first semester marking EWR assignments at the university though she had experienced the same model for about five semesters at a sister institution that had adopted the same EWR model.

Data collection and analysis

To explore the three teachers' positioning and agency, individual semi-structured interviews were conducted in semester 1 of 2021–2022. The interviews were divided into two parts: (i) stimulated recall and (ii) a follow-up interview. In the first part, the teacher and the interviewer looked at four feedback reports (two students, two reports per draft), with the teacher recalling what elements of the text they had commented on and the reasoning behind these comments. When needed, follow-up questions were asked to elicit further elaboration or to clarify elements of the feedback reports. After stimulated recall, the teachers were asked questions to obtain additional information about their experience and expectations (refer to **Appendix 1** to see these specific questions for all three teachers).

The collected data were analysed cyclically both separately by the two authors and the interviewer as well as together. The questions that guided our analysis were:

- Given the highly constricting institutionally assigned or imposed positions that our language teachers experience, which are 'difficult or impossible to reject or resist' (Kayi-Aydar, 2021: 7), how much agency do teachers have within the context of this university-wide writing programme and how do they exercise it?
- What can the positions the language teachers take, resist and ascribe to tell us about these teachers' agency?

In the first stage of our analysis, we discussed initial read-throughs of the transcripts and explored emerging positions, rights and duties. This initial analysis helped us develop a shared understanding of our approach, identify lexico-grammatical patterns frequently used by the teachers and trace preliminary storylines. Using the guiding questions, interview data were further examined to distil storylines of the teachers through an analysis of their speech acts that revealed their positions along with the rights and duties as they either claimed positions, ascribed these or were positioned by others in the storylines. While interpreting these storylines, we explored language teachers' acts of positioning in response to the assigned EWR feedback duties and whether they exercised their rights to redefine them. To do this, we relied on the four levels of positioning initially developed by Green (2020) and further refined by Kayi-Aydar (2021). This framework analyses speech acts from the narrators' point of view and describes how they reflexively or interactively position themselves exercising more agency (*by* and *with*) as well as when they are positioned by others which takes away their agency to a certain extent (*of* and *to*). See Table 11.1 for the framework we employed.

The grammar of agency framework (Arnold, 2011; Martin, 2016, 2020) was used as a secondary analytical lens in our study to enhance our understanding of how the teachers used language to construct agency for themselves and others. More specifically, we examined the teachers' use of language to attribute responsibility to themselves or others and how this related to their feedback practices. Table 11.2 summarizes key lexico-grammatical features that signal attributions of responsibility.

Ethical considerations

This study was conducted with the approval of the institutional ethics committee. The confidentiality and anonymity of the participants were ensured throughout the study, and their identities were kept confidential. The participants were informed that they could withdraw from the study at any time without any consequences.

Table 11.1 Four types of positioning

Type	Explanation	Examples of application to EWR
Positioning *by*	This refers to the positions individuals construct for themselves and others reflexively and take responsibility for their acts of positioning by exercising rights and duties, thus demonstrating agency.	EWR teachers may exercise their right to use their previous experience as a resource and self-position themselves as communication experts in relation to students and subject teachers. They may position students as novice writers who need explicit training in audience awareness.
Positioning *with*	Positions are agentively and interactively negotiated in a developing storyline. Individuals argue for their interpretation of the story, resisting, asserting, disputing or redefining rights and duties.	EWR teachers may choose to position themselves as teachers of grammar and language rather than genre experts and redefine and reinterpret the nature and type of EWR feedback accordingly.
Positioning *of*	Individuals are positioned by others with more authority but have some power to enact/negotiate alternative positions.	Positioning of EWR teachers as feedback providers by the institution, though somewhat restrictive, is something through which they can choose to enact other positions such as interpreters of EWR assignment guidelines.
Positioning *to*	Individuals' positions are imposed by the institution. These are difficult or impossible to reject or resist. Individuals are unable to redefine or dispute the assigned duties and obligations.	EWR teachers must offer two rounds of feedback to students within a set number of days.

Source: adapted from Kayi-Aydar, 2021: 6–7.

It is important to note that our roles within the programme may have impacted the results presented here. The first author was in charge of conceptualizing and coordinating the programme from its very inception while the second author was actively involved in the programme both as a teacher and deputy coordinator between 2012 and 2017. Our coordination duties involved interpreting the policies and translating them into the communication procedures and the tools described earlier in the chapter. Our aim has been to balance writing teachers' workload with meeting both students' learning needs as well as discipline teachers' expectations. As such, we are certain that we have had an impact on teachers' practices and agency.

To minimize our impact on the interviewees and the data presented in this chapter, we adopted two key strategies. First, an invitation to participate in the study was sent out to all the teachers working on the subject, with some of them choosing not to participate. The teachers who were eventually interviewed accepted the invitation to be interviewed as well as to share their feedback reports. Second, we hired a research assistant who was not familiar with the programme prior to

Table 11.2 The grammar of agency

Lexico-grammatical features	Examples
Pronouns	• The speaker's use of 'I' suggests personal responsibility for the utterance. • Use of 'we' suggests diffused or shared responsibility with others or collective agency. • Use of third-person pronouns suggests deflection of responsibility from the speaker to the general public.
Sentence modality	• The indicative, imperative and subjunctive moods and modal verbs mark the speaker's responsibility for a statement's reliability, authority or originality. • Modal verbs, for example, 'must', may indicate deflection of the speaker's responsibility for an action or obscure agency. • Verbs such as 'want' may suggest the speaker's strengthened personal commitment to action.
Verbs	• Emotive verbs can indicate speakers' feelings or motives which can provide useful insights regarding their acceptance or rejection of responsibility. • Epistemic verbs such as 'know' and 'think' index individual responsibility.

Source: adapted from Martin, 2016, 2020.

the interviews. He was able to ask questions from a non-specialist perspective, thus avoiding possible bias due to subject knowledge or the tendency for the respondents to acquiesce had the coordinators interviewed the respondents themselves (Bryman, 2016). The assistant was then involved in the initial coding and analysis of the data.

Findings and discussion

In line with the positioning theory framework, three storylines emerged in conversations with the three teachers that encompassed their description of the EWR and their positioning of themselves and others. These also shed light on teachers' agentive decision-making while giving feedback.

Storyline 1: Language teachers – EWR is not like 'regular teaching'

A recurrent theme across all the interviews was the teachers' comparison of their regular teaching duties with EWR. It was clear that the teachers felt more agentive in their own classes where they had more control over what they were teaching and how teaching unfolded.

Mike foregrounded the difference in terms of the process of engaging (or not) with students. He positioned EWR as a finite task with clearly defined start and end points ('two snapshots') while he described his regular teaching as an ongoing process ('a short video film').

EWR as two Polaroid snapshots

> M: You know they're going to submit a draft. You **don't know** the [EWR] students; you give them feedback ... They give you the second draft, and then you give them feedback. With students in a [regular] class you **know** who the students are. You see them every week. You can give them little bits of feedback all the time. It's an **ongoing** kind of **process** anyway ... EWR is two **snapshots**, whereas teaching regular class is **a short video film** as opposed to you know, **two Polaroid snapshots**.

This view of the programme as snapshots is tightly linked with the perceived lack of 'knowing' students. This exemplifies one of the positions Mike consistently assigns to EWR students – that of strangers who remain relatively unknown to teachers. This also suggests that he himself would like to get to know students, but his agency to do so is limited as he, like other EWR teachers, is *positioned to* respond to drafts on two separate occasions rather than having ongoing encounters with students.

Similar positioning emerged in Jane's description of her EWR work:

I am supposed to put in more energy

> J: I think also with my own ... courses ... my feedback is a lot **more detailed** because I've more time. I am supposed to put in **more energy** and effort into my own courses rather than this, to be honest. So there [are] a lot of things **I would love to** do with these [EWR] students, but **I can't** because of the time constraints and because of, you know, I just don't know whether or not my effort will be worth it because **I don't know** if the students ... even read [my feedback] report or not.

Like Mike, Jane highlights two rather different positions: that of a teacher working with her own courses and that of an EWR teacher. Unlike Mike, she relates her discussion to the amount of effort she gives to the two roles. The former position dictates more serious duties, indicated through her use of the comparative 'more': more detailed, more energy, more effort. The latter position is not described in terms of duties or rights but rather in terms of negative modality and epistemic constraints: 'I would love to do ... but I can't', 'time constraints', 'don't know'. The latter refers to not knowing how engaged students would be with teachers' feedback, a right that is again denied to EWR teachers.

Becca below uses the word 'passive' to suggest that EWR positions teachers as less agentive:

We are a bit more passive

> B: **I think** in the EWR marking initiative, language teachers are **a bit more passive** instead of **very active**. After all, we receive the draft from the

student. We read them, we provide them with feedback reports, but we **don't** actually reach out to those students like we do with **our own** students in our own subjects, **right?**

Here Becca's choice of the epistemic verb 'think', modifiers such as 'a bit' and the interrogative 'right?' shows a level of tentativeness indicative of uncertainty as to how much her agency to reach out to students and assess their engagement with teachers' feedback is restricted by the institution, thus suggesting *positioning of* by the institution.

While teachers described their agency within the EWR through their (in)ability to engage with students so far in this study, Jane's positioning is strongly influenced by her perceived duty to the EWR assignment. In response to the question about her approach to feedback, she reflexively engages in *positioning by* with regards to the assignment and the students and agentively defines her pedagogical approach as genre-based.

Fulfilling assignment requirements

> J: *My* approach . . . I think, [is] genre base[d] and I think [I] really try to . . . not take the focus away from what the students worry the most about which is . . . the **assignment** you know, [I] don't want to . . . distract them from **fulfilling** the task requirements, so I try to if possible. Like I always try to give them . . . advice based on . . . how much they've [ful]**filled** the **assignment** [requirements].

Jane's subscription to genre-based approach allows her to fulfil her duty to give students feedback or 'advice' that focusses on the assignment; she relies on the team-generated tools such as assignment checklists and reminds students about the requirements specific to the assignment. Jane interprets the EWR duty as ensuring students are conversant with the most likely unfamiliar genre they have been asked to write exemplifying *positioning by*, but with regards to her knowledge of student needs, she seems to be feeling a complete lack of agency and portraying *positioning to*. She says:

Giving focussed feedback

> J: There's a bunch of genres it seems they [students] have absolutely no idea about and will probably never need. So yeah, [I] just try to [give feedback] based on a very, very limited understanding of who these students are and what they might have [learnt].

Jane refers to her limited understanding of the students compared with her better grasp of the assignment requirements and agentively makes the decision to limit her feedback to aspects that might help the students (that she does not know about). In this excerpt, Jane's knowledge about the students' needs is limited and she feels **positioned to** in that respect.

Though all the teachers occasionally referred to membership categories when describing their feedback practices, Becca's narrative stood out because of the frequent use of the plural pronouns *we* and *our*. This was evident from the very beginning of the interview, when Becca was asked to talk about the areas she focussed on in her first feedback report and the reasons behind her focus. Right away, she started with the pronouns 'we' and 'our'.

Legitimacy through collective practice

> B: In the first draft, draft one, we primarily focussed on looking at some ... the structure, the organization, the content, so we looked at whether or not the student fulfilled the requirements in preparing the introduction . . . and we basically looked at also the structure and organization of each subsection in part one. So, as you can see, I commented on things like how the student was not really focussed on looking at the importance of the research questions.

Here, Becca starts with explaining her actual feedback at the end of the excerpt but she prefaces it with a detailed overview of the collective practice. She adopts a very similar pattern of explaining her feedback on the second draft. Her location of her own work within clear membership practices could be due to her extensive experience with the programme and with this particular assignment. By describing her agentic actions through collective practices, she is claiming legitimacy of her actions through membership of the bigger group of language teachers. This is an example of **positioning with**, that is, where she seems to be interactively negotiating and redefining a sense of *collective* agency by interpreting her personal practice as belonging to all language teachers.

Storyline 2: Students

Student–teacher relationships constitute the most typical general storyline for teachers. It is, therefore, not surprising that the data revealed consistent agentive attempts on the part of the three teachers to position EWR students in certain identifiable ways.

One common position constructed by the teachers was that of a general student, often signalled through the plural noun *students*, personal pronoun *they*, verb *tend to*, adjective *common*, quantifiers *a lot of* and *many* and adverbs *typically*, *often* and *generally*. In the excerpt below, Becca refers to her specific comments on a specific student's work, but then she quickly moves on to generalizing this to other students.

Students tend to

> B: And again, you can see comment #4 where the student did not include the importance of the RQs. Again, I think this is **very common**. You can see mistakes or oversight by **a lot of students** in draft one. **They tend to** focus too much on summarizing the research questions instead of also telling us why those research questions were worthwhile, you know.

Another common thread revealed through the analysis of the grammar of agency was the position ascribed by teachers to students as being less agentive. Jane's use of the passive voice and structures such as *were supposed* and *were assigned* when referring to students, often through the pronoun *they*, were reflective of this. The teachers' use of particular vocabulary positions EWR students as individuals with prescribed duties which are not always performed to satisfaction. Assigned duties include duties to be more involved in and more responsible for their learning, to understand and complete the subject assignment task, to correct mistakes after reading the feedback, to remember what to do and to do some independent work after receiving feedback (***positioning to***).

According to all the teachers, students also exercise certain rights within the EWR programme, such as the right to care or not, the right to prioritize their own activities and courses and, for example, the right not to submit a full draft or not to attend EWR consultations as examples of ***positioning by***.

They don't care

> J: But for a lot of other students, I can tell from the work that they **don't care**, because otherwise if you really care about my feedback, then you would at least show me your whole draft, right? You would finish your draft and give it to me, but a lot of them don't.

They have the discretion

> B: We don't reach out to them. It's the students. You know their responsibility, or **they have the discretion** to decide whether or not they want to sign up for a feedback section of feedback session. So, if the students are not going to be signing up for any of those feedback sections, that's the only report that [they are] going to get from us.

Another position ascribed to students was that of writers. Jane, for instance, talked about them as developing academic writers. Unlike Becca and Jane, Mike placed himself in the position of the reader and used noticeably more emotive language when talking about students as 'selfish' writers. When applying the grammar of agency to Mike's narrative, we noticed an interesting pattern in his use of negative adjectives and verbs of modality, signalling an element of emotionality.

Teachers as readers

> M: The first thing that I noticed is a quick kind of look through and I've just kind of said that they really, you know you're you're . . . you're presenting information in huge great big blocks of text, which is **not very reader friendly**. It **didn't** really kind of **make** me **want** to **read** it.

A few minutes later, when describing his report on the second student's writing, Mike returned to students' poor paragraphing skills, said that he expected students to 'write things in paragraphs' and then continued describing writers with a 'very selfish attitude':

Students as selfish writers

> M: One of the things that I **despise** about academic writing and business writing as well, is people who just kind of put things in large blocks of text because it shows a **disrespect** and **contempt** for the reader, 'cause they're not writing for the reader. They're just writing for themselves. So, it's a very **selfish** attitude.

Emotionality is an important component of Kayi-Aydar's framework for positioning analysis; Kayi-Aydar argues that analysing emotions has implications for our understanding of agency achievement and identity construction (Kayi-Aydar, 2019, 2021). Martin (2020), too, argues that '[e]motions experienced during the actual storytelling or emotions experienced in the narrated events enable narrators to position themselves or others in certain ways' (2020: 5). The excerpts above signal that Mike positions himself not as a teacher whose duty is to read students' texts no matter how well they are written (as teachers are typically *positioned to*) but, importantly, as a reader who has the right to want to or not want to read a student text and as a reader who may have strong emotional reactions to students' work. This self-position is in direct relation to the position Mike assigns to students, that of writers who have the duty to respect and write for the reader. Mike's self-positioning and positioning of students would fall under the category of *positioning by* which indicates agentic positioning determined by the narrator. This analysis of positioning explains why Mike focusses so much on text structure in his feedback to students and why he considers paragraph structuring to be so important.

Storyline 3: GE subject vs. language teachers

The third storyline involved language teachers describing their work with respect to GE subject teachers. GE subject teachers were often *positioned by* our teachers as the agentive 'owners' of the GE subjects who set up the ground rules for the assignment without necessarily engaging in the writing process. Jane, for instance, focussed on genre expectations when she said:

Genre they want

> J: I think their role is **just** to provide very clear expectations and guidelines and specifically . . . uhm, being very clear about the kind of genre that they **want**.

Jane then followed up with a lengthy discussion of how the guidelines given by GE teachers are not always detailed enough. This lack of detail creates potential for language teachers to clarify GE teachers' expectation and thus 'hold students' hands'.

It's not really their job

> J: [Access to subject teachers' guidelines] was useful for me, but I can imagine that **students get confused** because a lot of students [have] never written a book report before. They [subject teachers] just say oh, part one review. Summarize all the blah blah, which is very clear, but . . . students might need a bit more detailed [explanation], you know, **hold[ing] their hands**, tell[ing] them what to put in introduction and then how do you summarize . . . but then again. I **don't think** it's really their [GE teachers'] job. Their job is really **just** to **give the ultimate goal** of this task.

It appears from the two excerpts above that language teachers' agency lies in the pedagogic space created by GE teachers' insufficiently detailed guidelines and their contribution to 'just' defining the ultimate outcome. Even though language teachers are ***positioned to*** toensure students complete drafts according to specified guidelines, they can reflexively position themselves as those who clarify and support (***positioning by***). The teachers talked extensively about the way labour is divided between subject and language teachers. Becca, in the excerpt below, for example, positions GE subject teachers as the final readers and judges of students' work.

Readers of the final draft

> B: The subject teacher only reads the final draft if I'm not mistaken, they don't go through reading the first and the second draft, so I think subject teachers will be **more focussed** on the content rather than the language features of the report.

Becca differentiates the role of the subject teacher as she engages in *positioning with* them complementarily as the reader and judge of the final paper and not of the first and second drafts. In doing so, she talks about content and language as being separate focusses for two different types of readers, somewhat different from Mike who sees these to be overlapping to some extent.

A big overlap

> M: I think, probably subject teachers' **main focus** though [is] on the content ... Whereas what **we** have to do is to look **a little bit more** at the presentation. The structure, that cohesion, the grammar, the language. So, I'm not to say that there isn't a huge overlap between the two. There is **a big overlap** between the two, but maybe it's **more** content focussed from the subject teachers' POV.

In the above excerpt Mike, exemplifying *positioning with*, interactively and agentively negotiates the roles and duties of language teachers like himself in relation to the subject teacher in terms of extent of focus – more focus by language teachers on the presentation of content and by subject teachers on the content itself.

He later goes further into expanding subject teachers' role to include both content and language. As an example of *positioning by*, based on his pedagogical belief, Mike describes GE subject teachers' potential to integrate an approach traditionally associated with language teaching into their own pedagogy.

Content-language integrated teaching

> M: **Content-language integrated learning**. It's like it's the idea that if you're teaching engineering or radiography then **you can actually be taught** useful **strategies that enable you to integrate your subject content with the language learning**. So, the idea is that rather than have subject teachers teaching the subject and [language] teachers teaching English, **the subject teacher** can actually learn particular kind of strategies and skills, [to] **integrate language teaching into their style of subject teaching** ...That's the theory. I suppose **a lot of good subject teachers** do that already.

In this excerpt, Mike suggests that content subjects may be ideally positioned as the sites of language development if content teachers are trained to integrate language into their content teaching. Mike's use of the pronoun *you* positions subject teachers by him with relation to himself as potential beneficiaries of the CLIL (Content & Language Integrated Learning) approach.

The analysis here shows that subject teachers were reflexively *positioned by* the three EAP practitioners in our study as owners of the subject and the assignment who may not be experts in language and genre and who therefore may not always provide sufficient details about their expectations. This positioning limited language teachers' agency in terms of their ability to own the assignment, but, at the same time, created an opportunity for agentive action and reflexive repositioning (by) to clarify and to provide active assignment support. This analysis also shows that language teachers, though they are **positioned to**to offer language support, may not see language and content as a clear-cut dichotomy. Instead, they see the two overlapping and potentially being integrated.

Conclusions and the way forward

This study set out to understand language teachers' agency in the context of a policy-driven highly structured writing programme where language teachers are positioned to provide two rounds of feedback on a range of discipline-specific assessments within a short period of time, in addition to their regular teaching duties. We applied the four levels of positioning – **positioning by**, **positioning with**, **positioning of** and **positioning to** – to understand the three teachers' agency depending on how they were positioned by others or how they positioned themselves and others. Although the EWR programme is highly constricting in terms of time and the types of roles teachers play, we have found evidence that not only are the three participants able to agentively negotiate their positions to play the roles that they are assigned to but also to redefine and resist their positions and roles or ascribe positions and roles to other participants in their discursive recount of the process of giving feedback. The three participants had clear justifications for the roles they played and the positions they found themselves in or redefined for themselves as well as how they managed to effectively and agentively perform their duties.

One key finding was that our teachers wanted to engage with students on a deeper level and get to know them through a more personalized process. To address this finding, the programme needs to be redesigned in the future to include more opportunities for engagement with students such as longer consultations. Another finding is the teachers' uncertainty regarding the uptake of their feedback. While the current set-up has a mechanism for understanding this area through students' reflective comments on their revision, reflection can be emphasized further through more targeted training in reflective practice. Students need to be given more responsibility to engage with their teachers and their feedback synchronously and asynchronously.

Going forward the outcomes of this study could be operationalized into staff development sessions where language teachers working on the English Writing Requirement programme (EWR) share how they exercised their agency so that a community of practice could be developed and common ways of coping with institutional constraints could be adopted in the interest of all three stakeholders' professional and learning needs. Such sharing of approaches could also allow teachers to not feel constrained but instead to adopt pedagogically sound practices of agentively making decisions to enhance the quality of feedback and align their practice with the rest of the teachers' approaches thus providing students and subject lecturers more standardized writing support.

While we focussed on the participants' narration and recount of their rationale for giving feedback via stimulated recall method, it should be interesting in the future to explore how the language teachers' positions and their agentic decision-making impacted the feedback they provided their students in terms of the revisions made and the quality of the final papers.

References

Arnold, J. (2011), 'Operationalising Agency for Classroom Research', in *Proceedings of Contemporary Approaches to Research in Mathematics, Science, Health and Environmental Education Symposium*. Deakin University, Melbourne Burwood Campus, 221 Burwood Highway, Burwood.

Bomer, R. and T. Laman (2004), 'Positioning in a Primary Writing Workshop: Joint Action in the Discursive Production of Writing Subjects', *Research in the Teaching of English*, 38 (4): 420–66.

Bryman, A. (2016), *Social Research Methods*, Fifth edition, Oxford: Oxford University Press.

Burns, C., S. Chigaeva-Heddad and M. Leung (2019), '"Otherwise Good Luck . . .": Patterns of Use Associated with *Good* in Teacher Feedback', *Asian EFL Journal*, 3 (4): 293–315. https://www.elejournals.com/1963/asian-efl-journal/asian-efl-journal-volume-23-issue-3-4-may-2019/

Craig, J. L. (2012), *Integrating Writing Strategies in EFL/ESL University Contexts a Writing-Across-the-Curriculum Approach*, New York: Routledge.

Davies, B. and R. O. M. Harré (1990), 'Positioning: The Discursive Production of Selves', *Journal for the Theory of Social Behaviour*, 20 (1): 43–63. https://doi.org/10.1111/j.1468-5914.1990.tb00174.x

Ding, A. and I. Bruce (2017), *The English for Academic Purposes Practitioner: Operating on the Edge of Academia*, Palgrave Macmillan. https://doi.org/10.1007/978-3-319-59737-9

Gardner, S. and H. Nesi (2013), 'A Classification of Genre Families in University Student Writing', *Applied Linguistics*, 34 (1): 25–52.

Green, J. L., C. Brock, W. D. Baker and P. Harris (2020), 'Positioning Theory and Discourse Analysis: An Explanatory Theory and Analytic Lens', *Handbook of the Cultural Foundations of Learning*, 119–40, New York: Routledge.

Harré, R. (1979), *Social Being: A Theory of Social Behavior*, Totowa: Littlefield, Adams.

Harré, R. (2009), 'Selection from Personal Being', in John P. Lizza (ed.), *Defining the Beginning and End of Life: Readings on Personal Identity and Bioethics*, Baltimore: Johns Hopkins University Press.

Harré, R. and F. M. Moghaddam, eds (2012), *Psychology for the Third Millennium: Integrating Cultural and Neuroscience Perspectives*, Thousand Oaks: Sage Publications.

Harré, R. and P. F. Secord (1972), *The Explanation of Social Behaviour*, Oxford: Blackwell.

Kayi-Aydar, H. (2015). 'Multiple Identities, Negotiations, and Agency Across Time and Space: A Narrative Inquiry of a Foreign Language Teacher Candidate', *Critical Inquiry in Language Studies*, 12 (2): 137–60. https://doi.org/10.1080/15427587.2015.1032076

Kayı-Aydar, H. (2019), *Positioning Theory in Applied Linguistics: Research Design and Applications*, Cham, Switzerland: Palgrave Macmillan.

Kayi-Aydar, H. (2021), 'A Framework for Positioning Analysis: From Identifying to Analyzing (pre)Positions in Narrated Story Lines', *System (Linköping)*, 102: 102600. https://doi.org/10.1016/j.system.2021.102600

Langenhove, L. V. and R. O. M. Harre (1994), 'Cultural Stereotypes and Positioning Theory', *Journal for the Theory of Social Behaviour*, 24 (4): 359–72. https://doi.org/10.1111/j.1468-5914.1994.tb00260.x

Lughmani, D., S. Gardner, J. Chen, H. Wong and L. Chan (2016), 'English across the Curriculum: Fostering Collaboration', *Journal of English Language Teaching World Online*, Centre of English Language and Communication, NUS.

Martin, J. (2016), 'The Grammar of Agency: Studying Possibilities for Student Agency in Science Classroom Discourse', *Learning, Culture and Social Interaction*, 10: 40–9. https://doi.org/10.1016/j.lcsi.2016.01.003

Martin, J. (2020), 'Researching Teacher Agency in Elementary School Science using Positioning Theory and Grammar of Agency', *Journal of Science Teacher Education*, 31 (1): 94–113. https://doi.org/10.1080/1046560X.2019.1666628

Chapter 12

POWER AND THE CANADIAN EAP PRACTITIONER

MULTIETHNOGRAPHY AS RESISTANCE?

James N. Corcoran, Jennifer J. MacDonald, Jonathan Mendelsohn and Leonardo Gomes

Introduction

Canadian post-secondary institutions have orchestrated a dramatic increase in the population of international students, contributing to a domestic language education sector worth billions in revenue (Languages Canada, 2021; McKenzie, 2018; Russell et al., 2022). The 'internationalization' of Canadian higher education continues, bringing increased linguistic and cultural diversity to campuses as well as corresponding English for academic purposes (EAP) programmes that support these students' academic language needs. Alongside the expansion of EAP programming across post-secondary institutions globally and domestically, a field of research has emerged that attempts to better understand EAP (Bruce and Bond, 2022; Charles, 2022; Hyland and Jiang, 2021). In Canada, recent EAP research has focussed on and informed EAP assessment practices (Huang, 2018), pedagogical approaches (Bhowmik and Chowdhuri, 2021), writing instruction (Marshall and Walsh Marr, 2018) and curriculum design (Zappa-Hollman and Fox, 2021), to name but a few major areas. Recent work has also provided both emic (Van Viegen and Russell, 2019) and etic (Douglas and Landry, 2021) perspectives on EAP programmes across the country. However, though this body of work has been insightful, little attention has been paid to the lived experiences of those who design and deliver EAP. Our study adopts a critical storytelling approach that considers four practitioners' experiences working across Canadian institutions of higher education with an eye towards better understanding how they navigate an educational sector perceived as rife with precarity and marginalization (Walsh Marr, 2021; Corcoran, Williams and Johnston, 2022).

In order to situate our experiences, we must recognize that EAP is (and one might argue has always been) in lock step with a broader, international trend of neoliberal-oriented education (Litzenberg, 2020). In Canada, as in the UK, EAP programmes are frequently lucrative, revenue-driven ventures expected to financially support not only their own existence, but often the activities of other departments or activities within the post-secondary institutions (Ding and Bruce, 2017; MacDonald, 2016). Within this milieu of post-secondary language support EAP practitioners have often been positioned as non-academic staff (Ding, 2019) commensurate with (but not solely responsible for) the low status of EAP within the university (Bell, 2021; Bond, 2020; Charles and Pecorari, 2016; Fenton-Smith and Gurney, 2022; MacDonald, 2022; Sizer, 2019) as well as a sense of alienation and disarticulation of identities among practitioners (Hadley, 2015). Paradoxically, despite the lucrative nature of EAP programmes, many EAP practitioners suffer from employment precarity, which has been noted not only in the UK (le Roux, 2022) but also in Canada (Breshears, 2019; Corcoran, Johnston and Williams, forthcoming), where arguably little research has taken place on EAP practitioners.

Attempting to better understand the social phenomena associated with EAP in Canada, we have adopted a critical applied linguistics (CALx) lens (Pennycook, 2021) that draws upon both neo-Marxist (Hadley, 2015) and post-structuralist (Canagarajah, 2017; Sousa Santos and Menezes, 2020) approaches to language (teaching) and (social relations of) power. In essence, we are taking the best of two (critical, yet competing) theoretical positions on language and power in EAP: one that forefronts a critique of systemic inequities, and another that demands a recognition of social and historical situatedness. We argue that adopting this multifaceted CALx lens affords an interrogation of power-imbued issues related to 'the contingent and contextual effects of power in relation to access, exclusion, reproduction, and resistance' (Pennycook, 2021: 162) within Canadian EAP. For our study, we are interested in reconciling social structures with EAP practitioners' perceived professional agency or capability to 'act, initiate, self-regulate, or make differences or changes to their situation' (Liddicoat and Taylor-Leech, 2021: 1). In invoking this lens to interrogate perceived relations of power within Canadian EAP, we draw upon previous work in Canada that has taken the EAP sector to task for its neoliberal orientations and inequitable systemic features (Breshears, 2019; Haque, 2007; MacDonald, 2022; McCartney and Metcalfe, 2018; Morgan, 2016). We contend that one way to critically engage with localized, situated questions of power, agency and identities is to amplify the voices of those living and working in the EAP field. As Canadian EAP practitioners with diverse personal and professional histories, we look to share our perceptions of the field via analysis of thematically driven conversations. As outlined below, our critical conceptual lens and multiethnographic methodology are synergetic in providing the conditions for the investigation of Canadian EAP practitioners in order to (i) better understand the material conditions of EAP practitioners; and (ii) challenge asymmetrical social relations of power in Canadian EAP.

Context, participants and methodology

The four author–participants – James, Jennifer, Leo and Jon – bring a range of cultural, linguistic and professional identities to this project. Relevant to the topic of power in EAP, we occupy varying roles, levels of job security, autonomy or scope of decision-making and influence, and engagement with teaching, curriculum development and scholarship in our day-to-day roles. Figure 12.1 outlines intersecting professional identities, including our teaching histories and linguistic repertoires, all of which inform our spectrum of perspectives on the complex and multifaceted issues of power in Canadian EAP.

Although not yet widely embraced in the field of applied linguistics, duo/multiethnography is rooted in a qualitative paradigm that seeks to better understand social realities and individual agency/identity through collective reflection and storytelling. Drawing on William Pinar's (2022) concept of 'currere', or life histories, this methodological approach affords the critical juxtaposition of several individuals who experience the same phenomena. Interestingly, in a multiethnography, the author–participants are both the researchers and the researched. In essence, the researchers explore their respective currere through conversation, making meaning through storytelling and discussion, which include the presentation of theses and antitheses (Sawyer and Norris, 2015). This storytelling enables researchers to recall and reinterpret

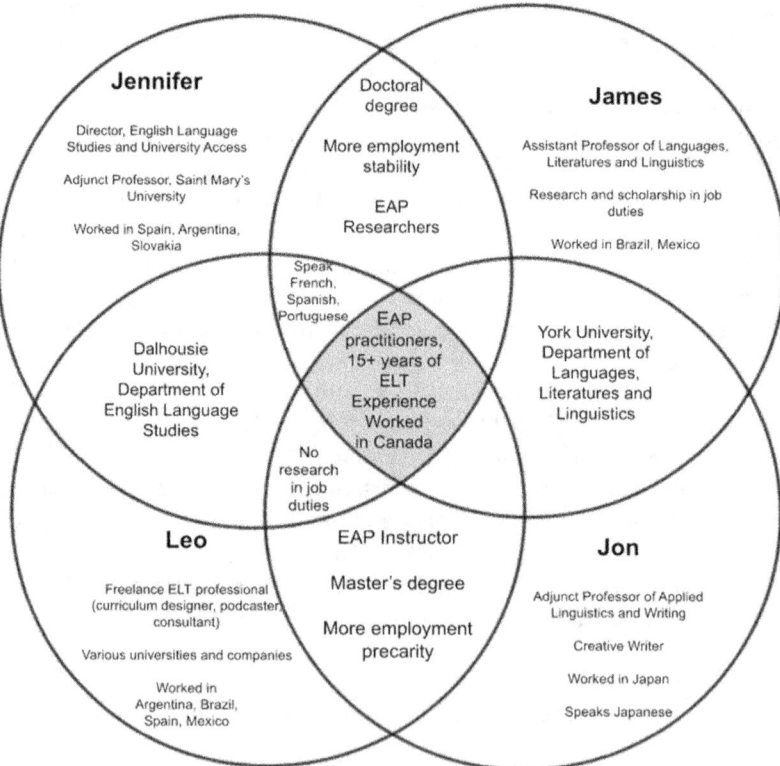

Figure 12.1 Our professional intersections.

past events and experiences, followed by cycles of interpretation that potentially lead to new perspectives and insights. In our case, this dialogic process has allowed us to trace connections between our life trajectories, work experiences and perceptions of power and agency in Canadian EAP. We have adopted this dialogic approach as we work together to question our beliefs, discourses and onto-epistemologies.

Over the past decade, multiethnography has been increasingly embraced in language education in Canada (Ahmed and Morgan, 2021; Corcoran, Gagné and McIntosh, 2018; Heng Hartse, Lockett and Ortabasi, 2018; Huang and Karas 2020), as well as a range of global contexts (Adamson et al., 2019; Banegas and Gerlach, 2022). Most recently, this novel methodological approach has been adopted in service of facilitating critical reflection on the part of language teacher educators and language teachers at different stages in their academic/professional trajectories (Kennedy and DeCosta, 2023; Smart and Cook, 2020; Tjandra et al., 2020). In the following sections, we present conversations that bring to the fore salient themes emerging from our study, followed by highlighted discussion in a conversational format that invites readers to consider not only our accounts, but also their own. Data collection involved synchronous Zoom meetings and asynchronous exchanges via Google Docs, resulting in qualitative data that was reviewed by all participants and coded into emergent, salient themes as part of a three-step, systematic analysis (Saldaña, 2021; Silverman, 2020) informed by our CALx conceptual lens that forefronted issues of access, exclusion, reproduction and resistance.

Findings: Our perspectives on power in Canadian EAP

In this section we present our findings as a set of conversations related to salient, power-imbued themes in Canadian EAP, followed by brief discussion of our positions in relation to extant literature in the field. What emerged from our conversations were convergent perspectives regarding certain features of EAP, such as the dedication of EAP practitioners to student life and learning outcomes, the challenges of carving out a career in EAP, as well as, at times, divergent perspectives on, for example, the optimum qualifications for EAP instructors, the benefits of professional development within EAP programmes and the place of unions as a potential bulwark against increasingly neoliberal-oriented ways of knowing and doing language education. As is traditional when writing up a multiethnographic study, our conversations have been re-jigged and pared down to maximize reader engagement.

EAP competencies, credentials, professional development and autonomy

> James: So, what do you all think is most important with respect to EAP instructor competencies?

Leo: Not to get too negative right away, but I'll never forget, I had this one practitioner approach me after a meeting and say, 'You don't belong here, you are not an academic', and I was really taken aback.

James: Sigh. I agree that there are entrenched hierarchies within EAP. How they manifest is what interests me.

Jennifer: I find it weird when structures of power reproduce themselves within a marginalized environment. There's a lot of gatekeepers within the university and you see this ethos reproducing itself within the EAP environment. I'm just like, why? We are all professionals here.

Leo: I've been teaching in this [university] programme for, maybe seven years, and classroom teaching is how you learn most. Experience is key.

Jon: Totally agree.

Jennifer: From the EAP director point of view, providing regular PD and teacher development in-house to complement classroom teaching experience is essential . . . alongside the usually non-existent formal EAP training that most people have never had . . . it is really hard to meet practitioners where they are.

James: In my opinion, competent professional practice requires more than experience. Ideally, all EAP practitioners would have a graduate degree and TESOL specialization. Speaking of which, what do you think is the importance of education and credentials for EAP practitioners?

Jon: Dunno, but I do have a story. In my first EAP job at a top Canadian university, we were given textbooks. Yet all the experienced teachers said, 'If you're a good teacher you shouldn't be using the textbook'. New to the programme, I was at a complete loss how to even begin. I'm not sure a master's or PhD would have helped.

James: Well, I love teaching, period . . . but my graduate degrees have opened the door to a broader EAP experience. In my faculty role, I can do research and some theorizing, both of which allow me to understand and engage with my professional practice in ways that would not be possible otherwise. I'm still unsure, though, which teaching credentials and degrees should be mandatory for EAP instructors.

Jennifer: I'm so with you, James. I'm a massive nerd, I actually like reading and writing and researching – that's a big part of my motivation for doing this. And I think to myself, how can you have an ounce of credibility teaching thesis writing to a PhD student if you have a bachelor's degree that you did twenty-five years ago and you haven't written anything academic since? There's just not any credibility there, even with TESOL specialization. This is a very Canadian EAP problem: unevenness across programmes with respect to education and credentials.

James: Yeah, I've seen programmes where those with only an undergraduate degree are team leads and others where you can't even get hired without a graduate degree in applied linguistics.

Leo: Brings to mind when I worked at an institution where a lot of the people had master's degrees, but in things like architecture, history, or Germanic

studies. How is that person more qualified to teach than a person who has, let's say, a CELTA or DELTA?
Jennifer: That said, Leo, applicants come to me and claim the DELTA is a master's level qualification and I'm like, you're back in Canada now, no one gives a shit about the DELTA.
Leo: Is it because universities are hierarchical places? A person with a PhD is normally seen as a god but do such degrees actually make someone a better EAP teacher?
James: Good question. I'm going to say usually but not always.
Jon: I don't know. I would say sometimes, but usually not. I've thought about doing a PhD, but there's no guarantee of better work, is there?
Leo: That's the problem.
Jen: I feel you. I guess I understand that undertaking a PhD is too much to ask of all practitioners, especially given the time and cost involved – not to mention the soft job market – but I also don't know how we get respect as a field without all being scholar–practitioners.

Our discussions surrounding EAP education and credentialization displayed clear fault lines in perspectives, potentially driven by our differing personal and professional histories and identities: James and Jennifer advocated for advanced credentials whereas Leo and Jon pointed to classroom-teaching experience as the most important competency. Extended conversations on these topics displayed this divergence of perspectives while also showing how James and Jennifer (in particular) sympathized with the lack of incentives for practitioners' scholarly engagement, moving off their originally established positions. Lack of consensus here highlighted a recurring theme: reduced perceived agency among those with less 'capital' to wield, that is, fewer credentials and, perhaps more importantly, lack of PhDs (Bell, 2021). The question of how the requirement of a PhD might impact internal (within the field) and external (outside the field) perceptions of EAP is very much an open one, and though our positions converged to an extent – we all agreed that a graduate degree should be the bare minimum – there remained an unbridgeable divide in perspectives within our group.

James: I also wanted to bring up this idea of instructor autonomy versus a more prescriptive model of course design and delivery.
Jon: If I can speak to losing autonomy . . . can you imagine you've been teaching a particular course alongside a team of other contract instructors for close to a decade, one that you've had a hand in designing and suddenly someone brand new comes in, and because they are hired as a full-timer, and have more degrees than you, they are given authority to revamp the course and are incentivized, be it financially or in working towards tenure, to do so? Totally demoralizing.
James: I'm torn on that one. I can see how that could cause frustration among experienced instructors, but I also think there is a need for research-driven curriculum design. Makes me wonder if that type of situation

could be approached in a more grounded way that takes feedback and suggestions from those who have experience teaching this course in this context.

Jon: In fairness, the powers that be did allow anyone to help revamp the course, but it was volunteer work for contract faculty, with no financial or career benefit that my full-time colleagues get.

Jennifer: You know, as a teacher, I like to have full reign of creativity, but from a director's perspective, no EAP course exists in its own vacuum. Depending on the course, there are a whole other set of requirements and stakeholders to consider. Some stuff, such as outcomes, is necessarily prescriptive. However, what we're trying to do at my centre is a massive curriculum overhaul shaped by lots of people, not just a few at the top.

Jon: That sounds reasonable, but still . . .

Leo: Spinning it back to the teacher's perspective for a moment, I am comfortable with my ideas about language education, and I decided I'm no longer comfortable using a set curriculum. That's one of the reasons why I recently decided to leave [university EAP].

James: Wow, that's a bombshell! Sorry to hear you're that dispirited with the profession.

Leo: It's not only the question of lack of autonomy, but also earning potential. I am going to focus on my language teaching activities that can make more money (i.e. the company I've recently started).

The issue of EAP instructor autonomy once again highlighted deep divisions in perspectives, pitting Jennifer's administrative concerns about the need for managerial guidance for EAP instructors (echoed in Simpson, 2022) against Jon and Leo's positions that there should be less imposition of curriculum design and professional development on instructors. Following extended conversations, a convergence of perspectives took place here, with participants collectively agreeing that there should be a model where EAP leadership considers more fully the perspectives and experiences of EAP instructors. However, power-imbued issues like required education, credentialization, professional development and instructor autonomy clearly demarcated the entrenched hierarchies and asymmetrical relations of power among EAP practitioners who identify as instructors versus those who identify as scholar–practitioners or administrators, highlighting the sense of exclusion and lack of access to power and decision-making perceived by EAP instructors such as Jon and Leo. (Lack of) access to decision-making may have implications for practitioner agency (Ding, 2019; Hadley, 2015) and lead to apathy and alienation among EAP instructors who are marginally employed (le Roux, 2022), a recurring theme stemming from our discussions and a troubling feature of EAPers working in a 'third space' (Bond, 2020; MacDonald, 2016). Conversely, Jen and James' perceived access and inclusion with respect to decision-making (and thus greater perceived agency) raise the spectre of an ethical responsibility of EAP programme directors and scholar–practitioners to instigate change on behalf of (or alongside?) those more marginalized in the profession.

Neoliberal EAP

>Jennifer: Canada is the Wild West for EAP, with a lot of instructor precarity.
>James: Having worked in four or five different EAP programmes, I can attest to the uneven conditions for EAP instructors . . . everything from hiring to professional development.
>Leo: It would be great if we could have better work conditions.
>James: Well, maybe I'm way off base here, but I'd say the UK is miles ahead of Canada in that EAP practitioners often seem to have PhDs and seem like they're lifers – this is their pursuit, and they probably have a permanent job somewhere.
>Jon: To that point, I've worked at institutions where you see this MBA-ification of these EAP programmes, where the administration is valued above pedagogy, above teaching and teachers. I'll never forget a certain Christmas work party. The newly hired head of the EAP programme was up on stage giving her big end-of-year speech, thanking the web designers, and the marketing team. She goes on and on, and never once mentioned the teachers. She just plum forgot. It just summed up the whole thing for me.
>James: EAP programmes are almost inevitably looking to maximize profit and that is a deeply problematic model to superimpose on educational activities. Not all programmes are the same, though, nor are the experiences of those working therein. In my university's case, we have credit-bearing EAP courses, which is different than yours [Jennifer] which is a pre-sessional language programme.
>Jennifer: That being said, yours is an academic unit, with central funding, and so I think it's a bit different than a cost recovery model, where when you get more students, your centre gets more revenue, and you can hire more teachers, and employ people to do other things.
>James: One of the perks of being junior faculty is I am not responsible for programme administration yet! And yes, I feel fortunate to have a permanent position in what feels like a safe set of programmes in our department. However, if we didn't have hundreds of students doing our ESL courses each year, the rest of the university would likely listen to us even less; they already undervalue what we do.
>Jennifer: Well, pre-pandemic there were so many examples of our institutions using international students as cash cows and unbridled recruitment to just to bring in the foreign tuition dollars without providing necessary support for students to thrive. With the pandemic, things have changed.
>James: Not to mention the recent encroachment of multinational corporations into post-secondary EAP.
>Jennifer: Don't get me started! They have come into several universities in Canada. These private companies are vultures, and they keep swooping around trying to convince new institutions to outsource. So that's the importance of an institution valuing and recognizing the expertise and

language work associated with EAP programmes and writing centres, because if the value of the work isn't seen, then why not outsource to these private companies?

James: I think a lot of what we see in our field reflects a wider reality in post-secondary education – the marketization or commodification of [language] education in the knowledge economy. Companies like these multinationals are a symptom of the wider neoliberal educational illness. Anyway, I think there's a reckoning that needs to take place more broadly, but maybe it starts here with us!

Leo: For some reason I see it getting worse, not better, in the future.

Jon: Yep, and it feels like it's out of our control.

Interestingly, these discussions on 'neoliberal EAP' highlighted the diversity of Canadian EAP programmes (e.g. sessional vs. pre-sessional; credit-bearing vs. certificate; variety of 'bridging' and 'pathway' models) as well as practitioner subjectivities within our group. Our perspectives seemed largely aligned from the start; for example, we all perceived the negative impacts on our professional lives from the way language (education) is commodified at universities across Canada (MacDonald, 2020). Not for the first time though, discussion turned to the issue of employment precarity linked to these macro-structural issues. A noteworthy difference in perspectives here was that Jon and Leo, who both inhabit more precarious positions, expressed an inability to impact this perceived state of affairs, whereas James and Jennifer sensed more optimism in how individuals and groups could resist these macro-level impositions that potentially constrain EAP practitioners' meaningful, agentive practice (Bruce and Bond, 2022; Ding and Bruce, 2017). Again, these fissures raise the issue of the ethics of instigating change for those with greater perceived professional power.

Unionization

James: As we discuss neoliberal EAP, it occurs to me that we should be discussing ways to combat the disposable labour model that allows for EAP instructors to potentially be mistreated at their institutions. Unions, anyone?

Jon: Ok, but I'm gonna take the other side here regarding unions. You sometimes get [EAP practitioners] who haven't been to a meeting in years because there is no way of forcing them and they, I imagine, don't want to come also because they feel their voices do not carry the same weight as their tenured or tenure-stream colleagues.

Jennifer: On the topic of unions, when COVID hit in the spring of 2020, at some centres, certain unionized instructors refused to do anything online – it wasn't in their collective agreement. I heard people saying, 'I can't wait to for this online crap to be over, so I can get back to REAL teaching', as if online teaching wasn't teaching. And I was like, 'Do you realize that you have dozens of students and by refusing to teach you're preventing them from graduating?!'

James: Seriously, people? We need more and more powerful unions as a bulwark against the advanced capitalist assault on language education, no? I am proud to be part of an institution with unions that fight for my rights and the rights of those around me.

Jon: That's the problem, right? The extremes. I'm deeply grateful for my union and its benefits but am so conflicted about it because we go on strike a lot and I'm constantly terrified they're going to do it again, which could mean far fewer students and my not getting enough work to support my family. One of these days they're [the union] going to make our university the place that nobody wants to go, and then none of us have work.

Leo: Unions are complicated.

Jennifer: They certainly are complex.

James: Complex, yes, but unionization of instructors should be seen as a potentially effective tactic of resistance. I've seen it done recently at a large Canadian university EAP programme and I hope it results in better, more satisfactory working conditions for practitioners. I also think there is a role for a progressive national organization or association that might better support EAP instructors (e.g. BALEAP in the UK), something we lack in Canada.

Leo: I dunno – what have our unions or associations done for us during the pandemic?

Once again, there was much convergence regarding the identification of impacts of neoliberal organization and management in higher education, leading to a shared sense of camaraderie in resistance. Nevertheless, while we all agreed on the deleterious impact of neoliberal (mis)management of EAP, our proposed solutions and forms of resistance were not aligned. Specifically, the idea of unionization as a form of resistance against precarious living conditions for EAP instructors raised a divergence of perspectives between James and the rest of the group. After extended discussion over time, despite repeated problematization of unions as impediments to efficiency, it was only grudgingly agreed that they may be an effective means of protection for EAP instructors. Further, the idea of creating another organization (e.g. a Canadian EAP association akin to BALEAP) was (disappointingly for James) met with little fanfare all around. Our differing life experiences and trajectories and professional backgrounds most certainly contributed to our (ideological) positions. Given the repeated reflections on employment precarity and the rapid encroachment of multinational EAP corporations in Canadian EAP, entrenched ideologies regarding tactics of resistance may be unhelpful in protecting those most marginalized in the profession (Breshears, 2019; Morgan, 2016). So, what is to be done? Walsh Marr (2021) identifies the 'opportunity for deeper dialogue, relations and learning' (2021: 139) between institutions and EAP practitioners. To this point, perhaps multiethnographic engagement may act as a site for cultivating critical reflection and awareness (Lowe and Lawrence, 2020). However, without all institutional stakeholders at the table, are these types of conversations sufficient to achieve critical (transformative) praxis, that is, substantive change to marginalized EAP instructors' material employment conditions?

Native speakerism?

> Leo: I googled the term precariousness, and the term originates from Latin, which basically relates to the act of praying or asking for favours. I think a lot of teachers feel like their fate is in the hands of . . . people who can make or break their lives and probably don't give it much thought. You know, I immigrated to Canada because I wanted more challenge in my work. But when I first arrived, I couldn't find a job teaching even though I had taught in Argentina and the US and Brazil. I'm like, 'what do you mean Canadian experience? Because it sounds like a catch 22 to me. How am I going to get Canadian experience if you never offer me a job?'
> Jennifer: Sounds like a bit of native speakerism.
> James: Native speakerism was definitely present at private language institutes in Brazil, where I started my ELT career. In order to get my first job in ELT, all I needed was to look and sound like a native speaker. I think there is a growing recognition from those in the field, though, that the days of native-speaker dominance are in the rearview. For example, I have seen culturally and linguistically representative EAP staffs at most programmes in Canada.
> Jennifer: Yes, I like to think our hiring practices are equitable.
> Leo: I also think the problem is what you said, James, when a hiring committee automatically assumes that just because your place of birth is an English-speaking country that automatically makes you more qualified. As if a native English speaker is cognitively more predisposed to teach a language that they never had to learn as an adult!
> James: I understand the critique of hiring and connection to native-speaker privilege, I really do. And I guess even though I think it's less of a problem, it does still exist.
> Leo: Oh, it definitely does, and I can speak from experience.
> James: I hear you. Perhaps we also need to recognize, though, that many so called 'native English-speaking' instructors are also multilingual, as evidenced by this group,[1] so we should probably also problematize the stereotypical monolingual NES while recognizing privilege bestowed upon those that look and sound the part.

Unsurprisingly, our polyvocal data clearly point to power being unequally distributed within Canadian post-secondary EAP. A focus on access and inclusion affords insight into how EAP practitioners navigate their professional lives in more or less agentive ways within a field impacted by professional incentives and disincentives connected to neoliberal orientations of language (and) education

(Block, Gray and Holborow, 2012; Hadley, 2015;. Our various anecdotes and critical incidents painted EAP as a field where, unfortunately, precarity and uncertainty are an economic reality for many (see also Breshears, 2019; Walsh Marr, 2021), and where we all feel – to greater or lesser extents – a certain sense of powerlessness and alienation (le Roux, 2022). Nevertheless, our conversations bring to light the plain fact that employment conditions reflect a (reproduced) hierarchy in the field, where those with tenure or tenure-track positions or permanent contracts appear to experience far more agentive lives within Canadian EAP. By contrast, those on part-time, part-year or sessional contracts perceive far less agency as they struggle with issues of access and exclusion (Corcoran, Johnston and Williams, forthcoming).

However, agency is complex and although these hierarchies (hopefully not reproduced by this framing) are clearly identified by EAP practitioners, even those considered (or who consider themselves) more marginalized can at times have a strong sense of professional agency (e.g. perceived impact on student lives and learning outcomes.) Further, not all of us working in the field perceive ourselves as acutely marginalized, and many of us do not feel pigeonholed into the 'butler stance' (Raimes, 1991) at all, but rather feel a sense of agency in advancing what we rightly recognize as a branch of knowledge and pedagogical practice that is often dismissed as something less than academic (Ding, 2019; Flowerdew, 2019).

What may inspire hope is the fact that, though there was less movement in our individual positions following our storytelling and critical reflection than we may have desired, participants felt affirmed, validated and engaged by this form of research. Given that issues of access (e.g. to doctoral education and secure employment contracts) and exclusion (e.g. having a say in professional development topics and curriculum decisions) appeared repeatedly during our conversations about the field, this methodology may just provide the conditions for more collaborative (rather than coercive) professional relations of power (Cummins, 2021) among EAP practitioners by engaging and elevating the voices of those who are less frequently heard in the literature. As such, multiethnography may be considered a form of 'doing' critical applied linguistics that actively challenges unequal relations of power (Pennycook, 2021).

Reflections on multiethnography

> James: As we come to the end of this project, I am curious as to how you all view your experiences with multiethnography. Also thank you for being here; during COVID times this academic and social engagement has been a lifeline for me.
> Jennifer: Why do therapy when you can just do a multiethnography? My favourite part of conferences is going for beer and shooting the shit. This project, and these conversations, for me, fill that hole.
> Jon: This has been huge for me to just have my voice heard and to say this is what matters to me. So many people are in positions like Leo has been,

that I am in, and that's valuable. Also, these conversations have made me think more about my role as a language teacher and how I can best support students while dealing with all the other bullshit that comes with being a part-timer.

James: It's interesting because I think we're incentivized to not talk about certain aspects of our profession, but during this project we have been able to air our grievances and talk about uncomfortable and unequal distributions of power in a comfortable space, despite our different personal and professional subjectivities. I think another sort of systemic thing that goes along with the EAP is we're necessarily put in competition with each other. And so, rather than be collegial or collaborative, it's competitive. I haven't felt that with this group. When I make decisions these days, I often reflect upon our conversations.

Leo: I'll be very honest with you guys, I'm really burnt out and almost quit on this project, but I have to admit that these chats have actually helped me reflect on my experiences in the profession while sharing perspectives that I really couldn't share with anyone, especially management.

James: That's really gratifying to hear, folks.

Multiethnography has rarely been employed to investigate the lived experiences of EAP professionals. Our conversations, which traversed a range of power-imbued topics related to our professional lives, led to not necessarily novel but nonetheless valid insights with respect to the differing lived experiences of those working in EAP. The nature in which we were able to share with each other was cathartic and validating, suggesting that this type of methodological approach can yield affective benefits for participants. Next, while it would be naive to think that this methodology could achieve a completely level playing field, we argue it did allow for a bending of the artificial boundaries between EAP practitioners with differing levels of perceived professional status and power (Lowe and Lawrence, 2020; Smart and Cook, 2020). Further, as our project hopefully demonstrated, polyvocal approaches to research can afford meaningful engagement with scholarship, as well as the challenging of entrenched hierarchies and asymmetrical power relations, potentially leading to a level of critical praxis (Hoggle and Bramble, 2020; Pennycook, 2021).

However, although there was some evidence to suggest that engaging in these conversations resulted in enhanced agency on the part of participants, the occasional lack of willingness to 'dig deeper' with respect to entrenched viewpoints suggests the potential limitations of this work when bringing together those who are impacted differently by systemic issues of access and exclusion. Self-reflexivity as a critical endeavour in EAP can clearly lead to improved awareness of systemic barriers and heightened social agency; however, it also necessarily leads to uncomfortable moments of heightened tensions (Kennedy and DeCosta, 2023). One of the limitations of this study, as well as a pressing question for those who might adopt this critical reflective approach, is how this type of project could more explicitly afford discussion of difference that leads to praxis. Might this type of critical, reflective work be best suited to take place primarily among those occupying similar perceived levels of status and power? These remain open questions.

Conclusions and future directions

Based on this project, we suggest that multiethnographic approaches to research can provide not only meaningful insights into the lived experiences of language teachers, but also an accessible form of research engagement for those with differing levels of research experience and professional status. Though not a panacea, multiethnography may thus afford more collaborative relations of power between EAP stakeholders, potentially leading to transformative perspectives for those engaged in this critical self-reflection as well as praxis in the form of measures to reduce issues of access and exclusion. As such, this methodology might be usefully adapted for use by EAP programmes and practitioners. To wit, one interesting feature of our data analysis is that there emerged from our conversations areas where incremental changes might be made to improve the agentive nature of EAP practitioners' work lives:

- Transparent hiring criteria (e.g. education, certification, experience).
- Improvements to working conditions for EAP instructors (e.g. permanent status, regularization, unionization and/or other forms of collective mobilization).
- Incentives for engagement with research and pedagogical innovation.
- Practitioner-driven professional development.
- Collegial exchange of research- and classroom-teaching inspired learnings.
- Programme leadership which builds relationships between EAP and other units (e.g. writing centres; disciplinary and administrative units).
- Collective curricular (re)design that includes practitioner input.

Drawing on our critical lens, collective experiences and a growing body of research into EAP in Canada, we argue that there exist clear tensions and territories that reflect asymmetrical relations of power in Canadian EAP. However, the time has come to do more than theorize power and recognize the reproduction of inequality and inequity; as Pennycook (2021) argues, 'we need alternative visions of how things can be, as well as potential ways of getting there' (2021: 140). To wit, our polyvocal engagement displays how these types of critical, socially situated conversations might be replicated by those in the field to inform contextually appropriate policy and practice. Further, though multiethnography may not benefit all participants, these types of conversations may provide an outlet for more 'marginalized' practitioners to have their voices heard as they critically reflect upon the politics of EAP in a manner that could lead to a shift in their sense of professional agency. There are no guarantees with respect to the emancipatory or transformative nature of this methodology; however, we argue that our findings point to multiethnography as a potentially effective tactic of resistance in EAP during these advanced neoliberal times.

Note

1 See Figure 12.1.

References

Adamson, J., A. Stewart, C. Smith, B. Lander, N. Fujimoto-Adamson, J. Martinez and M. Masud (2019), 'Exploring the Publication Practices of Japan-based EFL Scholars through Collaborative Autoethnography', *English Scholars Beyond Borders*, 5 (1): 3–31.

Ahmed, A. and B. Morgan (2021), 'Postmemory and Multilingual Identities in English Language Teaching: A Duoethnography', *The Language Learning Journal*, 1–16. https://doi.org/10.1080/09571736.2021.1906301

Banegas, D. L. and D. Gerlach (2022), 'Critical Language Teacher Education: A Duoethnography of Teacher Educators' Identities and Agency', *System*. https://doi.org/10.1016/j.system.2021.102474.

Bell, D. E. (2021), 'Accounting for the Troubled Status of English Language Teachers in Higher Education', *Teaching in Higher Education*. https://doi.org/10.1080/13562517.2021.1935848

Bhowmik, S. and A. Chaudhuri (2021), '"I Need My Instructor to Like Sit with Me": Addressing Culture in L2 Writing Instruction', *BC TEAL Journal*, 6 (1): 11–28. https://doi.org/10.14288/bctj.v6i1

Block, D., J. Gray and M. Holborow (2012), *Neoliberalism and Applied Linguistics*, London: Routledge.

Bond, B. (2020), *Making Language Visible in the University: English for Academic Purposes and Internationalisation*, Bristol: Multilingual Matters.

Breshears, S. (2019), 'The Precarious Work of English Language Teaching in Canada', *TESL Canada Journal*, 36 (2): 26–47.

Bruce, I. and B. Bond, eds (2022), *Contextualizing English for Academic Purposes in Higher Education: Politics, Policies and Practices*, New York: Bloomsbury.

Canagarajah, S. (2017), *Translingual Practices and Neoliberal Policies: Attitudes and Practices of African Skilled Migrants in Anglophone Workplaces*, New York: Springer.

Charles, M. (2022), 'EAP Research in BALEAP 1975-2019: Past Issues and Future Directions', *Journal of English for Academic Purposes*, 55: 101060. https://doi.org/10.1016/j.jeap.2021.101060

Charles, M. and D. Pecorari (2016), *Introducing English for Academic Purposes*, London: Routledge.

Corcoran, J. N., K. Johnston and J. Williams (forthcoming), 'EAP Practitioners across Canada: Diversity, Agency, and Employment (dis)Satisfaction', *TESL Canada Journal*, 40 (1).

Corcoran, J. N., A. Gagné and M. McIntosh (2018), 'A Conversation on the Ethics of Plurilingual Graduate Students' Thesis Writing Support', *Canadian Journal for Studies in Discourse and Writing /Rédactologie*, 28: 1–25. https://doi.org/10.31468/cjsdwr.589

Corcoran, J. N., J. Williams and K. Johnston (2022), 'EAP Programs and Practitioners in Canada: Results from an Exploratory Survey', *BC TEAL Journal*. https://ojs-o.library.ubc.ca/index.php/BCTJ/issue/view/38

Cummins, J. (2021), *Rethinking the Education of Multilingual Learners: A Critical Analysis of Theoretical Concepts*, Bristol: Multilingual Matters.

Ding, A. (2019), 'EAP Practitioner Identity', in K. Hyland and L. Wong (eds), *Specialised English: New Directions in EAP and ESP Research and Practice*, 63–76, London: Routledge.

Ding, A. and I. Bruce (2017), *The English for Academic Purposes Practitioner*, London: Palgrave Macmillan. https://doi.org/10.1007/978-3-319-59737-9

Douglas, S. R. and M. H. Landry (2021), 'English for Academic Purposes Programs: Key Trends across Canadian Universities', *Comparative and International Education/Éducation comparée et internationale*, 50: 1. https://doi.org/10.5206/cieeci.v50i1.10925

Fenton-Smith, B. and L. Gurney (2022), 'Collaborator, Applied Linguist, Academic, Expense? Exploring the Professional Identities of Academic Language and Learning Professionals', *Higher Education Pedagogies*, 7 (1): 160–78. https://doi.org/10.1080/23752696.2022.2130390

Flowerdew, J. (2019), 'Power in English for Academic Purposes', in K. Hyland and L. L. C. Wong (eds), *Specialised English*, 50–62, London: Routledge.

Hadley G. (2015), *English for Academic Purposes in Neoliberal Universities: A Critical Grounded Theory*, New York: Springer.

Haque, E. (2007), 'Critical Pedagogy in English for Academic Purposes and the Possibility for "Tactics" of Resistance', *Pedagogy, Culture & Society*, 15 (1): 83–106. https://doi.org/10.1080/14681360601162311

Heng Hartse, J., M. Lockett and M. Ortabasi (2018), 'Languaging about Language in an Interdisciplinary Writing Course', *Across the Disciplines*, 15 (3): 89–103.

Hogle, L. A. and C. Bramble (2020), 'Teacher Agency through Duoethnography: Pedagogical DNA in a Community of Learner-Teachers', *International Journal of Education & the Arts*, 21 (15): 1–20.

Huang, L. S. (2018), 'A Call for Critical Dialogue: EAP Assessment from the Practitioner's Perspective in Canada', *Journal of English for Academic Purposes*, 35: 70–84. https://doi.org/10.1016/j.jeap.2018.07.005

Huang, P. and M. Karas (2020), 'Artefacts as "Co-Participants" in Duoethnography', *TESL Canada Journal*, 37 (3): 66–74.

Hyland, K. and F. Jiang (2021), 'A Bibliometric Study of EAP Research: Who Is Doing What, Where and When?' *Journal of English for Academic Purposes*, 49: 1–12. https://doi.org/10.1016/j.jeap.2020.100929

Kennedy, L. M. and P. I. De Costa (2023), 'Reflexivity, Emerging Expertise, and mi[s-step]s: A Collaborative Self-study of Two TESOL Teacher Educators', in S. Consoli and S. Ganass (eds), *Reflexivity in Applied Linguistics*, 153–70, New York: Routledge.

Languages Canada (2021), *State of the Language Education Sector in Canada*, Languages Canada. https://www.languagescanada.ca/en/research

le Roux, M. (2022), 'The Predicament of PEAPPs: Practitioners of EAP in Precarity', in I. Bruce and B. Bond (eds), *Contextualizing English for Academic Purposes in Higher Education*, 165–80, New York: Bloomsbury.

Liddicoat, A. J. and K. Taylor-Leech (2021), 'Agency in Language Planning and Policy', *Current Issues in Language Planning*, 22 (1–2): 1–18. https://doi.org/10.1080/14664208.2020.1791533

Litzenberg, J. (2020), '"If I Don't Do It, Somebody Else Will": Covert Neoliberal Policy Discourses in the Decision-Making Processes of an Intensive English Program', *TESOL Quarterly*, 54 (4): 823–45.

Lowe, R. J. and L. Lawrence (2020), *Duoethnography in English Language Teaching: Research, Reflection, and Classroom Application*, Bristol: Multilingual Matters.

MacDonald, J. J. (2016), 'The Margins as Third Space: EAP Teacher Professionalism in Canadian Universities', *TESL Canada Journal*, 34 (1): 106–16.

MacDonald, J. J. (2020), 'Monolingualism, Neoliberalism and Language-as-Problem: Discourse Itineraries in Canadian University Language Policy', Doctoral dissertation, UCL (University College London).

MacDonald, J. J. (2022), 'The Differing Discursive Constructions of EAP within the University: Contrasting Institutional and Language Centre Perspectives', in I. Bruce and B. Bond (eds), *Contextualizing English for Academic Purposes in Higher Education: Politics, Policies and Practices*, 131–47, New York: Bloomsbury.

Marshall, S. and J. W. Marr (2018), 'Teaching Multilingual Learners in Canadian Writing-Intensive Classrooms: Pedagogy, Binaries, and Conflicting Identities', *Journal of Second Language Writing*, 40: 32–43.

McCartney, D. M. and A. S. Metcalfe (2018), 'Corporatization of Higher Education through Internationalization: The Emergence of Pathway Colleges in Canada', *Tertiary Education and Management*, 24 (3): 206–20.

McKenzie, A. M. (2018), 'Academic Integrity across the Canadian Landscape', *Canadian Perspectives on Academic Integrity*, 1 (2): 40–5. https://doi.org/10.11575/cpai.v1i2.54599

Morgan, B. (2016), 'Language Teacher Identity and the Domestication of Dissent: An Exploratory Account', *TESOL Quarterly*, 50 (3): 708–34.

Pennycook, A. (2021), *Critical Applied Linguistics: A Critical Re-introduction*, 2nd edn, New York: Routledge.

Pinar, W. F. (2022), *A Praxis of Presence in Curriculum Theory: Advancing Currere Against Cultural Crises in Education*, New York: Routledge.

Raimes, A. (1991), 'Out of the Woods: Emerging Traditions in the Teaching of Writing', *TESOL Quarterly*, 25 (3): 407–30.

Russell, B., C. Barron, H. Kim and E. E. Jang (2022), 'A Mixed-Method Investigation into International University Students' Experience with Academic Language Demands', *Frontiers in Education*. https://doi.org/10.3389/feduc.2022.934692

Saldaña, J. (2021), *The Coding Manual for Qualitative Researchers*, Thousand Oaks: Sage Publications.

Sawyer, R. and J. Norris (2015), 'Duoethnography: A Retrospective 10 Years After', *International Review of Qualitative Research*, 8 (1): 1–4. http://doi.org.myaccess.library.utoronto.ca/10.1525/irqr.2015.8.1.1

Silverman, D., ed. (2020), *Qualitative Research*, Thousand Oaks: Sage Publications.

Simpson, R. (2022), 'Perspectives on Directing an EAP Centre', in I. Bruce and B. Bond (eds), *Contextualizing English for Academic Purposes in Higher Education: Politics, Policies and Practices*, 149–64, New York: Bloomsbury.

Sizer, J. (2019), 'Is Teaching EAP a Profession? A Reflection on EAP's Professional Status, Values, Community and Knowledge', *Professional and Academic English: Journal of the IATEFL English for Specific Purposes Special Interest Group*, 52: 26–34.

Smart, B. and C. Cook (2020), 'Professional Development through Duoethnography: Reflecting on Dialogues between an Experienced and Novice Teacher', in R. Lowe and L. Lawrence (eds), *Duoethnography in English Language Teaching: Research, Reflection and Classroom Application*, 91–111, Multilingual Matters. https://doi.org/10.21832/9781788927192-007

Sousa Santos, B. and M. P. Meneses (2020), *Knowledges Born in the Struggle: Constructing the Epistemologies of the Global South*, London: Routledge.

Tjandra, C., J. Corcoran, M. Gennuso and A. R. Yeldon (2020), 'Digital Autobiographical Identity Texts as Critical Plurilingual Pedagogy', *Journal of Belonging, Identity, Language, and Diversity*, 4 (1): 81–100.

Van Viegen, S. and B. Russell (2019), 'More than Language: Evaluating a Canadian University EAP Bridging Program', *TESL Canada Journal*, 36 (1): 97–120. https://doi.org/10.18806/tesl.v36i1.1304

Walsh Marr, J. (2021), 'The Promise and Precarity of Critical Pedagogy in English for Academic Purposes', *BC TEAL Journal*, 6 (1): 132–41. https://doi.org/10.14288/bctj.v6i1.449

Zappa Hollman, S. and J. A. Fox (2021), 'Engaging in Linguistically Responsive Instruction: Insights from a First Year University Program for Emergent Multilingual Learners', *TESOL Quarterly*, 55 (4): 1081–91. https://doi.org/10.1002/tesq.3075

Conclusion

Engaging with Identity and Agency in a Collaborative Project

Laetitia Monbec

The idea of bringing together a group of EAP practitioners in a collective scholarship project around identity and agency came to Alex a few years ago. The constitution of the group was a difficult task; we received over eighty abstracts, all of which could have made for a valuable contribution to the volume. We selected as best we could to reflect the diversity of the field through voices less often heard, different positions and contexts. Although unfortunately, due to a lack of submissions from South America, we could not include any authors from the region, we hope the studies in the chapters provide a rich variety in terms of contexts and field status, habitus and capitals of the authors or practitioners portrayed. What we feel happy about is that the volume provides a diverse, both a broad and close, view of the field, each chapter presenting EAP and its practitioners as embedded in various societies and cultures, with different remits, expectations, conditions, students, colleagues and pedagogical practices. Overall, we also find much commonality in concerns and aspirations.

The project consisted of monthly online meetings which each author or teams of authors used to present and discuss their studies in progress. The project was challenging; it started during a pandemic, we met at odd hours due to time differences, some of us had internet access issues, some were pressed for time to conduct their studies and write, and each and everyone's lives were affected by a range of professional and personal events. Over the months, however, as we discovered each study, their context and the different issues related to identity and agency, the group became a source of intellectual engagement and feedback, as well as support and encouragement. We would like to thank all the authors for their dedication throughout. Each chapter in the collection is a unique contribution to the overall volume, in terms of context, but also in relation to the different ways authors engaged with the themes, theoretically and methodologically. This collection is a highly original engagement with identity and agency and manages to avoid the myopic theoretical hegemony that plagues TESOL identity research. It is this originality and this variety which will be picked up below in a short discussion which highlights what the volume achieves and what remains to be done.

Engaging with identity and agency

Ding (2019) discusses neoliberalism, marketization, socialization into the field, epistemic and cultural capital, associations and professionalism as the main structural forces that shape practitioner identity. For example, socialization in EAP is ad-hoc and post-hoc, with vague entry requirements impacting practitioners' cultural capital and agency within the university at large. At the end of the same chapter, Ding (2019: 72) concludes : 'We need to first dissect the conditions that shape us as a community and begin to collectively consider the identities we wish to forge and commit to, which enable us to better respond to the avaricious and mercantile vision of EAP which is looming large.' The authors in this volume provide a valuable attempt at doing this. They illustrate this range of structural influences and the impact they have on negotiating identity and agency. They provide a fascinating insight into ways these broad issues are realized and experienced in local contexts through the meso and micro interactions they analyse. Neoliberal pressures on higher education are felt throughout the volume, yet they do not impact status, position and outcomes in the same way in Pakistan, Singapore, Hong Kong or Zimbabwe, where EAP centres are not profit-making, as they do in Canada, the UK or South Africa. There, a range of additional factors are prioritized including practitioners' social and educational backgrounds and race (in Pakistan, Zimbabwe and Singapore) or governmental and institutional regulations' impact on scholarship and pedagogic practices (Hong Kong, South Africa). Many of the chapters discuss a sense of dislocation, of marginalization within the broader HE field, with its various impacts on recognition, well-being, self-esteem and sense of purpose (see chapters by Taylor; Corcoran, MacDonald, Mendelsohn and Gomes; Joubert and Clarence; Matthews; and Lughmani and Chigaeva-Heddad), but they also consider marginalization within EAP, in one's own department (see chapters by Muchena; Anbreen and Ayub; and Winiarska-Pringle and Rolińska) or ethical entanglements with colleagues when power relations are unequal (see Bond's chapter). Interestingly, not all see this marginality as negative; on the contrary, some find it a perfect space to hide in the Panopticon and to be the types of academics they want to be, the *'fulcrum'* of the field (see Tilakaratna's chapter) or to adapt to the conditions to find a way forward that preserves their own values (see Cheung's chapter). One of the first achievements of this volume then is that it illustrates concretely that the way we engage with agency and identity is itself contingent on the specific structural forces at play in our contexts and our own position within this context.

In a blog post, Ding (2016) proposed the framework, or guiding questions, below, to avoid the pitfalls of narcissism which (he bemoans in several paragraphs and in this volume's introduction) plagues TESOL and teacher education identity research. I follow this with a reflection on how the chapters in the volume take up or address these issues/questions.

My positive theory of identity discusses the following elements:

1. Provide a link from identity to agency.

2. Have explanatory powers to articulate the relationship between structure and agency and specifically account for morphostasis and morphogenesis i.e. to account for how agents are shaped by structural forces and how agents change structure over time.
3. Account for, at least theoretically, how professional identity is shaped. What are the discourses, knowledge bases, practices and social material contexts and forces that intersect to influence professional identity?
4. How does personal identity relate to social identity (or which one aspect is professional identity)? How do our personal concerns and commitments manifest themselves in the social sphere?
5. What connects or affiliates one practitioner to another? Is there such thing as a profession? Is there an essence to EAP? Something that binds all practitioners?
6. How do we account for recognition, distinction, social stratification and boundaries in defining a practitioner? Who makes these distinctions? And how do we change them?
7. How do neoliberal values impose themselves in universities and how do these values transform practitioner identity? (Ding, 2016)

First, a reader interested in theoretical approaches to identity and agency will have found a rich range of perspectives in the volume, including Field Theory (Bourdieu), posthumanism, Legitimation Code Theory, Critical Realism, Positioning Theory, Symbolic Interactionism, Critical Applied Linguistics and the ecological model of teacher agency. The reader can then discover how these approaches enable certain questions to be explored and insights to be generated.

Many of the chapters foreground identity rather than agency. They develop 'the discourses, knowledge bases, practices, and social material contexts and forces that shape practitioners' identities', but overall, the volume probably develops morphostasis more than morphogenesis. Yet, agency is present – central in some chapters, and only tangential in others (sometimes taking the form of a comment or an aspiration expressed in the conclusion). In Tilakaratna's chapter, the participants reject (*curse*) the labels that are assigned to them, as 'Global South' within the field or 'marginal' within the university, and argue their epistemic capital enables them to impact their students and make them into the *fulcrum* of the field. In Chapter 1, Ding and Monbec argue that the way to develop agency is to first understand the power struggles and underlying ideologies that persist in the field. In Chapter 2 Bond shares her reflections and a concrete way forward to shape ethics in EAP scholarship. In Matthews' chapter, several participants show agency in their interaction with technology. Corcoran, MacDonald, Mendelsohn and Gomes propose suggestions to develop practitioner agency in the closing of their chapter. Joubert and Clarence explain how they locate agency in their symbolic travelling between borderlands and heartlands, pushing back at times and sailing with the tide at others. In Cheung's chapter, agency is shown in the participants' determination and passion for scholarship in the face of unclear expectations and precarity in the new research track implemented in the institution. Lughmani and Chigaeva-Heddad's chapter explains how practitioners, despite a restrictive role on the English Writing Requirement programme, were able to resist and redefine their position in relation to students and subject lecturers. In other chapters, while participants show clear-sightedness about their position in the field, this is not always a way to develop more agency, as some of Anbreen and Ayub's participants recognize. If they disrupt the behavioural norms of their class, they 'face the music', showing that the weight of powerful structures and the pressure exerted by a collective class habitus are difficult to resist.

The methodologies used are also varied. As a few of the authors adopt an auto/multi/duoethnographic approach, this led to discussions around the challenges involved in using lived experience. With the promise of bringing rich, 'thick' data, exploiting one's lived experience is fraught with challenges: for example, it can be presented as unfiltered, true, authentic, and yet there is nothing less true than a subjective lived experience (Bourdieu, 1987). How we understand and interpret our lived experience is layered with ideology and prone to misreadings. It can also turn into a narcissist exercise where the simple fact of sharing details of one's life is believed to be of interest to others. Yet access to the lived experience and bearing witness are essential in order to make visible inequalities and discriminations and to understand the forces which shape the field. A personal narrative can be very impactful in achieving this, when it manages to make visible the elements that constitute the individual's modes of seeing, thinking and being and how the social world shapes their lives. The most transformative personal narratives (for the reader) are traversed by other voices and social contexts (Ernaux, 2011). There is however probably nothing more difficult to write. Authors of the volume approached this challenge differently. Tilakaratna provides a mini socio-analysis of the self at the start of her chapter, which says all that is needed to understand her trajectory and experience in EAP as it clearly shows how the intersectionality of gender, race and class have impacted her identity and agency. In other chapters, we clearly see how talking about one's lived experience has cathartic value. In this project, which started during different types of social distancing due to the global pandemic, some of the authors such as Winiarska-Pringle and Rolińska as well as Corcoran et al. were explicit that this was one of the outcomes of their methodology.

Overall, in this volume, the authors have shown a field which is made up of a constellation of worlds, each with its own logic, but importantly a world with no centre. We hope the volume has presented ideas and concepts that have intrigued, educated, perhaps challenged, maybe inspired or at least echoed with the reader. Personally, working on this project has left me hopeful that practitioners can be agents of change when they ground their action in ethical principles and act for a less competitive, more collaborative and solidary field with an aim to include and widen access to all types of practitioner. Alex is an excellent embodiment of this deliberate mode of action and I am grateful he invited me to co-edit this volume and for his commiseration following the delegitimising incident he describes in the introduction. We hope the reader sees in the authors' work many ideas to develop their own understanding of the field and their position within it and that it may open new spaces for imagination and action.

References

Bourdieu, P. (1987), 'The Biographical Illusion', *Working Papers and Proceedings of the Centre for Psychosocial Studies*, 14: 1–7.

Ding, A. (September 2016), 'The Limits of Identity Theory', *Teaching EAP* (Blog). https://teachingeap.wordpress.com/2016/09/03/the-limits-of-identity-theory/

Ding, A. (2019), 'EAP Practitioner Identity', in K Hyland and L. L C. Wong (eds), *Specialised English: New Directions in ESP and EAP Research and Practice*, 63–76, London: Routledge.

Ernaux, A. (2011), *Ecrire la Vie*, Paris: Quarto Gallimard.

INDEX

Archer, Margaret   4, 126–9, 174–5
autoethnography   112–13

Bourdieu, Pierre
   capital   94
   cultural capital   95–6
   doxa   14
   field   15, 93–4
   habitus   96–7
   hysteresis   12, 32
   illusio   13–15, 29
   metanoia   13
   reflexivity   31
   social surface   39
   symbolic capital   16

capital   94
critical applied linguistics   223
cultural capital   95–6

Deleuze, Gilles and Guatarri, Félix   48–9
doxa   14
duoethnography   140

English Medium of Instruction (EMI)   92, 187
ethics of EAP   36–7
   Affirmative ethics   49, 59, 61
   Code of ethics   36, 51
ethnography   112–13
   duoethnography   140
   multiethnography   224–5, 233–5
ethos   59–61

field   15, 93–4
   EAP field   18–19

Global North   30–3, 67–8, 76–8, 82, 108
Global South   37, 67–8, 74, 76–7, 108

Goffman Erving   158, 164
   stigmatized identities   158

habitus   96–7
hysteresis   12, 32

illusio   13–15, 29

labelling theory   157–8
language policy
   Hong Kong   186–7
   Pakistan   92
   South Africa   123
   Zimbabwe   108, 110
legitimation code theory (LCT)   68, 73, 110–12

metanoia   13
multiethnography   223, 233–5
multilingualism   24, 34

posthumanism   48–9
power   58–61
precarity   140, 188, 192, 195–6, 200, 222–3, 231

reflexivity   31, 126–7, 174
rhizome   48, 51

Social Actor Theory   22
social surface   39
SoTL (scholarship of teaching and learning)   49–53, 188
stigmatized identities   158
symbolic capital   16
symbolic interactionism   156–9
   impression management   157
   labelling theory   157
   the looking glass self   156, 159
systemic functional linguistics   22

www.ingramcontent.com/pod-product-compliance
Lightning Source LLC
Chambersburg PA
CBHW071820300426
44116CB00009B/1379